THE DEFINITIVE MIDDLE SCHOOL GUIDE

A Handbook for Success

Revised Edition

by Sandra Schurr

Original Guide by Imogene Forte and Sandra Schurr

IncentivePublications

BY WORLD BOOK
a Scott Fetzer company

Graphic Organizers by Kathleen Bullock
Cover by Robert Voigts

Print Edition ISBN 978-1-62950-008-9
E-book Edition ISBN 978-1-62950-009-6 (PDF)
Library of Congress Control Number: 2009923056

World Book, Inc.
233 North Michigan Avenue
Suite 2000
Chicago, Illinois, 60601 U.S.A.

For information about World Book and Incentive Publications products, call **1-800-967-5325**, or visit our websites at **www.worldbook.com** and **www.incentivepublications.com.**

Printed in the United States by Edwards Brothers Malloy.

What Is the Definitive Middle School Guide?

Student-centered education is the most effective approach to meeting young adolescents' needs. Educators and researchers alike agree on this! Research further indicates that grouping these students together in a supportive environment provides the best climate for learning and growing. The **Middle School** concept has proven to be the ideal model for educating young adolescents.

The Definitive Middle School Guide is an essential tool for educators and administrators at the middle grade level. It provides middle level educators with the latest information on the state of the middle school concept. Its easy-to-reference tips and lists make the guide invaluable. It incorporates the latest research and integrates current best practices and effective techniques for the classroom.

This book is your ready-to-grab, everything-in-one-place handbook for middle level education. It offers a complete collection of relevant information concerning the middle school philosophy and its essential program components. It is intended to serve as a combination encyclopedia, dictionary, and almanac so that readers can quickly and easily find out "everything they ever wanted to know about middle schools."

The Definitive Middle School Guide features self-contained modules (sections) arranged in a sequence designed to present the evolution of an effective middle school organizational pattern.

Module I: School Structures and Climate

Module II: Interdisciplinary Teaming and Block Scheduling

Module III: Curricular Models and Instructional Methods

Module IV: Classroom Management and Discipline

Module V: Advisory, Advocacy, and Affective Education

Module VI: Student Assessment and Evaluation

Each module may also stand on its own to be used independently of the other modules should the need arise. For example, if the reader already understands interdisciplinary teaming or cooperative learning, but wants to learn more about advisory programs, he or she can go directly to the advisory module without first working through the previous sections. Information is organized in a *list format* to allow the user to unearth major concepts without having to sift through extraneous information. The authors have researched, analyzed, and summarized the literature on middle schools so that it is presented in a concise way to meet your needs. Whether you are a busy teacher, administrator, parent, or other educator, you will quickly find the information essential to understanding and success in middle schools.

Educators responsible for setting up or conducting workshops or in-service programs will be delighted to discover that the common format for each of the six modules provides a complete and workable training package:

- A one-page overview.
- A glossary of terms crucial to understanding the topic.
- A set of guiding questions that serve as learning goals, as well as pre-tests and post-tests of the material addressed in the module.
- A series of LISTS that present the most important and germane material on the module's topic or theme in the form of items, descriptions, references, tools, and techniques.
- Several graphic organizers to help educators think, plan, or discuss what they learn or find.
- A list of findings from the published literature to provide motivation and support for the implementation of significant changes in schooling at the middle grade level.
- A final wrap-up to review the module. The "Review and Reflect" section at the end of each module is presented in a graphic organizer format. Activities are presented for readers or teams—one at each level of Bloom's Taxonomy. These guide educators as they review, internalize, incorporate, and act on the information, concepts, and ideas included in the module.

Major Topics in the Definitive Middle School Guide

School Structures and Climate

- Common denominators of successful middle schools
- Characteristics of early adolescents
- Ways to develop and enhance school climate
- Optimal facility requirements
- Creating a master schedule

Interdisciplinary Teaming and Block Scheduling

- Forming teams, roles, and responsibilities of team members and leaders
- Ways to build team identity
- Developing a team handbook
- Evaluating a team's effectiveness
- Ways to establish, promote, and flex a block schedule

Curricular Models and Instructional Methods

- Detailed overview of different curricular models
- Methods for differentiating instruction
- In-class grouping
- Effective lesson planning
- Best instructional practices
- Tips for effective discussions

Classroom Management and Discipline

- Classroom management tips
- Establishing classroom procedures
- Useful homework policies
- Ways to avoid discipline and management problems
- Guidelines for handling disruptive behavior
- Effective disciplinary actions

Advisory, Advocacy, and Affective Education

- Goals for effective advisory programs
- Krathwohl's Affective Taxonomy
- Responsibilities of advisors
- Ways to schedule advisory time
- Instruments for evaluating an advisory program's success

Student Assessment and Evaluation

- Authentic assessment
- Helping students become test-wise
- Using portfolios, performance assessment, rubrics, checklists, and conferences to assess
- Assessment tips, tools, techniques, and test formats

Table of Contents

MODULE III
CURRICULAR MODELS AND INSTRUCTIONAL METHODS
◄ 111 ►

Instructional Methods

MODULE IV
CLASSROOM MANAGEMENT AND DISCIPLINE
◄ 211 ►

MODULE V
ADVISORY, ADVOCACY, AND AFFECTIVE EDUCATION
◄ 271 ►

MODULE VI
STUDENT ASSESSMENT AND EVALUATION
◄ 317 ►

APPENDIX
◄ 371 ►

Module 1

School Structures

and

Climate

Contents of Module 1

Overview of
School Structures and Climate

A school that meets the needs of middle grade students:

- is based on the unique needs and characteristics of the early adolescent, including physical, psychological, intellectual, social, and moral-ethical needs.

- has a well-developed mission statement that is understood and accepted by administrators, teachers, students, and parents.

- is structured around the widely varying characteristics of early adolescents.

- is student-centered rather than subject-centered.

- includes provision for pre-service and in-service teacher training to meet the exceptionalities in interests, abilities, and experiences of students in transition.

- accepts and respects each student and teacher as an individual of worth and dignity in his or her own right, celebrates differences, and encourages creativity and freedom of expression in reflection of ethnic heritage and personal experiences.

- requires the same teachers to share the same students over the same block of time in the same part of the building.

The effective middle school organizational structure affords:

- articulation between the elementary school and the middle school and between the middle school and the high school that is enhanced by increased communication and a student-centered focus.

- flexible block scheduling to allow for varied learning activities, grouping and regrouping students for instruction, and common planning time for teachers.

- interdisciplinary approaches in disciplines and integration of all curricular areas.

- a varied range of exploratory opportunities for students.

- opportunities for focusing on affective education as a regular part of the daily schedule.

- emphasis placed on intramural rather than interscholastic athletics, with cooperation and participation encouraged.

- educators who have been specially trained and are committed to the education of the early adolescent.

- classroom teachers who have mastered strategies that promote positive classroom management and active student participation.

- forward thinking, devotion to excellence in classroom instruction, student motivation, the quest for life skills, broad-based learning, and creative thinking.

Terms Important for Understanding School Structures and Climate

Activity period: a time during regular school day for students to enjoy a variety of experiences that extend and reinforce the classroom curriculum (Schools can use this time for advisory-advisee or advocacy programs, for intramurals, for student electives, for clubs and service groups, or for community-based activities.)

Advisory-advocacy programs: regularly scheduled times during which each young adolescent has the opportunity to interact with a small group of peers and a teacher advocate in relation to school-oriented and personal concerns

Block schedule: scheduling that provides large blocks of time for teams of teachers and students to arrange both flexible groupings of students and varied periods of time for instruction

Common planning time: regularly scheduled time within the school day during which a given team or group of teachers who are responsible for the same group of students is available for joint lesson planning, parent conferencing, and material preparation

Cross-grade grouping: grouping students of more than one grade level together (This is often employed in exploratory courses and advisory or advocacy programs.)

Early adolescence: the stage of development between ages of 10 and 14 when students begin to reach puberty

Early adolescence generalist teachers: the subject area specialists (math, science, social studies, language arts) in the school who make up the interdisciplinary team within a given cluster of students

Exploratory programs: regularly scheduled experiences in which students investigate special areas of knowledge and interests (often non-academic or non-achievement oriented) for the purpose of expanding the base of personal experiences, interests, and aptitudes

Interdisciplinary program: instruction that integrates and combines subject matter ordinarily taught separately into a single organizational structure

Interdisciplinary team organization: the practice of organizing two to five teachers for instruction, using a common group of students as a focus rather than a common academic subject (This teacher group shares the same students over the same block of time in the same location of the building.)

Intramural programs: sports-oriented activities in which all students are encouraged to participate and which take place during or after the school day (The focus of these programs is widespread participation of students in a collaborative rather than a competitive setting.)

Professional or school learning communities: collegial groups that are committed to enhancing student learning as their primary outcome (The learning community engages in a variety of activities, including a shared vision, working and learning collaboratively, visiting and collecting data from community learning-based classrooms, and participating in shared decision-making. These learning communities result in academic gains for students, reduced isolation of teachers, and teachers that are better informed and more committed.)

School climate: the overall atmosphere, ambiance, and behavior patterns and expectations that set the tone for the entire operation of the school

School mission statement: an important and concise statement that clearly conveys the overall intent and focus for the schooling process in a given educational setting

Student-centered school structures: the organizational patterns unique to middle school philosophy that include flexible block schedule, interdisciplinary team, advisory program, exploratory program, intrascholastic sports, and team space allocations

Transescence: the stage of development that begins prior to the onset of puberty and extends through the early stages of adolescence

The Definitive Middle School Guide, Revised Edition
Copyright © 2014 World Book, Inc./Incentive Publications, Chicago, IL

Guiding Questions for Thinking About School Structures and Climate

1 What are the unique needs and characteristics of the middle grade student?

2 Why have early adolescents in our society today been labeled "kids caught in the middle"?

3 What are some key structures that meet the needs of middle level students today?

4 What are some major differences between the middle school and the junior high school configurations?

5 What are the important common denominators of successful middle level schools?

6 What are some guidelines for establishing a student-centered rather than a subject-centered middle school mission statement?

7 How does one go about developing a positive middle school climate?

8 What are the special features of a full-service school?

9 What are some key factors to consider when putting together a school-wide master schedule?

10 What are the important qualities and skills required of an effective middle level teacher?

11 How does one go about assessing classroom climate in a given setting?

12 What role does creativity play in defining a good middle school program?

13 How should the physical plant best be arranged to facilitate the middle school philosophy and program?

Frequently Identified Goals of Public Education
(as Determined by Gallup Polls of Parents and Taxpayers)

1 Students who are able to form and maintain positive relationships with others

2 Students who can function as part of a community

3 Students who are good problem solvers, creative thinkers, and critical thinkers

4 Students who are literate

5 Students who are able to use technology constructively in and outside the classroom

6 Students who are motivated to learn

7 Students who are competent in a specific skill or curriculum area

8 Students who are lifelong learners

9 Students who are confident enough to take risks

10 Students who are independent and can be self-advocates

11 Students who are accountable for their actions and decisions

12 Students who are able to make wise choices in work, recreation, leisure, and continued learning

13 Students who contribute positively to society

14 Students who are responsible citizens

15 Students who are global stewards

The Definitive Middle School Guide, Revised Edition
Copyright © 2014 World Book, Inc./Incentive Publications, Chicago, IL

Points to Consider When Developing a School Mission Statement

1 A school mission statement is a brief, but essential, sentence that clearly communicates the overall intent and focus for the schooling process in a given educational setting.

2 A school mission statement is important to a school because it very clearly communicates the teaching and learning priorities that a school has established for its "work."

3 A school mission statement is developed through the collaborative efforts of a team that includes representatives from the administrative staff, the faculty, the student population, the parents, and the business community it serves.

4 A school mission statement must reflect the diverse cultures, beliefs, values, and purposes of the entire school population.

5 A mission statement should evolve from a series of data-gathering activities that include surveys or questionnaires, interviews, discussions, and town meetings or forums.

6 A mission statement draft should be written to reflect the input from the various stakeholders represented in the data-gathering process.

7 A mission statement draft should be circulated throughout the school community to elicit recommendations for revisions.

8 A final school mission statement should be written to represent the "best thinking" of all stakeholder groups in the school.

9 A sample middle school mission statement might read as follows: "The mission of XYZ Middle School is to provide our students with the opportunities, resources, and environment to be lifelong learners and productive, responsible citizens in a changing global society."

10 A school mission statement should be evaluated on a regular basis to determine the effect it is having on school practices and individual behavior of those associated with the school.

Characteristics of Schools as Learning Communities

1 **Shared Mission, Vision, and Values**

The essential element of a learning community is shared understandings and common values. What separates a learning community from an ordinary middle school is its collective commitment to guiding principles that articulate what the people in the school believe and what they seek to create.

2 **Collective Inquiry**

The foundation of improvement, growth, and renewal in a learning community is collective inquiry. People in such a community are relentless in questioning the status quo, seeking new methods, testing those methods, and then reflecting on the results. This process has four steps:

a. Public and introspective reflection by members of the team;

b. Shared meaning whereby team members arrive at common ground;

c. Joint planning that moves the team forward to design action steps; and

d. Coordinated action that is carried out both by joint action and independently by individual members of the team.

3 **Collaborative Teams**

The basic structure of the professional learning community is a group of collaborative teams that share a common purpose. Building a school's capacity to learn is a collaborative rather than an individual task.

4 **Oriented to Action and Experimentation**

Professional learning communities are action oriented. Members of such organizations turn aspirations into action and visions into reality. They recognize that learning always occurs in a context of taking action, and they believe engagement and experience are the most effective teachers.

5 **Continuous Improvement**

A persistent discomfort with the status quo and a constant search for a better way characterize the heart of a professional learning community. Each member of the organization is engaged in considering these key questions:

a. What is our fundamental purpose?

b. What do we hope to achieve?

c. What are our strategies for becoming better?

d. What criteria will we use to assess our improvement efforts?

6 **Results Orientation**

Finally, a professional learning community realizes that its efforts to develop a shared mission, vision, and values; engage in collective inquiry; build collaborative teams; take action; and focus on continuous improvement must be assessed on the basis of results rather than intentions.

Source: DuFour, R., & Eaker, R. E. (1998). *Professional learning communities at work: Best practices for enhancing student achievement.* Bloomington, IN: National Education Service.

Identifying Structures of a School That Meet the Needs of Middle Grade Students

1 The identity as a middle school is established, thus eliminating the concept of the middle grades as a mini part of a high school or as a "junior" high school.

2 The school provides a comfortable and supportive physical classroom setting conducive to learning.

3 The constraints and limitations of a rigid schedule and bell system are removed and replaced by a flexible block schedule with no predetermined time periods.

4 The school chooses a grade-level configuration based on the needs and characteristics of pre-adolescents.

5 The integration of subject matter is promoted through the interdisciplinary team and common planning period concepts.

6 "Smallness within bigness" is created by combining teams of teachers and students in surrogate families.

7 The school takes individual differences into account and uses them as one of the bases for planning curriculum and instruction.

8 Both teachers and students are empowered to make decisions.

9 An emphasis on cooperation and collaboration discourages the "winner–loser" or "star" system.

10 Variety in instruction and experience for students is provided through alternative delivery systems, multimedia resources, and exploratory offerings.

11 There is an evident balance between a student-centered program and a subject-centered program.

12 Potential student involvement is valued in all areas of the schooling, and high priority is placed on self-direction, self-description, and self-assessment.

13 A logical transition is provided from the self-contained classroom of the elementary school setting to the departmentalization of the high school setting.

Name _____ Date _____

So, You Think You Have a Great Middle School!

◄ Rate the Success of Your Middle School ►

Directions to School Staff Members: Here's a tool to guide you in taking a close look at your middle school. Sixteen essential elements most often associated with successful middle school programs are listed below. Read each statement and its qualifying sub points carefully. Then react to each statement in terms of its stage of implementation for your school setting. Be honest in your assessment and be ready to cite several examples that document or validate your implementation rating.

Common Denominators of Successful Middle Schools Rating Scale

1 Middle level educators are knowledgeable about the unique needs and characteristics of the early adolescent.

    a. Every educator in my building knows the needs and characteristics associated with the intellectual, moral, physical, emotional-psychological, and social development of the students they serve.

    b. Every educator in my building understands how the growth and development of their students affect student outcomes in these affective and cognitive areas.

    c. Every educator in my building plans and teaches around these developmental needs of the students they serve.

2 Middle level educators maintain a balance between cognitive and academic goals and non-cognitive or affective goals.

    a. Every educator in my building is knowledgeable about the philosophy of the middle school, which places equal value on a student-centered and a subject-centered environment.

    b. Every educator in my building works hard to meet both the cognitive and the affective goals of our program.

    c. Every educator in my building places a high priority on building a school, team, and classroom climate that is conducive to learning and a culture that accepts mistakes as an integral part of the learning process.

The Definitive Middle School Guide, Revised Edition
Copyright © 2014 World Book, Inc./Incentive Publications, Chicago, IL

3 Middle level educators support a wide range of organizational patterns or structures including block scheduling, multi-age grouping, interdisciplinary teaming, developmental or academic grouping, exploratory programs, flexible scheduling, and school-within-a-school options.

   a. Every educator in my building is supportive of the flexible block schedule and uses it appropriately.

   b. Every educator in my building is associated with an interdisciplinary team that has a strong team identity, regular team meetings and student conferences, team rules, team celebrations, and team roles.

   c. Every educator in my building is comfortable with grouping and regrouping students for instruction.

4 Middle level educators insist on both team planning and personal planning time for teachers, recognizing that cooperative planning is essential to the middle school philosophy.

   a. Every educator in my building is a willing and effective team leader or team member.

   b. Educators in my building make optimal use of their team planning time.

   c. Every educator in my building is committed to team planning sessions that focus equal time on both discipline and classroom management techniques, as well as integrated instruction and team-teaching opportunities.

5 Middle level educators are committed to a physical plant where teams are housed together to support interdisciplinary teaming, collaborative team planning, team teaching, and team gatherings or celebrations.

   a. Educators in my building strive to create an attractive and safe "house" for their team of students.

   b. Every educator in my building values the teaming concept that specifies "an effective team is responsible for the same students, for the same extended period of time each day, in the same part of the facility, and with the same team of teachers."

6 Middle level educators push for high academic goals and expectations through a challenging curriculum and through high performance standards for students.

    a. Every educator in my building accepts the rigors of their assigned discipline and strives to help each student reach his or her potential.

    b. Every educator in my building is computer literate and incorporates technology into instruction and student activity.

7 Middle level educators advocate varied instructional strategies and alternative delivery systems for the teaching and learning of the curriculum.

    a. Every educator in my building makes practical and effective use of the following instructional practices on a regular and consistent basis: lecture, discussion, cooperative learning, learning stations, role plays, case studies, games, simulations, independent study projects, technology, and other approved delivery systems.

    b. Every educator in my building understands and applies varied instructional models in the design of their lesson plans, including such models as Bloom's Taxonomy of Critical Thinking, Williams' Taxonomy of Creative Thinking, Gardner's Multiple Intelligences, de Bono's Colored Thinking Hats, Johnson and Johnson's Cooperative Learning Model, and Riegle's Questioning Model.

    c. Every educator in my building is able to differentiate instruction for students through manipulation of content, time, materials, complexity of learning tasks, expected outcomes, and assessment data.

    d. Every educator in my building emphasizes active learning experiences over passive learning experiences in the teaching of academic content and skills to students.

The Definitive Middle School Guide, Revised Edition
Copyright © 2014 World Book, Inc./Incentive Publications, Chicago, IL

8 Middle level educators encourage authentic assessment and evaluation tools and techniques that promote learning and that include portfolio, product, and performance-assessment measures.

   a. Every educator in my building takes standardized and mandated state tests seriously.

   b. Every educator in my building is knowledgeable about the characteristics of authentic assessment measures.

   c. Every educator in my building incorporates portfolio, product, and performance-assessment tools and techniques when evaluating student growth and development.

9 Middle level educators promote a full exploratory program that includes mini-classes, exploratory course options, service clubs, special-interest activities, independent study projects, and field or community experiences.

   a. Every educator in my building promotes the exploratory program as an integral part of our school's curricular offerings.

   b. Every educator in my building participates in one or more of the following exploratory options: mini-classes, service clubs, special-interest activities, study projects, or field and community experiences.

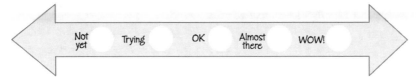

10 Middle level educators understand the need for positive adult-student relationships through a comprehensive advising and counseling program that recognizes teachers as student advocates and as members of an advisor-advisee or home-based advisor program.

   a. Every educator in my building has the opportunity to be an advisor to students.

   b. Every student in my building has a special adult advocate that she or he knows well.

   c. Every educator in my building sees himself or herself as an integral part of the guidance and counseling program in the school.

11 Middle level educators insist on strong parental involvement and community support through team conferences, student-led conferences, school advisory committees, learning communities for adults, community or business partnerships, shared decision-making, and community service programs.

    a. Every educator in my building works diligently at encouraging parental involvement in their classroom or program.

    b. Every educator in my building participates in team conferences and student-led conferences where appropriate to do so.

    c. Every educator in my building uses such communications as memos, newsletters, telephone calls, home visits, e-mail, tweets, invitations, websites, or message boards on a regular and consistent basis.

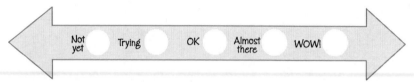

12 Middle level educators celebrate diversity among student, parent, and faculty or staff populations.

    a. Every educator in my building accommodates cultural differences and alternative learning styles.

    b. Every educator in my building promotes high expectations for students among all cultures.

13 Middle level educators place a high priority on violence- and drug-free schools, as well as programs and policies that foster health, wellness, and safety.

    a. Every educator in my building works hard to keep the school safe from violence, drugs, and crime.

    b. Every educator in my building fosters health, wellness, and safety within their domain.

The Definitive Middle School Guide, Revised Edition
Copyright © 2014 World Book, Inc./Incentive Publications, Chicago, IL

14 Middle level educators strive for high quality physical education and intramural programs that provide for differences in physical development.

    a. Every educator in my building is knowledgeable about the differences between intermural and intramural experiences for their students.

    b. Every educator in my building is concerned with appropriate physical development of students, including availability of free- and reduced cost-lunch programs and other health-related services.

15 Middle level educators ensure a smooth transition from elementary to middle school and from middle school to high school.

    a. Every educator in my building recognizes that the middle school setting is different and unique from the elementary school setting and the high school setting.

    b. Every educator in my building respects the need for a successful transition from the elementary school and to the high school, working hard toward those ends.

16 Middle level educators value a rigorous and quality staff development program that is comprehensive, ongoing, lifelong, and that provides alternatives for its participants.

    a. Every educator in my building seeks out and willingly attends most staff development options available to them.

    b. Every educator in my building has a personalized and individual staff development plan.

    c. Every educator in my building supports the need for specially prepared, trained, and qualified teachers and administrators at the middle school level.

Major Distinctions Between the Middle School and the Junior High School

A Middle School

1. is student-centered.
2. fosters collaboration and empowerment of teachers and students.
3. focuses on creative exploration and experimentation of subject matter.
4. allows for flexible scheduling with large blocks of time.
5. varies length of time students are in courses.
6. encourages multi-materials approach to instruction.
7. organizes teachers in interdisciplinary teams with common planning period.
8. arranges work spaces of teamed teachers adjacent to one another.
9. emphasizes both affective and cognitive development of students.
10. offers advisor-advisee teacher-oriented guidance program.
11. provides high-interest "mini-courses" during school day.
12. uses varied delivery systems with high level of interaction among students and teachers.
13. organizes athletics around intramural concept.

A Junior High School

1. is subject-centered.
2. fosters competition and empowerment of administrators.
3. focuses on mastery of concepts and skills in separate disciplines.
4. requires a regular six-period day of 50- to 55-minute periods.
5. offers subjects for one semester or one year.
6. depends on textbook-oriented instruction.
7. organizes teachers in departments with no common planning period.
8. arranges work spaces of teachers according to disciplines taught.
9. emphasizes only cognitive development of students.
10. offers study hall and access to counselor upon request.
11. provides highly structured activity program after school.
12. uses lecture styles a majority of the time with high percentage of teacher talk time.
13. organizes athletics around interscholastic concept.

The Definitive Middle School Guide, Revised Edition
Copyright © 2014 World Book, Inc./Incentive Publications, Chicago, IL

Contributions to the Middle School from the Junior High School

1 The original goal of the junior high school was to provide a separate transition between the elementary school and the high school.

2 Another initial goal was to provide a basis for the scientific study of adolescence.

3 A new grade level pattern (7-8-9 in the case of junior high schools) was implemented to meet the social and physical needs of the age group.

4 The junior high school successfully expanded and enriched the curriculum for early adolescents.

5 A variety of exploratory programs became available to seventh- and eighth-graders.

6 Guidance-oriented homeroom programs were developed and put into operation.

7 The junior high school structure provided clubs and student activities based on special interests and needs.

8 Junior high schools became centers for experimentation with curriculum and scheduling.

9 The structure provided opportunities for students to discover and explore special interests and aptitudes for future vocational decisions.

10 Students were exposed to possibilities for careers in the major fields of learning.

Questions to Answer
When Planning Transitions from Elementary, to Middle, to High School

Note: Use these questions to help develop a strategic plan for making school transitions—from elementary to middle school and from middle school to high school. Give your thoughts or opinions in answering each question.

1 How is the mission of the middle school different from the mission of the elementary school and the high school (or how should it be different)?

2 What is the ideal grade configuration for the elementary school, the middle school, and the high school? Give reasons for your answers.

3 What are the most difficult adjustments a student has to make when moving from the elementary school to the middle school?

4 What are the most difficult adjustments a student has to make when moving from the middle school to the high school?

5 What practices are in place now at your school for assisting students with the transition from elementary school to middle school? Are these practices successful? How could they be improved?

6 What practices are in place now at your school for assisting students with the transition from middle school to high school? Are these practices successful? How could they be improved?

7 What is the primary role of each of these individuals at your school for helping the students make a positive transition from the elementary school to the middle school setting: administrators, guidance counselors, advisory teachers, subject area teachers, and parents?

8 What is the primary role of each of these individuals at your school for helping the students make a positive transition from the middle school to the high school setting: administrators, guidance counselors, advisory teachers, subject area teachers, and parents?

9 What could elementary schools do better in preparing their students to move on to middle schools?

10 What could middle schools do better in preparing their students to move on to high schools?

11 Why do middle schools appear to suffer from a lack of clear identity when compared to both elementary schools and high schools?

12 As you reflect on your own transitions from one level of schooling to another, what problems were the most difficult for you to deal with or overcome?

13 If you had one piece of advice to give a student who is in transition from elementary school to middle school, what would it be?

14 If you had one piece of advice to give a student who is in transition from middle school to high school, what would it be?

The Definitive Middle School Guide, Revised Edition
Copyright © 2014 World Book, Inc./Incentive Publications, Chicago, IL

Needs and Characteristics of Early Adolescents

Physically, youth of this age tend to . . .

1. experience irregular growth spurts in physical development.

2. be self-conscious about trying to learn new physical feats.

3. experience fluctuations in basal metabolism, causing restlessness and listlessness.

4. be capable of initiating good personal hygiene habits.

5. have ravenous appetites.

6. experience periods of extreme fatigue and extreme energy.

7. mature at varying rates of speed.

8. be at a plateau in brain growth/development.

9. be disturbed by changes of the body and its rate of development.

10. tire easily and be reluctant to admit it.

11. be highly physical.

12. experience uneven bone/muscle growth, and as a result, exhibit a lack of coordination.

13. be very concerned with their rate of sexual development.

14. be lacking in good nutritional habits.

15. be easily upset if they are not physically coordinated and physically attractive according to existing cultural norms or standards.

Intellectually, youth of this age tend to . . .

16. be highly curious about life in general.

17. have difficulty acquiring new conceptual skills.

18. prefer active over passive learning experiences.

19. demand privileges but avoid responsibility.

20. relate to real-life problems, situations, and abstract ideas like "honesty, justice, and liberty."

21. develop "hero-like" figures as role models.

22. have interests that fluctuate frequently and sporadically.

23. experience metacognition (the ability to analyze complex thought processes).

24. like discussions of personal experiences with adults.

25. be easily discouraged if not able to achieve.

26. seek constant approval and reinforcement from adults they admire.

27. have a varying range of creative expression.

28. be intellectually curious about the real world and the environment around them.

29. be capable of exploring and selecting learning materials and experiences on their own.

30. be trusted to assume personal responsibility for their own learning.

Psychologically and emotionally, youth of this age tend to . . .

31 display erratic and inconsistent behavior.

32 worry over schoolwork, exams, and report cards.

33 be highly sensitive to criticism while possessing a desire for approval.

34 have ambivalent attitudes toward being independent while holding on to certain delights of childhood.

35 be moody, restless, and self-conscious.

36 vacillate among interests.

37 be searching for identity and acceptance from peers.

38 be easily angered and less able to recover than when they were younger.

39 seek independence from authority.

40 identify and relate to the behaviors inherent in sex roles.

41 be emotionally vulnerable.

42 rebel at the idea of having a baby sitter or other type of imposed supervision.

Socially, youth of this age tend to . . .

43 be rebellious and critical of parents and others in supervisory roles.

44 show independence in choice of friends.

45 be confused and frightened by new school or social settings.

46 crave periods of being alone.

47 show fierce loyalty to peer group values.

48 be concerned with presenting positive images to the peer group.

49 be aggressive and argumentative more often than not.

50 exhibit an indifference to adults, especially teachers and parents.

51 overreact when criticized or embarrassed.

52 change friends and peer groups often in response to changing interests, needs, and wishes.

53 experiment with new identities.

54 explore certain aspects of their own sexuality.

Morally and ethically, youth of this age tend to . . .

55 be idealistic.

56 have a strong sense of fairness.

57 be reflective and introspective in thoughts and feelings.

58 confront moral and ethical questions head-on.

59 ask large and ambiguous questions about the meaning of life.

60 show compassion for underdog situations and environmental or social issues.

61 be impatient with pace of change.

62 be slow to acknowledge own faults and flaws.

The Definitive Middle School Guide, Revised Edition
Copyright © 2014 World Book, Inc./Incentive Publications, Chicago, IL

Important Needs
Middle School Students Have
While in School

Students of all ages have several needs that must be met throughout the schooling process to be successful and productive. These needs impact both their behavior patterns and their academic achievements. As you read through these identified needs, discuss or write down some classroom or school activities, events, experiences, policies, procedures, or programs that directly address each need as stated. Be specific in your comments.

1 Students need to understand that they will be held responsible for their behaviors and their actions.

2 Students need to understand that personal property and the rights of others must be respected at all times.

3 Students need order, routine, structure, and fixed responsibility in their daily lives.

4 Students need attention and expressions of caring or nurturing throughout the school experience.

5 Students need an environment relatively free from anxiety, conflict, and unhealthy competition.

6 Students need assistance in standing up to peer pressures that move them to conform to the behavioral norms of outside groups.

7 Students need to realize that consequences follow behavior. (This amounts to, "If I do THIS, then THIS might happen.")

8 Students need sufficient rest, nourishment, and healthy practices.

9 Students need protection from television and Internet violence, crime, and the influences of advertising.

10 Students need the benefits of clear and positive communication between home and school.

High-Priority Areas to Consider When Creating a Master Schedule

1 Build in a 20- to 30-minute advisory class for all students.

2 Provide common planning time for interdisciplinary teams.

3 Place all core teachers on a single academic team with no cross teaming.

4 Maintain a student-teacher ratio of 150 students per four-person team.

5 Allow students to have options in choosing exploratory classes.

6 Offer a co-curricular program.

7 Plan for multi-age groupings in electives and mini-classes.

8 Organize electives and academic classes on a trimester schedule.

9 Program reasonable times for lunch periods.

10 Encourage a "school within a school" concept or a multi-age pilot team.

The Definitive Middle School Guide, Revised Edition
Copyright © 2014 World Book, Inc./Incentive Publications, Chicago, IL

Bits of Advice for Creating a Middle School's Master Schedule

1 Remember that the schedule for every school is unique because the demographics of every school vary.

2 Set priorities for scheduling and accept the fact that every schedule has its share of trade-offs or compromises.

3 Be aware that with more single or special classes or programs, more conflicts will surface during the scheduling process.

4 Limit or eliminate prerequisite courses in the exploratory areas.

5 Don't depend on scheduling software packages to solve all scheduling problems.

6 The master schedule must serve the students first, the teachers second, and the administrators third.

7 A school must have the courage to try new paradigms when setting up the schedule. Try something different.

8 A school must live with a master schedule to realize its limitations, advantages, and possibilities.

9 Keep a sense of humor.

Suggestions for Facility Requirements for Middle Schools

1 Team classrooms should be in close proximity to one another. This will allow instant communication and will cut down on time required for students to travel from one classroom to another.

2 These classrooms should adapt easily for grouping and regrouping of students. It may be necessary to vary class size, learning experiences, and delivery systems.

3 The environment must be safe and secure for students and staff at all times. This issue is of great concern to parents.

4 The furniture and equipment in classrooms should be functional, movable, and size-appropriate. Remember that flexibility is the key in middle school.

5 The media center should be the center of all curriculum and instruction, not just a library with books. The media specialist is the "expert" in curriculum, materials, equipment, and information.

6 Technological equipment and assistance should be readily available to classrooms and the media center.

7 The physical plant should be aesthetically pleasing and attractive. This enhances the setting for learning.

8 A large, well-lit group instruction or meeting area (with shades if necessary) should be made available for use by all teams. A good plan is to have a signup sheet posted at or near the entrance to the room and to ask team leaders to sign up in ink for no more than two consecutive days at a time.

9 It is desirable for teachers to have an assigned team meeting room for their use. A round table, comfortable chairs, and a bulletin board with a calendar enhance team-meeting space.

10 Plan effective traffic patterns so that the minimum number of students is changing classes at one time. The environment (both inside and outside of classrooms) should reflect the physical needs of students.

11 If lockers are provided, consider height and size. Assign lockers to students whose team classrooms are in the same area.

Ways to Maximize Space in a School Setting

All of these suggestions for better meeting the space needs of students to improve the delivery of content and instruction are relatively simple and inexpensive to implement. They do, however, require some creative thinking and openness to new ways of doing things.

1 Extend the school day by keeping the media center open for student and family use before school, after school, in the evenings, or on weekends. Use this time and space for special study sessions, tutoring sessions, remediation sessions, or enrichment sessions.

2 Decorate school hallways, corridors, auditorium stage areas, or cafeteria spaces and use foldout tables and stackable chairs as furniture.

3 Place television sets in the media center or in the cafeteria areas for teaching enrichment classes such as foreign language and extended art, drama, and music topics.

4 Use bulletin boards, bookshelves, hanging posters, and clotheslines for learning stations within the regular classroom.

5 Use outdoor courtyards or picnic tables or gazebos as extensions of classroom instructional spaces.

6 Use color as the foundation for separating room areas designated as learning spaces.

7 Use an empty conference room or classroom as a student lounge for enrichment activities or as an audiovisual room for showing movies or videos, using a signup schedule and a volunteer to run the equipment.

8 Encourage students to help reorganize classroom learning spaces and table or desk arrangements on a regular and consistent basis.

9 Provide a supply table where students can quickly replenish forgotten or broken pencils and misplaced or depleted packages of notebook paper without disruption of other students.

10 Use magnets to clip teacher notes and lecture outlines on the chalkboard during instruction. This helps to avoid misplaced papers and to give quick references to ideas while keeping teacher's hands free for instruction.

Characteristics of an Exemplary Middle School Building

1 The design of a developmentally responsive middle school facility should be first and foremost safe, inviting, and caring; it should promote a sense of community and encourage learning.

2 The overall purpose and functions of the exemplary middle school facility must center on the intellectual, social, emotional, moral, and physical developmental needs of early adolescents.

3 The overall size or scale of the building should be larger and less compact than an elementary school, but smaller than a high school. It should be made to accommodate the projected number of students through specialized spaces in a relatively compact facility so as not to overwhelm the students but rather to provide a gradual transition to the much larger high school facility.

4 The larger spaces, such as the gymnasium, learning resource center, and cafeteria, should be broken up into smaller parts in a number of ways by varying ceiling heights, by changing inside wall or floor construction materials, by arranging of furniture, and by providing alternative seating configurations.

5 Corridors should be relatively short in length to facilitate faculty monitoring and supervising of students as they move throughout the building.

6 The concept of "wayfinding" should be related to both scale and organization of the building. In other words, the building's spaces should be organized in such a way to keep students from getting lost or feeling overwhelmed by the enormity of the facility as they navigate from one space to another.

7 The building's physical appearance should inspire identification with and pride in the school by students, parents, faculty, and visitors alike. It should have a strong image which conveys a sense that "important business" is being conducted here at all times.

8 The ideal middle school facility should be comprised of classroom clusters (or pods) and activity centers, all of which are well-defined as separate entities as well as in terms of their relationship to one another. Clusters create small, supportive communities of learning. Classroom clusters should

a) be well-defined by grade level;

b) be separate from non-academic uses;

c) have corridors that support small-group learning, socializing, and locker usage;

d) have interconnected classrooms;

e) have centrally located team rooms with lockable storage and provisions for such machines as copiers, computers, or printers;

f) have a small meeting space for student groups; and

g) have physical or visual clues for defining boundaries between clusters.

Based on the case of the Central Tree Middle School.
Adapted from "Central Tree Middle School Post Occupancy Evaluation," http://www.designshare.com/Awards.

Suggestions for Developing a Positive Middle School Climate

1 Develop a school motto and logo and use them widely.

2 Create procedures for referring students to the office to recognize positive behaviors in addition to the usual office referrals for problematic behavior.

3 Reinforce good attendance at all school functions through individual and group incentives.

4 Display student work in all classrooms and throughout the building on a large scale.

5 Use marquees, school windows, and lobby showcases to convey positive messages.

6 Designate and maintain quality teacher, student, and parent lounges as "time in" rooms.

7 Take care when stating or promoting school rules so they take on a positive rather than a punitive flavor.

8 Support and encourage an active student council or government and parent advisory groups.

9 Seize opportunities to augment school life with extracurricular activities.

10 Form an "academic boosters" group to promote academics within the school.

11 Issue many invitations and encourage people to visit your school.

12 Draw attention to personal and professional growth of staff members.

13 Develop a positive marketing plan for your school that includes a multimedia presentation; regular newspaper, radio, TV, and web promotions; and parent communications.

Ways to Further Enhance Your School Climate
(Tips for the Principal)

1 Order business cards for all staff members and print the school's mission statement on the back. Encourage teachers to distribute these at parent conferences, professional workshops, national meetings, and community events.

2 Place an electronic reader board in the teacher's lounge or student cafeteria to pass on information, humor, and personal messages.

3 Consider labeling your hallways with street signs that promote positive thoughts and that help visitors find their way around the school. Consider such street names as "Friendly Freeway, Learning Drive, Empowerment Lane, Fun Way, Academic Avenue," etc.

4 Hold occasional staff meetings in unusual locations, such as local tourist attractions, community library, shopping mall, museum, or corporate conference room.

5 Organize a "brown bag breakfast" day once a month for staff. Stuff the treat bags with a carton of juice, a bagel and cream cheese, and a piece of fruit for a mid-morning snack.

6 Prepare stick-on labels for school telephones that carry such messages as "Attitudes are contagious. Is yours worth catching?"

7 Once a month, appoint a teacher, student, or parent to be your ASSOCIATE OF THE DAY. Have them follow you around and do everything you do including sharing in telephone calls, reading the mail, visiting classrooms, or attending meetings. Present them with a certificate celebrating their position as "Associate of the Day."

8 One day a month, organize LUNCH WITH THE PRINCIPAL DAY and invite a dozen students to have lunch with you in a unique place on campus. Focus on different groups such as ESOL students, at-risk students, honor students, troubled students, or specific grade of students.

9 Insert a "Dear Gabby" column in the school newsletter for staff and parents that encourages them to send in anonymous questions to be answered by the principal. These could center on "hot topics" or "controversial issues."

10 Schedule a "school fair" to be held at the local shopping mall. Include booths for each classroom or grade. Plan to promote your school's curriculum, student work, student demonstrations, teacher lesson plans, and displays of instructional materials. Promote a positive message: "YOUR TAX DOLLARS AT WORK."

11 Construct a series of "sandwich board" announcements to place strategically throughout the school and community announcing special events or accomplishments of the school populations.

12 Organize a traveling poster display for your school. Obtain a variety of commercial or handmade posters that promote positive messages and behaviors. Hang this collection in each wing of the building for a month at a time until all parts of the building have housed the poster collection for at least 30 days.

13 Borrow or rent a motor home, bus, or large van for one day or week and turn it into a "traveling road show" that promotes your school throughout the community. Include written materials, DVDs, podcasts, Power Point presentations, enlarged photographs, and displays of student work. Schedule visits for the "school mobile" at highly visible sites, such as shopping centers, voting polls, government buildings, local festivals, and sporting events.

The Definitive Middle School Guide, Revised Edition
Copyright © 2014 World Book, Inc./Incentive Publications, Chicago, IL

Questions to Use to Assess Creativity in Your School

How does your school feel about innovation and creativity in the curriculum and in the assessment process that drives the curriculum? Use this list of questions to determine your school's Creativity Quotient (or C.Q.).

1 Is creativity highly regarded by your school's administration and faculty members?

2 Is creativity included in your school's mission statement, goals, and objectives?

3 Are creative ideas implemented quickly in your school setting?

4 Does your school encourage brainstorming sessions as part of its agenda for in-service days?

5 Do you have staff meetings to discuss opportunities and successes as frequently as those to discuss problems and procedures?

6 Is your school's student assessment program designed to generate qualitative as well as quantitative information about your students?

7 Do you combine creative enterprises and innovative programs with your best and brightest teachers?

8 Do you maintain the notion that faculty is here first and foremost to meet the creative- and critical-thinking skill needs of the students?

9 Do you celebrate creativity in your school with ceremony, traditions, and rewards?

10 Are innovators in your school treated like heroes?

Important Standards for Effective Middle Level Teachers

Standard 1: Early Adolescent Development

The effective middle school teacher

- understands the range of developmental characteristics of adolescence within social, cultural, and societal contexts and uses this knowledge to facilitate student learning.
- creates learning opportunities that are appropriate and challenging for all early adolescents.
- creates positive classroom environments where developmental differences are respected and where individual potential is encouraged.
- adapts curriculum, instruction, resources, and assessment to provide for the range of differences in early adolescents.

Standard 2: Healthy Development of Early Adolescents

The effective middle school teacher

- demonstrates an understanding of the risk behaviors of early adolescents and the changes in family setting and society that affect their development by establishing a learning environment that promotes positive, productive, and healthy development.
- creates opportunities for early adolescents to make decisions, create personal goals, and identify their place within the context of the larger society.
- engages students in activities related to their interpersonal, community, and social responsibilities.
- creates a supportive classroom environment for discussion of issues of healthy development.
- utilizes school and community resources to support the health, social, and personal development of early adolescents.

Standard 3: Middle School Philosophy and School Organization

The effective middle school teacher

- understands the philosophical foundations of developmentally responsive middle schools and the unique school organizational features that these schools employ and carry out successfully.
- cooperates with other teachers to schedule instructional time effectively, matching learning priorities with the blocks of time necessary for student mastery.
- teams with colleagues to discuss students' needs and to develop units and programs that address developmental needs of young adolescents.
- creates interdisciplinary learning experiences that allow students to link knowledge, skills, and tools of inquiry from several subject areas.

- serves in an advisory capacity to early adolescents, advocates healthy development of students and makes appropriate referrals to professionals within the school and community.
- designs and implements exploratory activities to engage students in a variety of learning experiences.
- provides orientation to students in transition from an elementary school, from another middle school, or to a secondary school.

Standard 4: Middle School Curriculum

The effective middle school teacher

- understands and can successfully implement the established middle school curriculum.
- integrates current knowledge and skills from multiple subject areas and includes literacy and critical- or creative-thinking skills in designing the curriculum.
- plans curriculum activities that address varied intelligences, learning styles, and modes of expression.
- encourages multiple uses and applications of technology throughout the curriculum on a regular and consistent basis.
- incorporates learners' ideas, interests, and questions into a curriculum that expands students' understanding of the world.
- develops curriculum that encourages students to observe, question, and interpret ideas from diverse perspectives.
- develops assessment strategies as a part of curriculum planning.

Standard 5: Middle School Instruction

The effective middle school teacher

- understands the breadth of instructional options available to her or him and employs a variety of instructional strategies that are developmentally appropriate for the varying learning abilities and styles of early adolescents.
- uses a variety of instructional tools, techniques, methods, and resources that are motivational and appropriate for adolescents.
- incorporates technology as an instructional tool wherever feasible to do so.
- uses a variety of formal and informal assessment techniques to evaluate the progress of students and to modify teaching and learning strategies.
- creates learning experiences that encourage exploration and problem solving so that the learner is actively engaged in applying ideas.
- plans effective instruction individually and in cooperation with colleagues.
- participates in professional development activities to be current in his or her practice.
- establishes a positive learning climate in the classroom and works to maintain such a climate through a classroom management plan.

Standard 6: Family Involvement

The effective middle school teacher

- has a thorough understanding of the role of the family in a student's educational development and is able to use this knowledge to assist and support early adolescents and their families in the early adolescent's education.

- identifies and uses community resources to foster student learning.

- acts as an advocate for students in the larger community, as well as in school.

- participates in activities designed to enhance educational experiences beyond the school walls.

- encourages student participation in activities designed to enhance educational experiences beyond school walls.

- establishes respectful and productive relationships and partnerships to support students' learning and well-being.

Standard 7: Teacher Roles

The effective middle school teacher

- understands and performs the complex role of the teacher of early adolescents within the context of early adolescent development, middle school curriculum, instruction, and school organization.

- models positive attitudes and appropriate behaviors for the early adolescent.

- serves as an advisor to a small number of early adolescents.

- acts as an advocate and mentor for early adolescents.

- works as a member of a team on an ongoing basis.

- engages in and supports appropriate professional practices for self and colleagues.

Standard 8: Collaborative Behavior

The effective middle school teacher

- understands the importance of collaboration with families, resource persons, and community groups, and collaborates to improve schools for adolescents.

- collaborates with colleagues and other professionals to reflect on best practices, problem solving, and new ideas to improve education.

- teams with colleagues to develop interdisciplinary curriculum and instruction.

- participates in team and school activities designed to create a positive and productive learning environment.

- collaborates with community groups and other resource persons to promote education and achieve common goals for early adolescents.

Adapted from: Indiana Professional Standard Board (1998). Early adolescence generalist standards. Retrieved from: http://web.archive.org/web/20041001162020/http://isu.indstate.edu/ruebel/eagstand.htm

Findings from the Published Literature Related to School Structures and Climate

FINDING #1:

NMSA's 2005 update of *This We Believe* states that the developmentally responsive middle schools are those that have these characteristics:

. . . Curriculum that is relevant, challenging, integrative, and exploratory

. . . Assessment and evaluation that promote quality learning

. . . Multiple learning and teaching approaches that respond to their diversity

. . . Students and teachers engaged in active learning

. . . Organizational structures that support meaningful relationships and learning

. . . An adult advocate for every student

. . . Multifaceted guidance and support services

. . . A shared vision that guides decisions

. . . Courageous, collaborative leadership

. . . High expectations for every member of the learning community

. . . An inviting, supportive, and safe environment

. . . Educators who value working with this age group and are prepared to do so

. . . School-wide efforts that foster health, wellness, and safety

. . . School-initiated family and community partnerships

Source: Erb, T. O. (Ed.). (2005). *This we believe in action: Implementing successful middle level schools.* Westerville, OH: National Middle School Association.

FINDING #2:

Turning Points 2000 makes the seven following recommendations for schools:

. . . Curriculum is based on rigorous, public academic standards for student knowledge and performance, is relevant to adolescents, and is centered on how students learn most effectively.

. . . Use teaching methods aimed at preparing students to reach higher levels of achievement and become lifelong learners.

. . . Middle grade teachers must excel at teaching early adolescents, and be provided with various and continuing professional development opportunities.

. . . Cultivate relationships for learning that lead to a climate of intellectual development and a cohesive community of common educational purpose.

. . . Govern democratically, through participation by all school staff members.

. . . Create and ensure a safe and healthy environment, which leads to better academic performance and fosters supportive and ethical citizens.

. . . Involve parents and communities in reinforcing student learning and positive development.

Source: Jackson, A., Davis, G. A., Abeel, M., Bordonaro, A., & Carnegie Council on Adolescent Development. (2000). *Turning points 2000: Educating adolescents in the 21st century.* New York: Teachers College Press.

FINDING #3:

John H. Lounsbury points out that the following research-based generalizations can serve as guideposts for deciding on ways that early adolescents might be better served by home, school, and community:

. . . Early adolescence is a distinctive developmental stage of life.

. . . The general public has limited understanding of these 10- to 15-year-olds.

. . . The accelerated physical and personal development that occurs during this period is the greatest in the human life cycle and is marked by great variance in both the timing and rate of growth.

. . . These are the years during which each individual forms an adult personality, basic values, and attitudes—those things that determine one's behavior.

. . . Adolescents reach physical maturity at an earlier age than their grandparents did and they acquire apparent sophistication earlier than in previous generations.

. . . They seek autonomy and independence.

. . . They are by nature explorers, curious and adventuresome.

. . . They have intellectual capacities seldom tapped by traditional schooling.

. . . They learn best through interaction and activity rather than listening.

. . . They seek interaction with adults and opportunities to engage in activities that have inherent value.

. . . Their physical and social development become priorities.

. . . They are sensitive, vulnerable, and emotional.

. . . They are open to influence by the significant others in their lives.

. . . A significant portion of today's teenage population is alienated from society.

Source: Lounsbury, J. H. (2002). *Understanding and appreciating the wonder years.* Retrieved from http://web.archive.org/web/20020701045805 /http://www.nmsa.org/moya/new2002/pk_related_understanding.html.

FINDING #4:

As explained by Dr. Neila Connors:

"Creating the ambiance" of a school has seven key components:

. . . Ensure the physical, intellectual, emotional, and social safety of all teachers, students, and administrators.

. . . Embrace change and remain open to the notion that change enriches personal and professional lives.

. . . School leaders must project a positive attitude daily.

. . . Clear communication school-wide through the process of listening, speaking, reading, writing, thinking, and providing feedback.

. . . Practice good human relation skills since "positive and caring relationships are the heart of what makes a school extraordinary."

. . . Active participation by all directs the focus on what needs to be done, how to do it, and what outcomes will be celebrated.

. . . Positive public relations create a school where community members feel welcomed and supported by educators.

Source: Connors, N. A. (2000). *If you don't feed the teachers, they eat the students!: A guide to success for administrators and teachers.* Nashville, TN: Incentive Publications.

Review and Reflect

on School Structures and Climate
That Successfully Meet the Needs of Middle Level Students

Level 1: Remembering   Your Reflections

Task

List at least three unique needs and characteristics of the early adolescent in each of the following categories.

Intellectual Development

Moral Development

Physical Development

Emotional-Psychological Development

Social Development

Level 2: Understanding   Your Reflections

Task

Summarize the major benefits a middle school organizational structure can provide (over that of a junior high configuration) to meet the personal and educational needs of the 10- to 14-year-old.

In your own words . . .

Level 3: Applying   Your Reflections

Task

Assume that you are preparing to interview the principal of an exemplary middle school. Write four questions you would want to ask about the factors that make that school a successful one.

1.

2.

3.

4.

continued on page 48

continued

Review and Reflect
on School Structures and Climate
That Successfully Meet the Needs of Middle Level Students

Level 4: Analyzing   Your Reflections

Task

It has been said that all middle level students are at risk. Explain why this is likely to be true from your perspective and experiences.

Level 5: Evaluating   Your Reflections

Task

Use the Middle School Rating instrument and its common denominators of successful middle schools to judge the effectiveness of your middle school. (See pages 22–27.) Briefly summarize your thoughts about the results.

Level 6: Creating   Your Reflections

Task

Get ready to create an observation checklist or anecdotal record form that a teacher could use in the classroom to identify and document special needs, characteristics, and interests of the students in the class. Jot some ideas here to get started.

The Definitive Middle School Guide, Revised Edition
Copyright © 2014 World Book, Inc./Incentive Publications, Chicago, IL

Module II

Interdisciplinary Teaming

and

Block Scheduling

Contents of Module II

Overview of
Interdisciplinary Teaming and Block Scheduling

Interdisciplinary teaming encourages:

- conservation of time and space in an ever-expanding curriculum.
- elimination of overlap in varied subject areas.
- promotion of collaboration among students and teachers.
- coordination of assignments.
- reduction of fragmentation of learning from one discipline to another.
- relevance of motivational and enrichment projects.
- multiple use of resources, teaching tools, and instructional techniques.
- recognition of interrelationships among different subjects.
- promotion of critical and creative thinking through the application of skills and concepts across subject area boundaries.

Teachers' advantages include:

- improved intellectual stimulation provided by closer association with colleagues.
- improved discipline because of varied teacher personalities, styles, and strategies.
- improved delivery system provided through flexible schedules and group sizes.
- improved colleague support through shared goals, esprit de corps, and communication.
- improved evaluation through team input and assessment techniques.
- improved time management through team meetings and common planning periods.
- improved instruction through diversity in teacher talents, styles, and interests.
- improved coordination of curriculum through interdisciplinary instruction and joint planning in areas such as homework, texts, grades, and field trips.

Students' advantages include:

- improved student-teacher relationships through sense of belonging to established team or school family with special identity, customs, and rituals.
- improved motivation and enthusiasm for learning through varied instructional materials, techniques, and personalities.
- improved attendance and behavior because of consistent environment with common rules, guidelines, and procedures.
- increased academic, social, and Individual support from a wider number of adults who know and care about each student.
- improved opportunity for achievement through flexible grouping and scheduling options.
- improved self-concept through team-initiated advisory groups.
- improved chances for matching teaching styles with learning styles.

Terms Important for Understanding Interdisciplinary Teaming and Block Scheduling

Collaboration: a relationship between individuals or organizations that enables the participants to accomplish goals more successfully than they could have separately (Educators are finding that they must collaborate with each other to deal with increasingly complex issues.)

Common planning time: an arrangement of planning time that provides for teachers on the same team to have a common planning period during which they can meet together on a daily basis to hold team meetings, student or parent conferences, and plan interdisciplinary instruction

Conflict resolution: a process for recognizing that conflict exists and is a pathway to personal growth, that one can learn to solve problems effectively, and that there are alternative solutions to a problem for one to consider

Data-based decision making: a decision-making process that involves analysis of existing sources of information (class and school attendance, grades, test scores) and new data (student portfolios, surveys, interviews) to make decisions about the school and its programs (The process involves organizing and interpreting the data and creating action steps.)

Empowerment: enabling teachers to manage themselves and their students in pursuit of organizational and instructional goals

Flexible block scheduling: scheduling based on time blocks (A flexible block schedule is a "chunk" of uninterrupted teaching time allocated to a given group of students and teachers on an interdisciplinary team.) It allows the team to do one or more of several things:

a) Vary size of instructional groups of classes;

b) Vary frequency or number of times a group or class meets;

c) Vary length of instructional time for a group or class;

d) Vary order or sequence of meeting and planning times; and

e) Vary number of groups or classes that meet within an established block of time.

In short, block time scheduling assigns a group of students to a team of teachers and provides a period of time in which two to four class periods of 45 to 60 minutes each are in session. The team usually becomes responsible for instruction in math, science, social studies, and language arts. The goal is to establish a school within a school, which nurtures a bonding between students and teachers.

> *Note: This differs from the typical high school block schedule model which typically schedules a four-period day, in which students take two core and two elective courses in one semester to earn a year's credit. Usually, the high school instructional blocks are approximately 90 minutes long.*

Goals: statements of expected outcomes that represent the desirable end results of education as described by individual schools, districts, states, or government agencies

Interdisciplinary instruction: an instructional delivery system by which teams of teachers combine their expertise and course content to integrate the disciplines and correlate common areas of the curriculum

Interdisciplinary teaming: an instructional delivery system in which a mixed-discipline group of teachers shares the same group of students for an uninterrupted block of instructional time (Teams vary in size from two to five teachers and serve student groups ranging from 70 to 150 in number.)

Looping: the practice of keeping a teacher and a class together for two or three years (Sometimes called teacher rotation, teacher cycling, or student-teacher progression, it has been practiced at the elementary level for many decades.)

Norm: a system of shared beliefs (These beliefs produce patterns of behavior within a group of people, organizational structures, and control systems. A norm is to a group what a habit is to an individual.)

Participative leadership: shared leadership that creates interdependency among its team members by empowering, freeing up, and serving others

Shared responsibility: a system and environment in which all team members feel as responsible as the administrator for the performance of the work unit

Stages of middle school team development: five basic stages through which teachers ordinarily progress when establishing a specific interdisciplinary team, which are:

a) **Forming Stage** .... Insecure members depend on the leader for direction;

b) **Storming Stage** .... Members encounter conflict in working toward consensus;

c) **Norming Stage** .... Members finally work together as a team;

d) **Performing Stage** .... Members see increased student achievement and experience job satisfaction; and

e) **Transforming Stage** ..... Members welcome and enjoy change as teams constantly re-create themselves.

Synergism: a phenomenon in which simultaneous actions of separate entities together have greater total effect than the sum of their individual efforts

Team handbook: a handbook for the students and parents served by the interdisciplinary team (The purpose of this handbook is to share the team's philosophy, mission statement, goals, policies, procedures, rules, expectations, events, and plans for the school year.)

Team leader: the interdisciplinary team member who facilitates the teaming process for its members by coordinating the team's meetings, activities, budget decisions, and communications with the school's administrative team

Team meeting: daily team meeting held during the team's common planning time in order to carry on the assigned duties and responsibilities of the team itself

Team rules and discipline plan: a meaningful set of team rules and discipline procedures that are consistent throughout the school day and throughout the interdisciplinary team regardless of the varied teacher personalities, styles, and disciplines

Guiding Questions for Interdisciplinary Teaming and Block Scheduling

1 What is the single most important reason for teaming in the middle school?

2 How are teams best organized?

3 What are advantages and potential disadvantages of the teaming process for teachers?

4 What are advantages and potential disadvantages of the teaming process for students?

5 What are the characteristics of a successful team?

6 What are the roles of team leaders and team members?

7 What are some different tools or techniques that might be used to place teachers on a team?

8 What are some things that team members can do to support the concept of interdisciplinary teaming?

9 How can teachers determine their own readiness for interdisciplinary teaming?

10 What are some things team members can do to create a team identity?

11 What are some factors that can create friction and cause a team to be unsuccessful in meeting its goals?

12 What are some good reasons for a joint team planning period?

13 What goes on in a productive team meeting?

14 How is student achievement affected by interdisciplinary instruction?

15 How do teams integrate curriculum and instruction?

16 How does block scheduling contribute to the effectiveness of interdisciplinary teams?

17 What are the advantages of block scheduling for teachers?

18 What are the advantages of block scheduling for students?

19 How does research support interdisciplinary and block schedule teaming in the middle school setting?

20 What are some things teachers and administrators can do to "sell" the concept of interdisciplinary teaming and block scheduling to parents or guardians?

The Definitive Middle School Guide, Revised Edition
Copyright © 2014 World Book, Inc./Incentive Publications, Chicago, IL

Things to Remember
When Developing Teams

1 Team development is evolutionary. It does not happen quickly.

2 Team members must be trained in the "art and science" of teaming so they share the same vision and understanding of what teaming is all about.

3 Team effectiveness and team activities will vary from site to site because implementation of interdisciplinary teams is unique to each location.

4 Not every team member will embrace the teaming concept (and the resulting empowerment) to the same degree.

5 All team members must be assured that the teaming concept will improve work life and the performance of students.

6 Team development will not follow a straight path, but will encounter ups and downs in its evolution.

7 Team leaders and administrators must model the behavior they want their team members to display.

8 Teams are often highly motivated at the beginning of their teaming experience, but require ongoing, consistent guidance, training, and support from leaders.

9 Team members should complement, not clone, one another's styles, temperament, skills, talents, and interests.

10 Teams should have procedures or provisions for changing work assignments in situations where team members do not work well together.

11 Teams should begin making easy decisions before they tackle difficult decisions.

12 Operating policies, procedures, and systems, once developed, may need to be changed over time to allow for continued growth and empowerment.

13 Teams should emphasize communication as the "soul" of their existence, both within the team and outside the team.

14 Teams must be rewarded for their successes.

Name _____ Date _____

Questions to Ask of Individual Teachers
When Forming Teams

> *Directions: When forming teams, each teacher should be asked the questions below. Make a copy of the page for each teacher. Use the space beneath each question to write your answer.*

1 What subjects are you certified to teach?

_____

_____

2 What subjects would you like to teach? Please list in priority order.

_____

_____

3 What grades would you like to teach? Please list in priority order.

_____

_____

4 What special interests, talents, or hobbies do you have?

_____

_____

5 What special skills do you bring to the team?

_____

_____

6 How would you describe your basic teaching style?

_____

_____

7 Who are some staff members you would like to work with on a team?

_____

_____

8 Who are some staff members you would prefer not to work with on a team?

_____

_____

9 Where do you see yourself professionally in three to five years?

_____

_____

10 What else would you want your team members to know about you?

_____

_____

Possible Team Member Traits to Consider

Directions:

> a. *Form a small group of three or four members.*
>
> b. *Suppose your group has been given the responsibility of selecting four persons to serve on an interdisciplinary team in a middle level school for the next year.*
>
> c. *Read through the descriptions of potential team members and choose your ideal coworkers.*
>
> d. *Record your choices in the spaces provided at the end of the descriptions.*
>
> e. *Work with your group to reach a consensus on who should be on the team. Be prepared to defend your choices!*

1 Helen Humorous

Helen is the funniest character in the group. She often makes everyone laugh with her keen sense of humor. When things get dull, you can count on Helen to liven things up. She always makes the best of a situation and helps others to do so as well.

2 Tom Truthful

Tom always tells what he feels. He never lies to the group or hides things from them. He will always tell team members the truth (and always with tact) when asked a direct question.

3 Laura Leader

Laura is a natural leader. She is well respected and most people listen to her. She's careful to include other points of view when trying to help make a group decision.

4 Carl Creative

Carl is the most creative teacher on the staff. He will stop at nothing to promote his innovative ideas and materials with the team. He tends to motivate both staff and students.

5 Ida Informed

Ida knows all about middle schools. She has a wealth of knowledge and experience in all areas of interdisciplinary teaming and instruction and will provide the group with information about every important middle school issue.

6 Frank Favorite

Frank knows the principal well and can get special favors. He is dedicated to the teaching profession and knows how to arrange his priorities when asking for budgetary support from the administration.

7 **Mary Motivation**

Mary knows the secret to inspiring both teachers and students. She is constantly using original tools and techniques for keeping her colleagues on task and getting the tough jobs done.

8 **Wanda Worker**

Wanda is a workaholic and never minds going the extra mile to complete a project or an assignment. She truly enjoys doing "more than her share" and will often bail out a teammate when necessary.

9 **Ernie Energetic**

Ernie is a beginning teacher who has more energy than ten teachers put together. He did his student teaching in an exemplary middle school setting that serves as a training ground for some of the best middle school teachers in the country. What he lacks in experience, he makes up for with enthusiasm.

10 **Polly Professional**

Polly is a highly experienced elementary teacher with a desire to become the best middle school teacher in the district. She received the "Best Teacher of the Year Award" for her ability to develop interdisciplinary units. She has expert knowledge of ways to vary delivery systems and grouping of students for optimal learning conditions.

My four choices for team members are:

_____   _____

_____   _____

because . . .

Our group's four choices for team members are:

_____   _____

_____   _____

because . . .

Is Middle Level Teaming Right for You?

(Teacher Self-Inventory)

Name_____   Date _____

Grade, Subject You Teach_____

Directions:
Use this self-check quiz to determine your potential as a middle level teacher working on an interdisciplinary team. Write an X in the appropriate column on the left. (In answering, give yourself the benefit of the doubt!)

Yes	No	Do You . . .
		understand your own strengths and weaknesses as a person?
		understand your own strengths and weaknesses as a teacher?
		interact constructively with other adults?
		interact constructively with early adolescents?
		feel that, as a teacher, you are approachable, responsive, and supportive to your peers and colleagues?
		feel that, as a teacher, you are approachable, responsive, and supportive to your students?
		readily acknowledge and appreciate the physical, intellectual, social, and emotional needs and characteristics of early adolescence?
		regularly apply different and varied methods and activities in the teaching-learning process?
		regularly use group processes and group learning techniques?
		organize your curriculum in a way that facilitates the interdisciplinary approach to instruction?
		willingly counsel an individual student with an identifiable need?
		design and conduct group activities that capitalize on individual differences and learning styles of students?
		have the skills required to work in cooperative teaching situations with other teachers, paraprofessionals, and resource persons?
		accept the responsibility of multidisciplinary instruction in planning thematic and coordinated studies with other teachers?

continued on page 60

Is Middle Level Teaming Right for You?

Yes	No	Do You . . .
		seek out and enjoy teaching subjects outside your own area of specialization?
		readily acknowledge there are many ways—not just "your way"— of teaching students?
		recognize that team members will have differences, disagreements, and conflicts, but also understand that these can and should be resolved?
		believe in weekly team plans and meetings?
		display a tactful honesty and willingness to work and plan together with team members?
		demonstrate a willingness to utilize differences between, as well as similarities among, team members?
		demonstrate a realization that your subject area is of no more or less importance than other subjects?
		demonstrate a realization that ability grouping may not be compatible with interdisciplinary team teaching?
		agree that team members ought to be flexible in individual scheduling to meet a particular student's needs?
		display an interest in (not necessarily an understanding of) the other academic subjects?
		show sensitivity to the feelings of the other team members? (Can you eliminate petty or personal complaints that may interfere with the primary objectives of interdisciplinary team teaching?)

Scoring: Give yourself one point for every yes response.

20 - 25 You are definitely a middle school person.

15 - 19 You are definitely leaning toward a middle school commitment.

10 - 14 You are mildly interested in learning more about middle schools.

0 - 9 You may be an elementary or high school teacher at heart.

Roles and Responsibilities
of a Team Leader

A team leader

1 functions as a liaison between the administration and team.

2 coordinates instructional programs within the team.

3 coordinates practices and procedures between leader's team and other teams.

4 serves on and appoints team members to various school or district committees.

5 schedules and coordinates administration of criterion-referenced and standardized tests.

6 prepares and submits the team budget for supplies, textbooks, audiovisuals, and equipment needs.

7 familiarizes new teachers and substitute teachers with the school program and the team practices and procedures.

8 disseminates information on trends, new approaches, and research findings to team members.

9 schedules and conducts team meetings.

10 assists in the selection of personnel that affects team activities including aides, volunteers, team members, substitute teachers, and support staff.

11 promotes public relations between team members and parent-school community.

12 facilitates communication among team members.

13 coordinates interdisciplinary instruction efforts.

14 works to maintains a high level of morale among team members.

Things to Consider
When Selecting a Team Leader

Directions: Prepare a mock application form that could be filled out by each team member who wishes to be considered for the team leader position. Encourage applicants to be as honest as possible in their responses. Use these questions to select the "best" person for the job, given the circumstances. Ten possible items are suggested below.

1 What would appeal to you most about being the team leader?

2 What bothers you most about the team leader position?

3 How do you think a leader influences a team?

4 What would be most stressful to you about being a leader of this particular team?

5 Why do you think the team would want to follow you?

6 What do you see as your leadership strengths? What are your leadership weaknesses?

7 How would you describe your leadership style?

8 What key tasks should be the responsibilities of the team leader?

9 How would you want the team members to evaluate your performance as the team leader at the end of the school year?

10 Who would make a good leader for your team? Why?

BONUS ACTIVITY:

As a potential team leader, think of several metaphors that could be used as the springboard for constructing a logo, creating a slogan, or inventing a cheer. Try these for starters:

A team that has a vision is like a superhighway because . . .

A team that works well together is like a symphony because . . .

A team that is student-centered is like a rain forest because . . .

The Definitive Middle School Guide, Revised Edition
Copyright © 2014 World Book, Inc./Incentive Publications, Chicago, IL

Are You an Effective Team Builder?

Team Member Self-Inventory

Name_____ Date_____

Directions:

How effective are you as a team builder? Rate yourself by responding honestly to these statements. Give yourself a score of 1 to 7 on each item, with 7 being the highest rating.

1 I spend sufficient time selecting team members with the appropriate skills and attitudes required to make the teaming concept work. ☐

2 I encourage ownership among team members by allowing them considerable independence and autonomy in goal setting, problem solving, and delivery of instruction. ☐

3 I nurture and practice the spirit of teamwork throughout the school setting. ☐

4 I insist on open and honest communication at all times. ☐

5 I keep my word, my agreements, and my promises to people. ☐

6 I respect the personality differences and cultural diversities of others. ☐

7 I provide quality staff development opportunities for enhancing the teaming process. ☐

8 I value constructive criticism. ☐

9 I believe that teaming and collaboration will maximize the learning that takes place. ☐

10 I will coach and counsel team members who are not able to meet reasonable standards and expectations. ☐

Scoring: Add the scores.

60–70 You are well aware of what it takes to be an effective team builder.

40–59 This score is acceptable, but you need to sharpen your team-building skills and attitudes.

20–39 You aren't really a team player yet, but you may be willing to give it a try!

0–19 You may want to consider a structure other than teaming.

> Write a summative statement expressing something you learned from doing this inventory.

The Definitive Middle School Guide, Revised Edition
Copyright © 2014 World Book, Inc./Incentive Publications, Chicago, IL

Roles for Team Members

1 **Team Leader-Facilitator:** Schedules and presides over meetings, coordinates items for agendas, manages conflicts, and provides leadership for team activities.

2 **Team Recorder:** Keeps a record of actions and decisions made by the team and serves as historian of the team's operations.

3 **Team Timekeeper-Gatekeeper:** Nurtures team relationships and keeps team members on task in a timely fashion.

4 **Team Gopher-Resource Person:** Locates and manages the multiple resources needed to plan, implement, and evaluate team activities.

5 **Public Relations-Marketing Person:** Prepares reports, news releases, and information fliers or memos to inform other faculty members, administrators, and parents of team's actions and accomplishments.

6 **Social Chairperson:** Organizes social and personal celebrations for students and teachers on the team.

7 **Curriculum Coordinator:** Keeps calendar of tests, major curricular projects, and weekly topics for each discipline represented on the team.

8 **Media Director:** Assumes major responsibility for files and organization of team resource, curricular, and reference materials.

9 **Treasurer:** Keeps accurate records of monies belonging to team and of fund-raising efforts.

10 **Liaison Link:** Communicates with other teams, administrators, and support staff to encourage communication between and among various groups and stakeholders of the school.

11 **Special Event Coordinator:** Coordinates plans and efforts for staging field trips, holiday celebrations, outside speakers, and award ceremonies.

12 **Action Researcher:** Maintains records of student growth and achievement levels for purposes of documenting the team's impact on the teaching and learning process.

Activity: Prepare a set of role cards for each of the jobs above. Write a description of each role on a single card. Have each person randomly draw a card for a team or staff meeting and play that role during the meeting. At the end of the meeting, redistribute the cards so that every member will play another role at the next meeting. Repeat this procedure until everyone has had a chance to play every role, as well as a chance to decide which person best fits each role. Encourage members to play the "best fit" role on the team for a year.

The Definitive Middle School Guide, Revised Edition
Copyright © 2014 World Book, Inc./Incentive Publications, Chicago, IL

Possible Causes of Team Failure

1 Failure to see that team organization is fundamentally different from traditional departmentalized or self-contained configurations

2 Dissemination of information that does not flow freely in all directions, but tends to flow from the top down

3 Lack of staff development in teaming skills or practices for all team members

4 Continuous conflict that focuses on persons rather than on issues

5 Failure to consider personalities and interpersonal variables when staffing teams

6 An atmosphere that is not participative and open, but that fragments members and compartmentalizes ideas

7 Failure to understand that new teams will need considerable time and practice before they can become fully functioning teams

8 Team decisions that emphasize manipulation and dissonance rather than consensus and compromise

9 Team members that lack self-discipline or who are unwilling to recognize the patterns and stages of the team process

10 Teams that reward individual achievements over group achievements

11 Failure to place team organization at the top of the scheduling priority list so that all else revolves around it

12 Performance appraisals that are subjective and arbitrary rather than collective and self-initiated

13 Failure to understand importance of team identity and the power of symbols, rituals, and ceremonies in the life of the team

14 Teams that have focused on task activities to the exclusion of work on team member relationships

Tools for Building a Team Identity

1. Team name, logo, mascot, colors, and slogan

2. Team decorations for door, hallways, and rooms

3. Team newspaper or newsletter

4. Team rules or codes of conduct

5. Team rewards

6. Team intramurals

7. Team birthday celebrations

8. Team government

9. Team recognition days

10. Team meals

11. Team assemblies

12. Team display of student work

13. Team T-shirts

14. Team bulletin boards

15. Team handbooks

16. Team student conference

17. Team contests

18. Team field trips

19. Team song or choral reading

20. Team parties

21. Team scrapbook

22. Team Open House

23. Team honor rolls

24. Team calendar

25. Team web page, podcast, or blog

26. Talent shows, spirit days, dress-up days

27. Team community projects

28. Team academic "brain bowls"

29. Team cheers

30. Team rituals

The Definitive Middle School Guide, Revised Edition
Copyright © 2014 World Book, Inc./Incentive Publications, Chicago, IL

Characteristics of Effective Teaming

1 Teams should be balanced and should include team members who have varied teaching and learning styles. Learning style inventories can be used to identify modalities, right-left brain tendencies, and preferred instructional modes.

2 Teams should include team members with the appropriate subject matter competencies. A four-member team should include the specialties of math, science, social studies, and language arts-English-reading. A three-member team should include any three of these areas, with a strong backup in the fourth area. A two-member team should include experiences, training, and degrees in a science-math combination and a language arts-social studies combination.

3 Teams should be assigned or housed in specific team areas with adjacent classrooms. School floor plans can be adapted to the teaming process by designating sections of the building for team assignments and reassigning space to accommodate those teachers working together.

4 Teams should have a common planning space so that team members can meet daily for team meetings, house shared materials for mutual accessibility, hold student or parent conferences, and store team records or files.

5 Teams should have a common planning time to facilitate daily meetings, which are needed to:

a) determine schedules,
b) discuss students,
c) evaluate programs,
d) design special team events or activities,
e) plan goals and objectives, and
f) develop interdisciplinary units.

6 Teams should designate a team leader, as well as key roles and responsibilities for both the team leader and team members.

7 Teams should hold regular team meetings with predetermined agendas and concise minutes.

8 Teams should strive to preserve team autonomy and flexibility in planning, implementing, and evaluating instructional practices for team members and their students.

9 Teams should share decision-making tasks with the administration whenever and wherever possible to do so. This requires both a mutual commitment and respect among all parties involved.

10 A team should be accountable for its own budget and supplies whenever possible. This encourages both wise spending and maximum use of resources by the team.

11 Teams should include specialists and other support staff members in team decisions and activities. Exploratory teachers and guidance counselors, for example, can add a great deal of valuable input when dealing with issues ranging from student behavior to interdisciplinary units.

12 Teams should respect the similarities and differences that exist among team members and practice the art of compromise or negotiation to accomplish team goals and objectives.

Things That Great Teams Do

1 Build a strong team identity, but be certain that the team's identity is compatible with and supportive of the school's overall identity.

2 Conduct regular team meetings with predetermined agendas and follow-up minutes. Appoint a team historian to maintain records of the team's progress throughout the year.

3 Hold regular parent and student conferences. Do not let a week go by without inviting some student(s) or parent(s) to become the focus of a productive discussion or action plan. Try to have conferences that "celebrate" an individual's success, as well as those that are scheduled for solving problems.

4 Maintain a team calendar. Distribute this weekly or monthly calendar to both students and parents. Include as many important dates, events, and deadlines as you can to communicate team member schedules.

5 Maintain and use a flexible block schedule. Spend considerable time grouping and regrouping students for instruction and scheduling and rescheduling blocks of time for that instruction. Take full advantage of the opportunity to expand or reduce predetermined blocks of time for the academic subject areas in order to maximize the learning process.

6 Celebrate team successes. Do not let a day go by without taking time to review the high spots of the day or the high points of the week for yourselves, your students, or your parent community. Remember that a string of minor successes can lead to sensational ones!

7 Integrate subject matter. Look for ways to correlate the different academic subjects every chance you get. Do not assume that students will automatically see the connections from class to class; you must help them understand the links between one content area and another.

8 Forget mistakes, but learn from them. All team members should feel comfortable in taking risks to tease their minds and stretch their imaginations. Some of your ideas or activities will falter, but develop the attitude that a group learns more from its failures than from its successes.

9 Plan "play" into the week. It is all right to allow some free time in a weekly schedule for both teachers and students. Use this time for reflecting and refocusing so that the week becomes both enjoyable and productive.

10 Hold team "professional reading-learning" sessions. Try to build a professional library of resources for the team so that team members can continue to grow in their careers. Do not limit the materials to educational themes, but include books, pamphlets, tapes, and journals in areas of business, economics, and politics.

The Definitive Middle School Guide, Revised Edition
Copyright © 2014 World Book, Inc./Incentive Publications, Chicago, IL

11 Develop common discipline procedures. Be certain that all team members enforce the same rules in the same way so that students can't "play one teacher against another."

12 Establish common grading guidelines. Agree on a grading system that will be used by the team and develop a specific set of descriptors for each point on the grading scale to avoid discrepancies from one team member to another.

13 Coordinate homework. Communicate daily to determine types of homework to be required in the core content areas. Avoid overloading students with unrealistic homework tasks on any given day.

14 Coordinate the administration of quizzes and tests. Create a plan for assessing student achievement in the core subject areas so that no student is required to study for more than one major quiz or test at any one time.

15 Encourage a standard paper heading. Although this may seem like a minor point, the students do not find it so. It can minimize the frustration of a student who has to remember if the name and date go in the upper right-hand corner for one class and in the lower left-hand corner for another class.

16 Hold team detentions. Handling student discipline problems within the structure of the team is a goal of the teaming process; therefore, time and procedures for dealing with student detentions must be built into the team's schedule.

17 Conduct team "help sessions" for students. It is important that the team try to build into the weekly and monthly schedule of team activities time for helping, tutoring, or coaching students in the academic areas. These sessions could vary according to the schedule, with time blocks set aside before school, after school, and within the school day.

18 Provide students with opportunities for extra credit work. A written team policy should encourage any student to complete extra credit work for enrichment or remedial purposes, regardless of that student's ability level.

19 Give frequent student academic and personal progress reports. A bank of tools and techniques for recognizing cognitive and affective achievements in the classroom should become an integral part of the teaming process. Progress charts, awards assemblies, recognition banners, personal badges or buttons, and happy-grams to the home can all be parts of this celebration.

20 Monitor student academic and personal progress. Student folders, portfolios, notebooks, and anecdotal records should all be considered parts of the accountability process for keeping track of where students stand both academically and personally. Learning logs, journals, and projects can all be parts of this data-collecting effort.

Barriers for Effective Teams to Overcome

1 **Personality conflicts**
Recognize and appreciate diversity and make allowances for different needs, characteristics, moods, and personalities within the team.

2 **Inconsistency in expectations for students**
Recognize that team members all view the teaching and learning process differently and that it is the team's responsibility to synthesize these expectations when making decisions.

3 **Inconsistency in expectations for teachers**
Recognize the individuality of team members when setting personal goals and objectives for the school year and work to reach consensus on goals and objectives, in keeping with teacher talents.

4 **Poor planning, organization, and goal setting**
Recognize that teams often take shortcuts in planning or goal setting for the school year, organizing resources, and preparing students and parents for the teaming process. It is critical that an effort be made in the opening weeks of school to set the tone for the next nine months.

5 **Lack of support for one another or disloyalty**
Recognize that there will be times when team members do not offer one another the degree of support or loyalty required for making interdisciplinary teams successful. This is often due to teacher stress or burnout. Remember that when team members begin to experience these difficulties, time must be set aside immediately to resolve the divisive issues and get back on track.

6 **Poor communication**
Recognize that communication is the very heart and soul of effective teaming and should become the first priority when dealing with the various members of the teaming process.

7 **Refusal to share ideas and materials**
Recognize that in the past, many teachers have been programmed to hoard materials and hide ideas rather than share resources and exchange information. Teaming requires collaboration on a daily basis to maximize learning and growing for students and for teachers.

8 **Difficulty with individual team members**
Recognize that on some teams there will be teachers who don't want to be there, for reasons ranging from individual feelings of inadequacy to ignorance of the teaming concept. For the good of the students, each team member must accept individual strengths and weaknesses within the team.

9 **Inability to vary delivery systems**
Recognize that it is not enough to group teachers and students into teams, but that the restructuring of instructional time and techniques is also critical to the redesign of middle-level classrooms.

10 **Poor public relations**
Recognize that teachers must do a better job of "tooting their own horns" and letting the public know the advantages that teaming brings to the schooling process. Teaming is compatible with today's workplace with its emphasis on quality teams, shared decision making, and empowerment of workers. Let the world know that today's middle school classrooms now represent a more realistic training ground for tomorrow's business settings.

The Definitive Middle School Guide, Revised Edition
Copyright © 2014 World Book, Inc./Incentive Publications, Chicago, IL

Components of a Good Team Handbook

It is very important for each interdisciplinary team to develop a handbook for use by both students and parents. The team handbook provides relevant information about the team to which a given student is assigned. Possible contents of a teaming handbook are given below.

1 **Profile of team members**

Start with short biographical sketches of each teacher on the team. This information can be written in an essay, outline, or short paragraph format. Teachers might want to tell something about their families, hobbies, special interests, travels, pet peeves, previous teaching experiences, educational degrees or awards, and future goals.

2 **Team mission statement**

Both the school's and the team's mission statements should be included in the handbook. It is important to share the overall philosophy of the middle school concept with special emphasis on the interdisciplinary teaming component.

3 **Team identity sheet**

An outline of the team's unique characteristics and plans for the year should be included. Briefly describe the team's name, color, logo, slogan, cheers, traditions, rituals, and celebrations, as well as anything else key and important to its special identity.

4 **Team guidelines and procedures**

An overview of the team's classroom behavior rules, as well as guidelines for student grades, for absences, for homework, for make-up work, and for disciplinary procedures should also be part of the teaming handbook.

5 **Team class schedule**

A brief explanation of how the students spend their time in school is appropriate for the teaming handbook. A copy of the block schedule with a brief explanation of how it works might also be part of this section.

6 **Team meeting agenda**

It is useful to include a sample team meeting agenda in the handbook as a reminder to both students and parents that much school-day time is spent planning and evaluating the team's instructional program. Another helpful item to include in this section of the handbook is a chart showing the team meeting times, dates, and locations.

7 **Minutes from team meeting**

A sample of minutes from a typical team meeting can be a useful tool in showing students and parents the kinds of tasks completed during the team's common planning periods.

8 **Calendar of team dates and special events**

Students and parents will appreciate a list of the planned rituals, celebrations, traditions, events, and special dates that will have an impact on their time and energies during the school year. This calendar can be used as a vehicle for planning both short-term and long-term activities.

9 **Team problem-solving and decision-making tools and techniques**

Most parents are interested in learning more about the various problem-solving and decision-making models that are used as part of the learning and instructional processes employed by the team. Information about how decisions are made, how problems are solved, or how concerns are addressed make good reading for both teachers and students alike.

10 **Student-parent conference planning sheet**

A sample of the student-parent conference-planning sheet should be part of the handbook so that students know what to expect when they attend a teacher-student conference. It should be noted that all teachers on the team should be present for a student-parent conference, which is generally held during the team's common planning period.

11 **Parent telephone report form**

A sample telephone report form should be part of the handbook so that parents can see that team teachers keep records of telephone contacts with the home.

12 **Study hints**

The teaming handbook is a good place in which to remind students and parents of the importance of cultivating good study habits while in school. This section might include everything from hints on how to study for a test to suggestions for writing an effective research paper or book report.

The Definitive Middle School Guide, Revised Edition
Copyright © 2014 World Book, Inc./Incentive Publications, Chicago, IL

Ways to Use Common Planning Time

1 Hold formal and informal team meetings to discuss students, parents, schedules, curriculum issues, school business, and team policies and procedures.

2 Plan grade level or departmental meetings or sessions with colleagues to foster communication and an appropriate level of shared decision making.

3 Offer special staff development activities or a mini-workshop for self-improvement, including short audiovisual training events, lectures by district personnel, or programmed texts and workbooks.

4 Develop interdisciplinary approaches or units. This could be a high priority for common planning time get-togethers. Try integrating a concept, skill, or topic on a daily basis in at least some small way to help students understand the correlation between their teachers, subject areas, and skills development.

5 Reward students. Celebrating student success should be a regular occurrence and should vary from appreciation roles and verbal praise to student work displays.

6 Conduct student and parent conferences. It is important to build "talking" time into the weekly schedule for dealing with both student and parent problems as they arise. Remember: "An ounce of prevention is worth a pound of cure."

7 Share teacher ideas, concerns, worries, failures, and successes to foster morale, emotional health, and well-being by providing outlets for sharing "war stories" or brainstorming creative ideas.

8 Update team records. Documenting team events, discussions, and decisions is important to team success. This includes everything from student records to team minutes so that paperwork does not become a burden at any given time.

9 Organize team events, celebrations, or field trips. Building a strong team identity depends upon a team's ability to plan and implement a wide variety of special happenings for all teachers and student members of the team.

10 Update team calendar to coordinate course requirements, test dates, class excursions, and special lesson plans. Avoiding duplicate or conflicting class requirements or regulations can pave the way for considerable academic achievement.

11 Brainstorm solutions to problems or alternatives for decisions. Holding short stand-up team meetings during the day can help solve short-term problems or aid in making short-term decisions as they come up.

12 Enjoy a social time with special treats or a potluck lunch. Take time for fun!

Advantages and Disadvantages of Varying Team Sizes

Choosing the size of teams to service students and teachers is a crucial decision for a school that is organizing for an interdisciplinary approach. There are both distinct advantages and disadvantages for teams ranging from two members to five members.

Two-Person Team

ADVANTAGES

1. Fewer students
2. Variety of subjects may be taught
3. Ease of integrating the disciplines
4. Ease of getting together for meetings
5. Fewer personality conflicts
6. No "odd man out"
7. More secure environment
8. Easier transition from single teacher at 5th grade level

DISADVANTAGES

1. Students deal with a limited number of teaching personalities
2. May burden teachers with too much preparation
3. Not as much backup for absenteeism
4. Limited diversity in teaching styles

Three-Person Team

ADVANTAGES

1. Diversity of instructional materials and methods (Three heads are better than one.)
2. Group will usually teach one subject in common and may integrate subject areas easily
3. Diversity in teaching styles
4. More opportunity to group students according to ability

DISADVANTAGES

1. Sometimes difficult to find a common subject to teach
2. Increased likelihood of "two against one"

The Definitive Middle School Guide, Revised Edition
Copyright © 2014 World Book, Inc./Incentive Publications, Chicago, IL

Four-Person Team

ADVANTAGES

1 Usually one major subject per teacher (requiring one preparation)

2 Good transition to high school

3 Teacher may specialize if so desired

4 More opportunity to ability-group students within a team

5 Greater diversity of instructional materials and methods (Four heads are better than one.)

6 Greater diversity in teaching styles

DISADVANTAGES

1 Sometimes more difficult for members to meet

2 Greater potential for personality conflicts

3 May be more difficult to gain and maintain consistency in program

4 Teachers may specialize too much and become departmentalized

Five-Person Team

ADVANTAGES

1 Usually one major subject per teacher (requiring one preparation)

2 Good transition to high school

3 Teacher may specialize if so desired

4 More opportunity to ability-group students within a team

5 Greater diversity of instructional materials and methods (Five heads are better than one.)

6 Greater diversity in teaching styles

7 Possibility of using one individual as remedial teacher with smaller groups of students

DISADVANTAGES

1 Sometimes more difficult for members to meet

2 Greater potential for personality conflicts

3 May be more difficult to gain and maintain consistency in program

4 Teachers may specialize too much and become departmentalized

Things on Which
Team Members Should Agree

Team members should meet during pre-school planning days. It is essential that the team members agree on . . .

1 times for regular team meetings.

2 the ways to schedule students into classes.

3 the continual sharing of curriculum objectives leading to the development of interdisciplinary units.

4 selecting and securing textbooks and other needed resources.

5 how and when to meet with parents and students.

6 a team classroom-management plan.

7 ways to communicate in writing to parents.

8 a homework policy.

9 schedules and policies for use of technology in the classroom.

10 procedures for sharing materials.

11 field trip plans to extend classroom experiences.

12 team assignments.

The Definitive Middle School Guide, Revised Edition
Copyright © 2014 World Book, Inc./Incentive Publications, Chicago, IL

Techniques for Effective Team Meetings

1 Plan the meeting cooperatively.

2 Acknowledge the schedules of others.

3 Provide ample lead-time.

4 Keep a portion of the agenda open.

5 Stay on task.

6 Keep presentations and discussions short and to the point.

7 Make space ready and presentable for the meeting.

8 Eliminate distractions.

9 Schedule time to socialize if possible.

10 Feed the troops.

11 Value humor.

12 Learn to read silence.

13 Manage hostility.

14 Respect differences.

15 Protect confidentiality.

16 Stretch for closure.

17 Invite participant feedback.

18 Retire useless practices.

19 Establish priorities.

20 Evaluate results.

Ways to Spend Team Meeting Time

1 Grouping and regrouping of students for instruction

2 Sharing major curricular thrusts with one another

3 Building a team schedule or calendar for the semester or year

4 Preparing for "teachable moments"

5 Integrating two or more of the discipline areas

6 Planning outside field experience or in-class speakers

7 Discussing problematic students or parents

8 Holding collaborative student or parent conferences

9 Setting consistent behavioral expectations for students

10 Engaging in self-renewal or staff development tasks

11 Discussing educational philosophies, hot issues, or national trends

12 Playing an active role in school policy making

13 Coordinating lesson plans to reinforce one another's subject areas

14 Brainstorming or bouncing ideas off one another

15 Planning to reinforce an academic skill across several subject areas

16 Sharing successful teaching experiences with team members

17 Teaching team members a new active learning strategy

18 Engaging in a problem-solving or decision-making session

19 Working to build team unity or team identity

20 Planning team celebrations

The Definitive Middle School Guide, Revised Edition
Copyright © 2014 World Book, Inc./Incentive Publications, Chicago, IL

Team Meeting Time Wasters

1 No purpose, agenda, or follow-up to the previous meeting

2 Too few people or too many people at the meeting

3 Key people or leadership missing from the meeting

4 Starting late

5 Ending late

6 No time limits to the meeting

7 People not interested, prepared, or willing to take an active part in the meeting

8 Redundant, rambling discussions that do not lead to decisions or solutions during the meeting

9 Hidden agendas introduced with side issues that dominate the meeting

10 Too many interruptions during the meeting

11 Participants who do not know what is expected or what procedures to follow at the meeting

12 Agenda topics at the meeting not relevant to one's personal, professional, or work needs

13 Short notice or lead-time for meeting

Name _____ Date _____

Difficult Situations in Meetings
or Teaming Situations

Directions: Use the following situations as springboards for discussing conflict or problem situations that sometimes arise during team discussions or team meetings. Try to role-play and determine what could be done to remedy the problem setting. Summarize a possible solution for each situation.

1 A team member tends to dominate the discussion.

Solution:

2 A team member wants to argue.

Solution:

3 A team member attacks the messenger and not the message.

Solution:

4 A team member starts a "side meeting" with a fellow teammate.

Solution:

5 A team member comes unprepared or is uninterested.

Solution:

6 A team member lacks interest in or shows little concern for the ideas of others.

Solution:

7 A team member fails to participate in or contribute to group discussions or decision making.

Solution:

8 A team member is lazy, careless, or fails to follow up on agreed upon tasks.

Solution:

9 A team member is antagonistic.

Solution:

10 A team member is extremely opinionated and strongly defends own opinions.

Solution:

11 A team member lacks tact or finesse.

Solution:

12 A team member resists change of any nature.

Solution:

The Definitive Middle School Guide, Revised Edition
Copyright © 2014 World Book, Inc./Incentive Publications, Chicago, IL

Team Decision Making and Problem Solving: Tips & Tools

1 **Brainwriting**

Write the issue or problem at the top of a sheet of paper and contribute three ideas for addressing or solving it. (Each team member does this individually.) Place all papers in a stack. Each team member draws a paper from the stack and adds three more ideas—either new ones or extensions of ideas already listed. Repeat this process eight more times. Then distribute a sheet to each team member and take turns reading aloud the list from one sheet while others cross out ideas that are repeated on their sheets. Ordinarily, 10 minutes of "brainwriting" generates about 75 new ideas to address an issue.

2 **Decision Chart**

This is a good tool to use when the team is not sure where to begin! Draw a long rectangle at the top of a sheet of paper or on a flipchart or whiteboard. Inside the rectangle, write "DECISION" followed by a brief description of the decision that must be made. Draw a vertical column down from the left side of the DECISION box. Label this "POSSIBLE RESOLUTIONS," and divide it into four to six rectangles. Work as a team to briefly summarize four to six ideas that could resolve the dilemma. Write the summaries in the rectangles. Next, decide on a set of three criteria for judging each of the alternatives (e.g., workability, extent to which it fits with team vision, willingness of team members to uphold it, potential to improve student progress). Create a 1-5 rating scale for each criterion. (Use a separate piece of paper or area of the flipchart or whiteboard.) Draw three lines out to the right of each alternative's rectangle. Work as a group to rate each of the alternatives on each criterion. Write the scores on the lines next to the idea. Compile the scores for each alternative decision; choose the one with the highest score.

3 **Planning Tree**

Use this tool to plan a task with a major goal and sub-goals that can be accomplished through a variety of sequential tasks. On a sheet of paper, a flipchart page, or a whiteboard, draw a tree with a thick trunk, major branches, and a few small branches growing from each large branch. Write the major goal on the trunk and the sub-goals on the large branches. On the small branches, write specific tasks that will contribute to reaching the sub-goal. When this is done, number the specific tasks in a sequential order for completion.

4 **Fishbone Model**

Use this model to explore the effects of a particular decision or problem solution. Draw (be imaginative!) or copy a fish skeleton large enough to fill a sheet of paper, a flipchart page, or an area on a whiteboard. Write the decision or solution option on the FISH HEAD. On each of the bones coming off the spine, write an effect, outcome, or result that would likely follow from that decision/solution. Go back and color the bones with the effects that are desirable. The number of bones colored (or not colored) will help you to evaluate the desirability of this decision/solution option.

5 **Flowcharts**

Use a flowchart to visually show and follow either the possible outcomes of a particular decision under consideration or the steps for solving a problem. A flowchart is also a great tool for carrying out a plan—organizing sequences of steps, actions, or decisions. Decide on a set of symbols that you will use (e.g., arrows, triangles, circles, boxes, dotted lines) and include an explanation for each symbol. The arrangement will vary according to the specific situation.

6 Opposing Forces Chart

Many problems or challenges involve forces that positively support movement toward a goal and others that impede movement. Getting these down in writing helps a team state, embrace, accept, and operate with these sometimes conflicting forces. Start by writing a heading that identifies the situation to resolve or decision to implement. Write two sub-headings: DRIVING FORCES and OPPOSING FORCES. Draw a broad arrow under each sub-heading. Working as a team, identify forces that you believe could move the team toward the goal or solution (e.g., positive actions, skills, people, tools, or procedures). Write these beneath the DRIVING FORCES arrow. Beneath the OPPOSING FORCES arrow, identify forces the team believes are keeping members from reaching a goal or solution (e.g., restraining actions, skills, people, tools, or procedures). Finally, prioritize the driving forces to be used and begin diminishing the number of opposing forces.

7 Discussion Guide

Start by gathering a list of statements about the decision or problem at hand. Each team member should contribute statements that support a decision/solution, oppose a decision/solution, define the issue, or offer a different solution. Write the statements on a flipchart page or whiteboard. Next, to show what value the team should place on a statement's relevance to the decision/solution, create a scoring system for rating each statement. (For example, 1-5, where 1 = "low" and 5 = "high.") Split into pairs, discuss each statement, and agree between the two of you on a score for each statement. Pairs then share their conclusions and scores with the entire team.

8 Delphi Method

Working independently of the other team members, each member writes suggestions of ways to deal with a particular problem or decision. Compile the suggestions into one list and distribute the list to the team members. Each member considers all the suggestions and reflects back to the team his or her reactions to each one. Finally, vote or discuss to reach a consensus on which decision/solution is most acceptable to the team.

9 Multi-Voting

After ideas are gathered for a decision or problem solution and written on a sheet of paper, a flipchart page, or a whiteboard, each team member votes for as many of the ideas as he or she likes. Tally the votes and circle all the ideas that have won at least a simple majority. Vote again, but, this time, each member has only half the number of votes to spend among the remaining (circled) ideas as there are remaining ideas. (I.e., if there are eight remaining ideas, each member has four votes to spend. In the case of an odd number of remaining ideas, round up— seven remaining ideas gives four votes.) Continue this multi-voting until the list is down to five ideas or fewer. As a team, discuss the remaining ideas to make a choice.

10 The Dot Technique

Start by distributing three press-apply dots (circular stickers) to each team member— one red, one yellow, and one green. A red dot is worth three points; green, two points; yellow, one point. After team members have brainstormed a number of possible decisions or solutions and have written these on a flipchart page, each member decides how to "spend" his or her dots. If a person feels strongly about one idea, all three dots may be placed on that item. But team members may distribute their dots over two or three different ideas. Tally and discuss the results as a team. Repeat the procedure as needed to reduce the number of ideas. All ideas with at least one red dot should remain on the list for further discussion and voting.

Questions to Answer When Observing a Team Meeting or Problem-Solving Session

To obtain an objective opinion about how a team is functioning, recruit an outside observer to sit in on a team meeting or problem-solving session. The following questions can be used to record the behaviors of the group members and the group processing outcomes.

1 Did the team get started on time, and, if so, how was this accomplished?

2 How well did the team set up its agenda and structure for the meeting?

3 How did the team establish its rules and follow its predetermined procedures?

4 How did the team share information and explore different perspectives or points of view?

5 How did the team handle conflict?

6 How did the team stay on task?

7 How were ideas accepted, rejected, or recorded?

8 How were decisions made?

9 How was consensus achieved?

10 How active and widespread was the participation of team members?

11 How did the team reflect on its own functioning?

12 How did the team leader or facilitator maintain order, control, and time on task?

13 What type of climate emerged?

14 What types of minutes or records were kept?

15 How were follow-up tasks and timelines delegated or handled?

Name _____ Date _____

Ways to Determine Whether You Are a Good Team Player

Directions: Determine whether or not you are a good team player by rating yourself on the following behavior tasks.

1 I am well aware of my team role and the functions of the team.

Never 1 2 3 4 5 6 7 Always

2 I express my willingness to cooperate with other group members and my expectation that they will also be cooperative with me.

Never 1 2 3 4 5 6 7 Always

3 I support the efforts of the team leader and other team members.

Never 1 2 3 4 5 6 7 Always

4 I follow the guidelines for gaining consensus and participate equally in making team decisions.

Never 1 2 3 4 5 6 7 Always

5 I am open and candid in my dealings with the team.

Never 1 2 3 4 5 6 7 Always

6 I recognize the relationship of planning periods to the effectiveness of the team's activities.

Never 1 2 3 4 5 6 7 Always

7 I respond to the needs of students through the teaming process.

Never 1 2 3 4 5 6 7 Always

8 I do my part in helping to resolve conflicts among team members.

Never 1 2 3 4 5 6 7 Always

9 I share materials and resources with other team members to promote the success of the entire group.

Never 1 2 3 4 5 6 7 Always

10 I collect and use data for purposes of improving the team's effectiveness and developing the instructional program.

Never 1 2 3 4 5 6 7 Always

11 I stick to agenda items at team meetings wherever possible to do so.

Never 1 2 3 4 5 6 7 Always

12 I complete team paperwork and tasks in a timely fashion.

Never 1 2 3 4 5 6 7 Always

13 I actively participate in parent and student conferences.

Never 1 2 3 4 5 6 7 Always

14 I communicate effectively with team members, parents, administration, and other support staff.

Never 1 2 3 4 5 6 7 Always

15 I regularly participate in staff development activities.

Never 1 2 3 4 5 6 7 Always

The Definitive Middle School Guide, Revised Edition
Copyright © 2014 World Book, Inc./Incentive Publications, Chicago, IL

Team Self-Evaluation

School_____ Team _____

Name _____ Grade Level_____

Each member of an interdisciplinary team should complete this evaluation.
Afterwards, the team leader should facilitate a meeting where responses are shared
and consensus is reached. The agreed-upon answers can be recorded on a master
sheet, kept in the team master notebook, and reviewed on a regular basis.

always   *frequently*   *infrequently*   *never*

_____ 1 Our team meets on a regular basis.

_____ 2 All team members are present at our team meetings.

_____ 3 All team members come to our meetings on time.

_____ 4 All team members stay for the duration of our meetings.

_____ 5 Our team talks about ways to best meet the needs of students.

_____ 6 Our team works effectively with resource personnel.

_____ 7 The members of our team support the efforts of our team leader.

_____ 8 Every member of our team participates in the decision-making process.

_____ 9 The team's decisions are implemented.

_____ 10 Our team keeps a team notebook that includes agenda, minutes, parent conference forms, student conference forms, and other information pertaining to our team.

_____ 11 Our team has goals and objectives for the school year.

_____ 12 Our team periodically evaluates its goals and objectives.

continued on page 86

continued

Team Self-Evaluation

always	frequently	infrequently	never

_____ **13** Our team members use team duty time to correlate subject matter and to plan for interdisciplinary instruction.

_____ **14** Our team members conduct face-to-face parent conferences during team duty time.

_____ **15** Our team members use team duty time to conduct student conferences.

_____ **16** Our team discusses ways to use our block time effectively.

_____ **17** Our team groups and regroups students for instruction within our team.

_____ **18** Our team changes our "regular" schedule to accommodate teacher and student needs.

_____ **19** Our team has an agenda for all team meetings.

_____ **20** Our team follows the agenda at our meetings.

_____ **21** Our team planning time is kept strictly for team business.

_____ **22** The team paces itself and allows for "ups" and "downs," cycles of hard work and relaxation.

_____ **23** The team regularly takes time to provide outlets for members to share ideas and frustrations.

_____ **24** Our team members inform the exploratory teachers about decisions reached at our team meetings.

_____ **25** Our team coordinates the amount of homework given to students so that it is spread throughout the week.

_____ **26** Our team coordinates test days so that students do not have more than one test on a given day.

_____ **27** Our team has established team procedures and policies for our students.

_____ **28** Our team has established a team identity through the use of a team name, team logo, team assemblies, etc.

_____ **29** Our team plans, implements, and evaluates at least two interdisciplinary units a year.

Name _____ Date _____

Ways to Assess Team Progress

1 Great Things We Have Done as a Team This Month	**2** Things We Have Done That We Wish We Had Not	**3** Things We Have Not Yet Done but Would Like to Do
• _____	• _____	• _____
• _____	• _____	• _____
• _____	• _____	• _____
• _____	• _____	• _____
• _____	• _____	• _____
• _____	• _____	• _____
• _____	• _____	• _____
• _____	• _____	• _____
• _____	• _____	• _____
• _____	• _____	• _____
• _____	• _____	• _____
• _____	• _____	• _____
• _____	• _____	• _____
• _____	• _____	• _____
• _____	• _____	• _____
• _____	• _____	• _____
• _____	• _____	• _____

The Definitive Middle School Guide, Revised Edition
Copyright © 2014 World Book, Inc./Incentive Publications, Chicago, IL

Student Growth and Achievement Factors for Teams to Track

It is important for teams to have a plan for documenting student growth, performance, and achievement levels during the school year, especially because there is growing evidence that the teaming concept does indeed enhance the teaching and learning process in the classroom. Some worthy goals to consider and document might be:

By at least _____ percent *(insert a realistic figure here)*, **our team plans to . . .**

1 decrease student tardiness or absence rates.

2 increase parent involvement through participation in school functions.

3 increase student participation in extracurricular academic clubs or activities.

4 increase student attendance at school sporting or social events.

5 increase student achievement on standardized test scores in a given subject area.

6 increase student achievement on criterion-referenced test scores in a given subject area.

7 increase averages of report card letter grades.

8 increase number of community service projects.

9 increase number of elective field experiences.

10 increase number of positive parent contacts by telephone calls, e-mails, or conferences.

11 increase number of communications sent home to parents or guardians.

12 increase number of interdisciplinary units implemented during a semester.

13 increase number of student-generated or student-led activities within the classroom.

14 decrease number of discipline referrals.

15 decrease number of in-school or out-of-school suspensions.

16 decrease number of drug and alcohol referrals.

17 decrease number of violent acts or acts of vandalism.

18 decrease number of missing homework assignments.

19 decrease number of inactive learning experiences in class.

20 decrease number of disruptive behaviors within the classroom setting.

The Definitive Middle School Guide, Revised Edition
Copyright © 2014 World Book, Inc./Incentive Publications, Chicago, IL

Steps for Implementing Team- or Site-Based Inclusion

1 Conduct a survey or needs assessment of special services available on your team or in your school for target populations of students requiring special assistance. Collect and analyze the data so that it is both manageable and usable for the teachers to interpret and internalize.

2 Define the concept of "inclusion" for your team or school and develop a mission statement that clarifies its purpose and philosophy.

3 Plan and implement a series of focus groups or information sessions that involve administrators, teachers, students, and parents. Use these sessions to share data collected and to establish a set of goals for an inclusion program. Decide on the steps necessary to develop an inclusion program for the team or school.

4 Examine the options or the continuums of placement alternatives identified for inclusion programs and select a strategy that best fits your team or school setting. Develop a rationale for your choice.

5 Outline a staff development program for training educators who will be involved with the overall inclusion program. Be sure to include suggestions for curriculum modifications and varied active learning strategies that work best for inclusion teams. Determine what external or outside support services will also be necessary to make the program work effectively.

6 Clarify the role and job descriptions for all technological support resources that will be required by teams or the school to make the inclusion program a success as well as the processes for requesting such services on a need basis.

7 Formalize a written inclusion plan for implementation of the inclusion process on a team or in the school that identifies timetables, procedures, training requirements, and methods for obtaining feedback on how things are going.

8 Establish a comprehensive method for collecting both formative and summative data on the implementation of the inclusion program that includes observations, interviews, surveys, and self-reflective tools.

9 Determine ways to use the evaluation results for improving the inclusion plan, making certain to consider both the benefits and the outcomes of inclusion on both student achievement and teacher performance.

10 Create multiple ways to celebrate the success of inclusion efforts that provide rewards for ALL who participate in the program.

Key Benefits of Teams

1 Improved work climate through a highly motivated environment

2 Shared ownership and responsibility for tasks

3 Conservation of time and space in an ever-expanding curriculum

4 Coordination of assignments, testing schedule, rules, guidelines, and classroom procedures

5 Common commitment to goals and values as result of complete buy-in

6 Reduction of fragmentation of learning from one discipline to another

7 Proactive approach to problems due to innovative and effective problem solving

8 Multiple uses of resources, teaching tools, technology, and instructional techniques

9 Better decisions and implementation and support of those decisions

10 Intellectual stimulation provided by closer association with colleagues

11 Skill development of staff through cross-training in roles and responsibilities

12 Delivery system improved through the use of varied teacher personalities, styles, talents, and strategies

13 Early warning system for problems

14 Effective delegation of workload and flexibility in task assignments

15 Improved time management through team meetings and common planning periods

The Definitive Middle School Guide, Revised Edition
Copyright © 2014 World Book, Inc./Incentive Publications, Chicago, IL

Drawbacks to Teaming

1 Can be time-consuming, especially in the beginning months

2 Sometimes results in personality conflicts, which lead to lack of support or disloyalty to one another

3 Requires people to change and reconceptualize their teaching roles

4 Inconsistency in teacher expectations, as team members all view the teaching and learning process differently

5 Requires a long time to produce significant results in attendance, discipline, achievement, and motivation of students

6 Inability or reluctance to share ideas and materials freely

7 Are viewed negatively by "old school" colleagues and parents who like order, control, and authority levels

8 Difficulty with individual team members who feel inadequate or uncomfortable with the teaming concept

9 Can cause role confusion, as members have difficulty leaving "traditional hats" at the door

10 Inability to vary delivery systems due to inexperience with the restructuring of instructional groups, times, and techniques

11 Can appear confused, disorganized, and ineffective to the outside observer

12 Poor communication due to time constraints, lack of commitment, or poor listening skills

13 Poor public relations, as team members are reluctant to "toot their own horns" and point out the compatibility of teams in school with teams in the workplace

14 Lack of consistent problem-solving or decision-making model to apply as needed

15 Lack of comprehensive team evaluation and reflection process

Block Scheduling Questions
That Decision Makers Must Answer

1 Will students retain more or less with the block schedule?

2 Will the curriculum have to be changed?

3 How will yearlong, sequential courses be handled, such as foreign language courses and Advanced Placement courses in U.S. History or Government?

4 Will students make the most of these extended classes?

5 Will teachers be able to adapt their instructional delivery systems for these longer blocks of time?

6 Will more intense schedules help students develop better decision-making, problem-solving, and creative-thinking skills than in a traditional 180-day schedule?

7 What impact does a block system have on class size?

8 Will absent students have a more difficult time catching up on missed assignments?

9 Will students be able to earn more credits under the block system?

10 How will retention rates of students be affected when there is a gap in sequential courses?

11 Is early graduation still a possibility with the block schedule?

12 How is content coverage affected by the block schedule?

13 What impact is the block schedule likely to have on the school climate?

14 What results have been reported by schools using the block schedule?

15 What is the major negative factor to overcome when implementing the block schedule?

16 What assurances do we have that students will be able to function effectively in these "macro classes" of two hours?

17 Will teachers suffer "burnout" from the drain of teaching two-hour sessions?

18 What impact will the block schedule have on electives?

19 What type of staff development is essential to make the block schedule successful?

20 How can the community best be informed about the benefits of the block schedule?

The Definitive Middle School Guide, Revised Edition
Copyright © 2014 World Book, Inc./Incentive Publications, Chicago, IL

Time Concepts Related to the Block Schedule

It is important to equate the concept of block scheduling with the concept of time. The primary focus of the block schedule is to make the best use of classroom time to affect positively achievement and performance of students.

1 Classroom Time

Block scheduling encourages interaction and individualization of instruction between the teacher and the student. In many high schools, students enter into a contract or an individual educational plan to ensure both student and teacher accountability.

2 Prime Time

Block scheduling allows for periods of "prime time" teaching, which is generally the first thirty minutes at the beginning of the period followed by a "down time" during the middle of the period and ending with another "prime time" block of minutes at the end of the period. It is important that the teacher directs instruction during the first "prime time" period, provides interesting and motivating practice or application during the "down time" period, and provides a creative and challenging summary during the final "prime time" period.

3 Transition Time

Block scheduling provides for a smooth transition between the "prime" and "down" time periods by emphasizing understanding and application of material learned rather than on content coverage.

4 Reflection Time

Block scheduling demands that teachers spend part of their prep or planning time reflecting on what happened in class and how well the established lesson plan was accepted by the students.

5 Personal Time

Block scheduling also demands that teachers take some part of their prep or planning time to regroup their own personal thoughts and energies so that it becomes the "pause that refreshes."

6 Preparation Time

Block scheduling promotes the idea of varied delivery systems and alternative instructional strategies that meet the diverse needs, interests, abilities, and learning styles of students. Quality lesson plans are essential to this process.

7 Consulting Time

Block scheduling has built-in time for teachers to consult with students who are at risk and who need special attention and academic assistance.

8 Facilitating Time

Block scheduling argues the fact that teachers must reconceptualize their roles in the classroom from "sage on the stage" to "guide on the side."

9 Team Time

Block scheduling builds a time in the school day for teams of teachers to meet and talk to one another about curriculum, individual students, and interdisciplinary options.

10 Professional Growth Time

Block scheduling encourages teachers to pursue professional growth experiences on school time. This can be done as part of the Preparation Time, Prime Time, or Team Time and should involve anything from observing colleagues in action (during Prime Time) to discussing professional journal articles (during Team Time) and critiquing one another's lesson plans (during Preparation Time).

"Must-Do" Actions When Promoting the Block Schedule

1 Conduct a needs assessment with teachers, students, and parents prior to the implementation of the block schedule.

2 Include teachers, students, and parents in the planning and decision-making activities and action steps.

3 Make the transition from the traditional to the block schedule for the right reason, which is to facilitate instruction and improve student performance.

4 Work to improve assessment measures that will enhance and not detract from the improved delivery systems for instruction.

5 Modify the curriculum to support the new block scheduling structure.

6 Remind teachers, parents, and students that many trial-and-error experiences are inevitable when making a major change, such as that represented by implementing the block schedule.

7 Create a school climate and environment that values change, promotes collaboration, and encourages risk taking to improve the schooling process for students.

8 Remember and remind others that it takes time and resources to make a major transition in the restructuring of any organization.

9 Keep in mind that whatever scheduling pattern you foster, it must promote the skills you are trying to teach and the concepts that are most important for your students to grasp.

10 Never forget that the workload and union issues must always be addressed throughout the change process!

The Definitive Middle School Guide, Revised Edition
Copyright © 2014 World Book, Inc./Incentive Publications, Chicago, IL

Potential Hindrances to Block Scheduling

1 Moving to a block schedule does not ensure that teachers will improve their instructional delivery systems and that students will learn more. Changing the schedule alone is not enough.

2 Many scheduling changes are done to benefit the administrative needs of the adults in the school rather than the academic needs of the students. Both must benefit.

3 Too many block schedules are developed around existing or established models rather than an honest diagnosis of problems embedded in the current scheduling system. Don't throw out the baby with the bath water!

4 A significant number of faculty members think that the schedule should drive the instructional and assessment process, rather than the other way around. It is imperative that curriculum, instruction, and assessment determine what schedule is most appropriate in any given situation.

5 Block schedules rarely involve representatives from all major stakeholder groups. Students must be involved in the decision-making process.

6 Decisions on what to do with student transfers from schools without the block schedule must be considered. It is critical to consider options for alternative enrollment problems.

7 Students may still find that even with a block schedule, there is too much lecture in the classroom, leaving too much independent work for students outside the classroom. Teachers need to become the facilitators of the learning process rather than the dictators of learning content.

8 Faculty and staff show reluctance to provide direct input and feedback into the planning and implementation process for the move to the block schedule.

9 District personnel are not willing or able to provide adequate training options and opportunities for teachers in the instructional areas of effective pacing and alternative delivery systems.

10 Teachers are not effective in applying either adequate pacing skills or active learning strategies within the block schedule, primarily because course material does not contain suggested lesson plans or pacing guides for doing so.

Reasons to Flex the Block

A flexible block schedule can have the following beneficial results:

1 The total team can test during the same time period to accommodate best testing time and better use of class time.

2 A film or DVD can be shown to a total team to make better use of instructional time.

3 A teacher can be relieved so that he or she can attend to the development of an interdisciplinary unit, conferencing, team teaching, or visitations.

4 Total team activities (such as a guest speaker, field trip, assembly, field day, or intramurals) can be arranged.

5 An extra period once or twice a week can be created for extended advisory periods, silent sustained reading, study skills, or other needs.

6 An extra period can be created for a guest teacher.

7 The schedule can be rotated within the block so that each teacher sees each group at different times of the day.

8 The schedule can be shortened to provide time for mini-courses.

9 Home-base, mini-, or maxi-classes can be created to accommodate an interdisciplinary unit.

10 A maxi-class period can be created to accommodate an extended period for science labs, projects, research, or presentations.

The Definitive Middle School Guide, Revised Edition
Copyright © 2014 World Book, Inc./Incentive Publications, Chicago, IL

Ways to Flex a Block Schedule

The block schedule is at the heart of the middle school. It is designed to accommodate a program that meets the needs and characteristics of the middle-grade student. It has three main parts: advisory, basic skills, and physical education-exploratory classes. The basic skills interdisciplinary team of teachers has a block of time for academic instruction that can be manipulated to meet the teachers' needs and the needs of their students.

The following ideas are based on a block of time consisting of five 45-minute "periods" for a total of 225 minutes.

1 Use one hour for a total team guest speaker experience, which leaves 165 minutes for:
   a. Five 33-minute mini-periods
   b. Four 41-minute periods

2 Create seven 32-minute mini-periods.
   a. Each regular block teacher teaches his or her normal class, while two guests teach additional classes.
   b. All regular block teachers plus two guests teach interest classes.

3 Create a 75-minute bonus class.

75	Science	Social Studies	Mathematics	Language Arts	Reading
37	Social Studies	Mathematics	Language Arts	Reading	Science
37	Mathematics	Language Arts	Reading	Science	Social Studies
37	Language Arts	Reading	Science	Social Studies	Mathematics
37	Reading	Science	Social Studies	Mathematics	Language Arts

4 Use the entire block of time for a combination large group or small group experience.
   a. Team meeting
   b. Guest speakers
   c. Mini-conference
   d. Drama presentation
   e. Advisory skit presentations
   f. Team awards assembly
   g. Team movie
   h. Trivia bowl
   i. Jeopardy bowl
   j. Field trip
   k. Career day
   l. Team students work at elementary school
   m. Science fair project displays and presentations
   n. Interdisciplinary unit group activity
   o. Team intramurals

5 Create an extra period one day per week (six 37-minute "periods").

    a. Sustained silent reading

    b. Introduction of skill of the week

    c. Introduction of vocabulary of the week

    d. Team meeting

    e. Current events

    f. Teaching skills for standardized testing

    g. Study and organization skills

    h. Mini-interest classes

    i. Any team unity-identity activity

6 Rotate schedule within the block.

Week One 1–2–3–4–5

Week Two 5–1–2–3–4

Week Three . . . . 4–5–1–2–3, etc.

7 Implement a drop schedule within the block.

A.	Week 1	Week 2	Week 3	etc.
	##	1	1	
	2	##	2	
	3	3	##	
	4	4	4	
	5	5	5	

    B. Periodically, run four classes instead of five to allow a team member to be engaged in one or more of the following activities:

        1) Team teaching

        2) Student remediation

        3) Student enrichment

        4) Planning future team activities

        5) Staff development activities

        6) Parent conferences

        7) Planning an IDU (Interdisciplinary Unit)

8 Switch teachers within the block! Periodically, and without telling the students beforehand, the team teachers switch teaching assignments for a day.

9 Place half of the class and two teachers with a guest speaker for half of the block time (112 minutes), while the other three teachers are teaching the other half of the class in 37-minute periods. After the 112-minute time interval, switch the two groups.

Sample Schedule: Flexing the Block

(Common Flexible Schedule for All Teams)

Grade 6

- Advisory 9:15 – 9:37
- P.E. or Exploratory 9:40 – 10:20
- Core Instruction 10:23 – 11:03
- LUNCH Teams A, B, C 11:03 – 11:33
- Core Instruction
- Core Instruction (Teams D, half E) LUNCH 11:35 – 12:05
- Core Instruction — LUNCH half Team E 12:56 – 1:26

Grade 7

- Advisory 9:15 – 9:37
- Core Instruction
- Core Instruction — LUNCH Teams A, B, C 10:30 – 11:00
- Core Instruction — LUNCH Teams D, E 11:35 – 12:05
- Core Instruction 2:07 – 2:27
- P.E. or Exploratory 2:50 – 3:30

Grade 8

- Advisory 9:15 – 9:37
- Core Instruction
- Exploratory / P.E. 11:33 – 12:13
- Exploratory — LUNCH Teams A, B, C 12:16 – 12:53
- P.E. — LUNCH 12:56 – 1:26
- Core Instruction
- LUNCH Teams D, E 12:56 – 1:26

Note option of splitting a team for separate lunch times if necessary (shown on Grade 6 schedule).

Ways to Use the Time Block Constructively

Using instructional strategies that are active, varied, motivating, and relevant for students is the key to making the block schedule effective. Here are eighteen tools and techniques that should be an integral part of the middle school program regardless of the discipline being taught or the diversity of students being challenged.

1 An interactive lecture that includes one or more of the following variables or other variations:

a. Feedback lecture
b. Guided lecture
c. Responsive lecture
d. Demonstration lecture

e. Pause Procedure lecture
f. Think-Write-Discuss lecture
g. Bingo lecture

2 A class discussion that is led first by the teacher and then by a student or group of students.

3 A media-based lesson that replaces verbal information with one or more aids to learning such as a movie, video clip, DVD, website, chart, transparency, pictures, artifacts, records, audiotapes, or a manipulatable set of objects.

4 A demonstration and hands-on lesson that actually shows students how to perform a new skill or apply a new concept.

5 A directed textbook reading lesson in which the teacher guides the reading and learning experience by pre-teaching key vocabulary, asking questions, and checking for understanding.

6 A writing lesson in which the teacher directs the writing experience by giving a series of directives on how to proceed and the students engage in a sustained writing task.

7 A field experience where the students learn directly from an outside expert or resource through observation of objects and situations.

8 A visit by a guest speaker in which a resource person uses one or more teaching techniques to share directly information or personal experiences not possessed by the teacher.

9 A cooperative learning small group activity, which can take any one of several formats, such as:

a. Think-Pair-Share
b. Three-Step Interview
c. Jigsaw
d. Roundtable

e. Team Learning
f. Circle of Knowledge
g. Numbered Heads Together
h. Co-op Co-op

10 A skills practice lesson in which the teacher provides instruction and materials so that the student can practice a previously learned skill in a context different from the one in which it was taught.

11 An industrial arts or construction lesson in which the teacher provides instructions and materials for the students to reproduce a product, construct an artifact, or engage in a work activity for an industrial process.

12 A role-play or case study lesson in which the teacher sets up a scenario for students to play the assigned parts and situations, which can either be prescribed by the teacher or left up to the creative interpretations of the students.

13 A simulation experience provided by the teacher that requires the students to engage in a situation that closely resembles a real-life scenario. The teacher provides directions and materials, monitors the simulation activity, and conducts a follow-up discussion or debriefing.

14 An action research lesson in which the teacher works with the students to design an experiment or hypothesis, collect data, record and tabulate data, and share their subsequent findings or results.

15 A series of learning stations in which the teacher develops a number of learning tasks around a central theme and sets up small group sites for these tasks to be completed by students on a rotating schedule.

16 A debate or panel discussion lesson whose topic and guidelines are provided by the teacher so that students can argue the pros and cons of an issue or controversial idea.

17 A survey, interview, or questionnaire lesson that provides students with the tools and techniques for developing and using an original instrument to collect and interpret data on a given topic.

18 A game-based lesson that models a popular game show or format such as Tic-Tac-Toe, Jeopardy, or Wheel of Fortune to review learned information.

Teacher Survey About the Block Schedule

Directions:
Use these twelve statements to review the effectiveness of your block schedule. Respond to each of the first ten statements with a 1, 2, 3, 4, or 5 according to the five-point scale described below. Complete statements 11 and 12. Compare results with all team members to evaluate the effectiveness of the block schedule to date.

1 = strongly agree   2 = agree   3 = not sure yet
4 = somewhat disagree   5 = strongly disagree

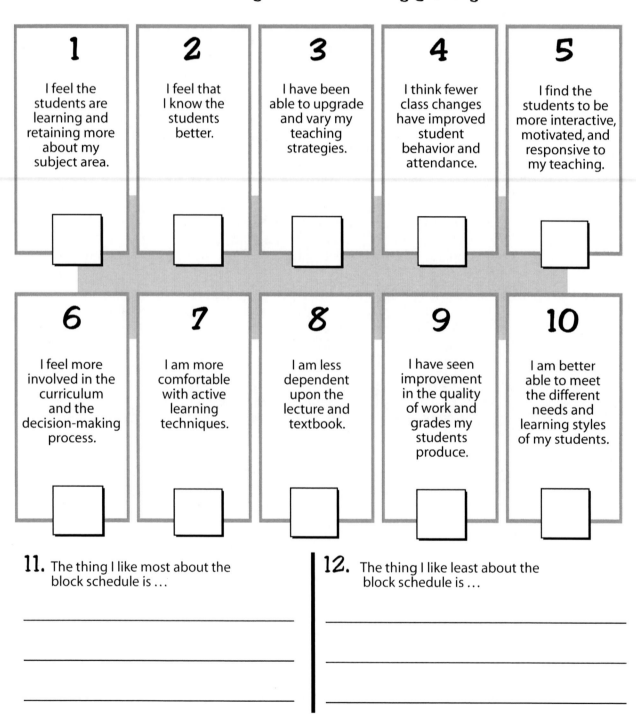

1
I feel the students are learning and retaining more about my subject area.

2
I feel that I know the students better.

3
I have been able to upgrade and vary my teaching strategies.

4
I think fewer class changes have improved student behavior and attendance.

5
I find the students to be more interactive, motivated, and responsive to my teaching.

6
I feel more involved in the curriculum and the decision-making process.

7
I am more comfortable with active learning techniques.

8
I am less dependent upon the lecture and textbook.

9
I have seen improvement in the quality of work and grades my students produce.

10
I am better able to meet the different needs and learning styles of my students.

11. The thing I like most about the block schedule is …

_____

_____

_____

12. The thing I like least about the block schedule is …

_____

_____

_____

The Definitive Middle School Guide, Revised Edition
Copyright © 2014 World Book, Inc./Incentive Publications, Chicago, IL

STUDENT SURVEY ABOUT THE BLOCK SCHEDULE

Directions:
Please use the five-point scale to respond to each of the following statements about your learning under the block-scheduling plan. The results of this survey will be used to help evaluate the effectiveness of the block schedule to date.

____ **a.** I enjoy coming to school and attending classes more than I did before.

____ **b.** I find the teachers vary class activities, which makes learning more interesting.

____ **c.** I seem to learn and retain more subject area content.

____ **d.** I feel the teachers are able to give me more individual attention.

____ **e.** I know my teachers better and they know me better under this system.

____ **f.** I am improving my work habits and my grades.

____ **g.** I find school more challenging and responsive to my needs.

____ **h.** I understand more because the teachers are able to cover the material more thoroughly.

____ **i.** I find that the time in class is more productive and moves by more quickly.

____ **j.** I feel the teachers are able to plan and teach their subject areas more effectively.

1 = STRONGLY AGREE

2 = AGREE

3 = NOT SURE YET

4 = SOMEWHAT DISAGREE

5 = STRONGLY DISAGREE

Please complete these two statements:

k. The thing I like most about the block schedule is . . .

l. The thing I like least about the block schedule is . . .

Name:_____Date:_____

Advantages of the Block Schedule for Students

1 Students of all abilities and special needs can meet graduation requirements in three years.

2 Students can complete college courses during their last two years of high school.

3 Students have only four teachers and only four classes to prepare for each day, instead of the traditional six or seven. Students have homework for four classes each night rather than for seven or eight.

4 Students have a greater range of classes from which to select.

5 Students develop more of a team spirit rather than an isolated or competitive spirit.

6 Students often report a better understanding of the lessons and are more likely to apply the new concepts learned.

7 Students often report higher Advanced Placement scores.

8 Students often report that the day is much less frantic and stressful because it is free of distractions, arbitrary time constraints, and student conflicts.

9 Students are more likely to experience varied instructional methods that better accommodate their individual learning styles.

The Definitive Middle School Guide, Revised Edition
Copyright © 2014 World Book, Inc./Incentive Publications, Chicago, IL

Advantages of the Block Schedule for Teachers

1 Teachers are required to teach only three courses, with one of the four daily periods used as a planning period.

2 Teachers see only 90 students per day, rather than 150 students per day.

3 Teachers are in control of the learning time, which allows for extended teaching periods and team teaching with colleagues.

4 Teachers have opportunities to develop varied instructional techniques that are more compatible with individual learning styles and needs of students.

5 Teachers can use the extra teaching time within a class for more complex lab experiences, more in-depth class discussions, more extended field trips and quality resource speakers, more effective use of technology, and more efficient cooperative learning group activities.

6 Teachers can better monitor at-risk students because they have fewer students in all.

7 Teachers can engage in more authentic student assessment due to reasonable time periods and student numbers for evaluation purposes.

8 Teachers will experience fewer attendance and discipline problems because students now find it harder to skip a class because they miss so much.

9 Teachers experience little or no negative impact on school budget allocations, because block scheduling does not require significant dollar amounts to implement.

10 Teachers experience a more relaxed and "user friendly" classroom climate and since students spend less time passing from one class ro another, there is increased time for instruction.

Findings from the Published Literature Related to Teaming and Block Scheduling

FINDING #1:

John Arnold points out this idea:

As compared to conventional departmentalized arrangements, well-functioning teams enjoy the following potential advantages relative to curriculum:

. . . Teams can create a more personal, positive climate where risk taking, initiative, and responsibility on the part of teachers and students can be cultivated.

. . . Teachers know student needs, interests, and abilities better and thus can tailor activities to meet individual and group concerns.

. . . Teachers have greater flexibility in the use of time and grouping of students.

. . . Teachers have colleagues with whom they can develop curriculum, share ideas and responsibilities, learn new skills, and receive support.

. . . Integrative and interdisciplinary curriculum, as well as special events, are more easily facilitated.

Source: Arnold, J. Teams and curriculum. (1997). In Dickinson, T. S., & Erb, T. O. (Eds.). *We gain more than we give: Teaming in middle schools.* Columbus, OH: National Middle School Association.

FINDING #2:

John Arnold and Chris Stevenson state:

We believe that "small partner teams" consisting of two or three teachers and forty to seventy-five students have some distinct advantages over larger groupings. With larger teams there is a marked tendency for such teams to divide the day into periods of less than an hour and to teach their subject separately, thus replicating the junior high school departmental format that deters curriculum integration. With partner teams virtually all of the potential advantages of teaming are magnified. In these smaller teams people get to know each other better and find agreement more easily. Because a two-teacher team has on average half as many students as a four-teacher team, there is a greater potential to create a strong spirit of belonging and community. Curriculum can be more easily attuned to students' interests and needs. Comprehensive student-centered assessment appears to be more easily accomplished. Occurrences of student self-government are notably more frequent and more highly developed among smaller teams, and students appear to take initiative and accept responsibilities more easily in these groupings. Discipline is also less external, rule-bound, and adversarial, and student advising appears to occur more naturally throughout the day. From the teacher's standpoint, partner teaming brings the advantage of more efficient communication between adults and more ease in flexing the schedule to accommodate the irregular time requirements of a more integrated curriculum.

Source: Arnold, J. F., & Stevenson, C. (1998). *Teachers' teaming handbook: A middle level planning guide.* Fort Worth, TX: Harcourt Brace College Publishers.

FINDING #3:

Paul George and Bill Alexander tell us:

During the period from 1981 through 1991, we have assembled the collective wisdom of hundreds of experienced middle school educators into what we might describe as the "ten commandments of interdisciplinary team organization at its very best."
Here they are:

1) interpersonal compatibility among team members;

2) balance of subject strengths, personality styles, ethnic backgrounds, sexes, ages, certifications, etc.;

3) planning time together;

4) skillful team leadership;

5) personal characteristics of members that include patience, tolerance, optimism, and enjoyment of teaming concept;

6) pro-attitudes toward students where they are treated like "customers";

7) attitudes toward teammates where members fit the expression "diverse but unified";

8) relative autonomy for their own policies, schedules, performances;

9) involvement of principals who are able to "keep a tight grip on loose reins"; and

10) continuing education aimed at team member interests and concerns.

Source: George, P. S., & Alexander, W. M. (1993). *The exemplary middle school* (2nd ed.). Fort Worth, TX: Harcourt Brace Jovanovich College Publishers. (Note: the 3rd ed. of this book was published by Thomson/Wadsworth in 2003.)

FINDING #4:

Donald G. Hackmann and Jerry W. Valentine write:

The following factors provide guidance to school faculties as they consider scheduling alternatives:

. . . The schedule should support interdisciplinary team organization. In middle level research, the worth of interdisciplinary teaming has been so thoroughly documented that the issue has become a "given" when speaking of organization expectations of a quality middle level program (Dickinson & Erb, 1997).

. . . The schedule should support an appropriate curriculum. The schedule should allow teachers to develop a curriculum that is responsive to the needs of their students and ensures that all students "have equal access to curriculum offerings" (Williamson, 1998).

. . . The schedule should support quality instruction in the disciplines through the expanded and flexible uses of time. The schedule must provide adequate periods of time to effectively implement active learning experiences. The effective schedule is defined by instructional responsiveness, allowing teachers to vary the time devoted to different subjects on different days, avoiding the necessity of giving equal time to unequal subjects (George & Alexander, 1993).

. . . The schedule should promote student development and supportive relationships. The quality schedule should achieve a balance between daily stability and creative variety that is developmentally responsive to young adolescents. (Schurr, Thomason, & Thompson, 1995).

. . . The schedule should promote quality teacher collaboration. Research studies have found three organizational characteristics that correlated significantly with teacher collaboration. Those were the extent of teaming in the middle school, the degree of flexibility of the schedule, and the presence of common planning times for the team member (Clark & Clark, 1994 and Steffes & Valentine, 1995).

. . . The schedule should promote teacher empowerment. The greater the degree of teacher autonomy for making decisions about their students and the team, the greater the degree of three variables:

  a) teacher innovation and creativity;

  b) varied instructional strategies and techniques; and

  c) ability to identify and address student needs and behavior (Steffes & Valentine, 1995).

Source: Hackmann, D., & Valentine, J. (1998). Designing an effective middle level school. *Middle School Journal, 29*(5), 3-13.

Review and Reflect
on Interdisciplinary Teaming and Block Scheduling

Level 1: Remembering	Your Reflections

Task	
List the most important advantages of interdisciplinary teaming and the block schedule for you as a teacher and for your students.	**For teacher** **For students**

Level 2: Understanding	Your Reflections

Task	
Explain how you would "sell" the concepts of teaming and the block schedule to a group of parents new to the school and unfamiliar with the ideas.	**Give a summary or outline.**

Level 3: Applying	Your Reflections

Task	
Construct a mock up for a teaming handbook that you might develop for parents of students on your interdisciplinary team.	**Jot down ideas for your Table of Contents.**

continued on page 110

Review and Reflect

on Interdisciplinary Teaming and Block Scheduling

Level 4: Analyzing   Your Reflections

Task	**Difficult Elements**
Determine what elements of teaming and the block schedule would be most difficult for you to accommodate. Think of ways you might address these concerns.	**Ways to Address**

Level 5: Evaluating   Your Reflections

Task	**Criteria**
List criteria you would use to judge the effectiveness of an interdisciplinary team. Or, list the criteria you would use to evaluate the effectiveness of a team's use of a block schedule.	

Level 6: Creating   Your Reflections

Task	**List major categories for your outline.**
Create an outline for an interdisciplinary unit that you could implement with a team of teachers and students.	

The Definitive Middle School Guide, Revised Edition
Copyright © 2014 World Book, Inc./Incentive Publications, Chicago, IL

Module III

Curricular Models

and

Instructional Methods

Contents of Module III

Overview of
Curricular Models and Instructional Methods

Effective planning and implementation of curricular models and instructional methods in the classroom depends on:

- the teacher's understanding and ability to incorporate key curricular models and instructional methods into the classroom program.

- the teacher's understanding and ability to differentiate instruction for the students.

- the teacher's understanding and accommodation of varied learning styles of the students.

- the teacher's willingness to incorporate flexible in-class grouping strategies.

- the teacher's ability to plan meaningful discussions and to respond supportively to incorrect student answers.

- the teacher's awareness of both the strengths and the potential weaknesses of the textbook as an instructional tool.

- the teacher's belief that active learning experiences result in more meaningful and lasting learning than content delivered by the teacher.

- the teacher's familiarity with a wide range of instructional strategies, including simulations, contracts, interdisciplinary units, controlled lectures, learning stations, and discussions.

- the teacher's commitment to cooperative learning experiences and activities based on a deep understanding of how students learn from one another.

- the teacher's skill at integrating thinking skills at all levels into the curriculum.

- the teacher's eagerness to employ technology as a major tool for teaching students what they need to know and do in order to be successful.

- the teacher's recognition that learners need consistent practice in setting and achieving long-term and short-range goals for themselves.

- the teacher's acceptance of the fact that students must have skills and concepts presented to them in varied yet specific objective-based situations.

Terms Important for Understanding Curricular Models and Instructional Methods

Acceleration: teaching advanced concepts to those students who are ready for them

Active learning: learning activities and experiences that have these characteristics:
  a) Students are involved in more than listening.
  b) Less emphasis is placed on transmitting information and more on developing students' skills.
  c) Students are involved in higher-order creative- and critical-thinking skills.
  d) Students are engaged in hands-on and learning-by-doing tasks or activities.
  e) Greater emphasis is placed on students' exploration of their own attitudes, values, and interests.

Authentic learning: learning experiences that have real-life applications and value so that learning is used to solve problems and complete open-ended tasks

Collaborative learning: learning that allows teams or groups of students at the same location to learn together as opposed to highly individualistic modes of learning

Computer-based learning (CBL): use of computers as a key component of learning environment where computer is used for teaching purposes

Core curriculum: curriculum that focuses on content and skills considered to be basic for all students, especially in the disciplines of reading-language arts, social studies, science, and mathematics

Curriculum: a set of predetermined work plans developed by or for teachers to use in the classroom by which the content, scope, and sequence of that content and the skills taught through that content are defined and configured

Curriculum alignment: alignment refers to the "match" or fit between the curriculum and the tests to be used to assess learners and measure what these learners know and can do

Curriculum compacting: compressing the required curriculum into a shorter period of time so students who master it ahead of their classmates can use the time they "buy back" for other activities

Distance learning: field of education that focuses on pedagogy, technology, and instructional design systems that deliver education to students who are not physically on-site to receive education (They communicate at times of own choosing and through electronic media.)

E-learning: an approach to facilitate and enhance learning through computer and communication technology, which includes use of Internet, e-mail, discussion forums, collaborative software, and team learning systems

E-portfolio: a personal digital record containing evidence and information through artifacts or evidence demonstrating what one knows and can do

Flexible grouping: students are part of many different groups and also work alone, based on the match of the task to student readiness, interest, or learning profile

Hidden curriculum: curriculum that is taught without formal recognition but includes lessons that reflect powerful conventions and norms at work in the schools, although not formally recognized as such

Independent study: process through which student and teacher identify problems or topics of interest to the student (Both student and teacher plan a method of investigating the problem or topic and identifying the type of product the student will develop.)

Instruction: systematized teaching that uses a variety of delivery systems and active learning strategies to teach the predetermined curriculum

Learning centers: stations or collections of materials learners use to explore topics or practice skills matched to their readiness, interests, and learning profiles

Learning contracts: an agreement between student and teacher designed to match skills or content to their readiness, interests, and learning profiles

Metacognition: the intrinsic process of learning about learning and thinking about thinking

Mind map: a diagram used for linking words and ideas to a central key thought

Motivation: an internal state that activates behavior and gives it direction

Program or content standards: the knowledge and skills expected of students at certain stages in their education that describe what students should know and be able to do

Rubric: a set of criteria and standards linked to learning objectives that are used to assess a student's performance

Scaffolding: a process that provides support needed for a student to succeed in challenging work (Examples of support include use of study guides, graphic organizers, manipulatives, assistive devices, and text-survey type strategies.)

Technology integration: term used by educators to describe effective uses of technology to support instruction in all subject areas

Tiered assignments: assignments focused on a key concept or generalization with tasks or resource materials adjusted to varying levels of complexity according to students' academic readiness

Virtual learning environment: software system designed to facilitate teachers in managing of education for their students, especially by helping teachers track learners' progress

Guiding Questions for Curricular Models and Instructional Methods

1 What is the academic purpose of schooling in the middle grades?

2 What steps can be taken to ensure that realistic outcomes are established so that all students can achieve these outcomes?

3 What types of instructional strategies are essential for ensuring academic success for all students and how can these be incorporated in daily lesson planning?

4 What are some major curricular models that are successful in teaching middle level students?

5 How does one develop a student profile and differentiation data sheet?

6 What are the characteristics of different learning styles?

7 What are the major characteristics of a differentiated curriculum?

8 What are some effective active learning models for differentiating instruction?

9 How does one manage a differentiated classroom?

10 What flexible in-class groupings are reasonable options for teachers to consider?

11 What are the steps for developing a quality lesson plan?

12 What are some good ways to give feedback to students and how should one respond to their incorrect answers?

13 What are some strengths and limitations of the textbook as an instructional tool?

14 What are some guidelines for developing and implementing successful simulations, discussions, lectures, interdisciplinary units, contracts, and learning stations in the classroom?

15 What are some creative product and performance options that one can suggest to students?

16 How does one "smuggle" thinking skills into the curriculum?

17 What are some tips for leading more effective discussions?

18 How can one infuse more technology into the classroom?

19 How can one evaluate and document Internet resources?

20 What are some curricular assessment tools for evaluating teacher effectiveness in the classroom?

Traits of Early Adolescents to Keep in Mind When Planning Lessons and Activities

As you plan activities, develop lessons, and deliver instruction, keep in mind that early adolescents . . .

1 have unique interests and varied abilities. They need opportunities to express their creativity.

2 identify with their peers and want to belong to the group. They must have opportunities to form positive peer relationships.

3 reflect a willingness to learn new things they consider to be useful. Therefore, they require occasions to use skills to solve real-life problems.

4 are curious about their world. They need varied situations for exploration and extension of knowledge.

5 experience rapid and sporadic physical development. They require varied activities, physical space, and time to be themselves during instructional periods.

6 are self-conscious and susceptible to feelings of low self-esteem. They need opportunities for success and recognition.

7 are at a time in their lives when they need adults but don't want to admit it. They need caring and flexible adults who like and respect them.

8 want to make their own decisions. They need many opportunities to do so within the learning setting. They also need consistency and direction as they engage in this process.

9 prefer active over passive learning activities. They need hands-on and cooperative learning experiences.

10 are idealistic and possess a strong sense of fairness; therefore, they require academic situations appropriate for sharing thoughts, feelings, and attitudes.

11 are inquisitive and continually seeking answers to questions about who they are and how smart they are. They benefit from assignments that encourage questioning tasks according to some organizational pattern or structure.

12 seek alternative ways to internalize information. They thrive on a philosophy that recognizes that the brain needs variety.

Overview of Curricular Models to Use for Designing Instruction

Model 1: **Taxonomy of Cognitive Development**	Model 2: **Taxonomy of Creative Thinking**	Model 3: **Multiple Intelligences**
This model provides a dynamic instructional tool for designing questions and tasks at six different thinking levels arranged in a hierarchy. It is also a two-dimensional model that identifies and describes four different forms of knowledge which are not hierarchical but that must be included when designing effective questions and tasks across disciplines.	This model promotes creative thinking skills throughout a subject area or discipline. It has eight different levels—four of which are cognitive in nature while the others are more affective in nature. It is also a model that serves as an extension of Bloom's highest level—the "creating" level.	The theory of multiple intelligences emphasizes a student's learning style or how one best internalizes new information and skills as part of the learning process. Howard Gardner has identified nine different intelligences. The information about these intelligences is useful to teachers when making curricular decisions and when developing a variety of instructional strategies for diverse student populations.
Model 4: **Cooperative Learning**	Model 5: **Six Thinking Hats**	Model 6: **SCAMPER Model of Creative Thought**
These collaborative models offer teachers a variety of structures for organizing small work groups for students. It is important that teachers understand and follow the five elements that must be present for authentic learning to occur when students are engaged in group work. It is also essential that teachers establish firm guidelines for small groups when it comes to roles, rules, social skills, and student measures of success.	This model is an effective problem-solving tool for use with students during discussions that examine issues, including controversial issues. Students play one of six roles during the discussion as they experiment with six different perspectives when examining alternative ways to solve a problem or make a decision.	This model offers an alternative tool for teasing the minds of students and stretching their imaginations. It has seven different levels of creative thought, which are all reflected in the acronym of SCAMPER (making it easy and popular for both teachers and students in the classroom).
Model 7: **Q-Matrix Questioning Model**	Model 8: **RAFT**	Model 9: **Brain-Based Learning**
This model provides an alternative structure to use when developing a set of varied and high-quality questions for everything from written tasks and tests to oral discussions and debates. It is also a quick template that connects well to Bloom's Taxonomy and that can even be used by students when developing independent research questions and quests for information.	This is a "writing-to-learn" model that improves students' thinking and writing skills. The RAFT acronym represents four categories predetermined by the teacher in a given curriculum area. The RAFT model gives students a specific outline to guide their writing assignments within a set of established criteria.	In this model, information and experiences in a teaching-learning setting are organized in a way that best suits the brain's natural operational principles.

The Definitive Middle School Guide, Revised Edition
Copyright © 2014 World Book, Inc./Incentive Publications, Chicago, IL

Curricular Model 1
Taxonomy of Cognitive Development (Bloom)

Bloom's Taxonomy is a structure for classifying educational objectives so that teachers and students have a common framework for determining the types of desired changes in student behavior as learning takes place. Bloom suggests that there are six distinct levels of behavioral outcomes related to thinking and that the levels are arranged in a hierarchy from the simplest to the most complex.

REMEMBERING LEVEL: This level focuses on the act of recalling when memory is used to produce definitions, facts, or lists and on the act of reciting or retrieving material.

UNDERSTANDING LEVEL: This level emphasizes one's ability to understand uses and implications of terms, facts, methods, procedures, and concepts.

APPLYING LEVEL: This level refers to new situations where one makes use of learned material through products like models, presentations, interviews, or simulations.

ANALYZING LEVEL: This level encourages one to analyze structure, recognize assumptions and poor logic, and evaluate relevance by creating charts, surveys, diagrams, or graphic representations.

EVALUATING LEVEL: This level involves the act of setting standards, judging or using standards, producing evidence, and accepting or rejecting evidence on the basis of sound criteria through products such as critiques, recommendations, and reports.

CREATING LEVEL: This level requires users to put parts together in a new way or synthesize parts into something different, resulting in a unique form, original product, functional whole, or coherent work such as a speech, experiment, essay, or drama.

The Revised Bloom's Taxonomy devised by Anderson and Krathwohl (2001) is also a two-dimensional model that identifies and describes the various forms of knowledge that are not hierarchical. They are as follows:

FACTUAL: Factual knowledge refers to stated facts, data, and definitive or statistical pieces of information.

CONCEPTUAL: Conceptual knowledge refers to generalizations, theories, or big ideas.

PROCEDURAL: Procedural knowledge refers to techniques and methods.

METACOGNITIVE: Metacognitive knowledge refers to strategies, cognitive tasks, and self-knowledge. A teacher can use every level of the taxonomy to specify a task or question for each form of knowledge.

Example: Here is a sample application of this two-dimensional model. The example uses the topic of the human body systems and gives tasks that might be assigned to students for the Remembering Level.

FACTUAL: Name the major organ systems of the human body.

CONCEPTUAL: Recall the primary function or purpose for each of these systems.

PROCEDURAL: Locate pages in your science book that tell something about each system of the human body.

METACOGNITIVE: Choose a human body system that is of special interest to you. State one reason why you chose this system.

Source: Anderson, L. W., & Krathwohl, D. R. (2001). *A taxonomy for learning, teaching, and assessing: A revision of Bloom's taxonomy of educational objectives.* New York: Longman.

Bloom's Taxonomy can be used to design a worksheet, mini-unit, an independent study assignment, a series of creative homework tasks, or a nontraditional assessment quiz can be designed around Bloom's levels. On page 122, find a sample assignment sheet for students of instructional tasks related to technology.

Bloom Action Verbs for Classroom Action

Level	Related Action Verbs
1. REMEMBERING *Learn the information.* Remembering is the recall or retrieval of previously learned material. All that is required is the bringing to mind of the appropriate information. This represents the lowest level of learning outcomes in the cognitive domain.	choose, count, define, distinguish, draw, fill in, find, identify, indicate, know, label, list, locate, match, memorize, name, pick out, point, quote, read, recall, recite, recognize, record, recount, repeat, reproduce, select, state, trace, underline
2. UNDERSTANDING *Comprehend the information.* Understanding is defined as the ability to grasp the meaning of material. This may be shown by translating material from one form to another, by interpreting material, and by estimating future trends. These outcomes are one step beyond the simple remembering of material.	associate, classify, conclude, demonstrate, describe, determine, differentiate, expand, explain, extend, find, generalize, give examples, give in own words, illustrate, interpret, measure, paraphrase, prepare, rearrange, recognize order, reorder, represent, restate, retell, reword, rework, rewrite, show, suggest, summarize, translate
3. APPLYING *Use the information.* Applying refers to the ability to use learned material in new and concrete situations. This may include application of such things as rules, methods, concepts, principles, laws, and theories. Learning outcomes in this area require a higher level of recollection than those associated with understanding.	apply, calculate, carry out, collect information, complete, compute, construct, convert, demonstrate, derive, develop, discover, discuss, dramatize, employ, examine, execute, experiment, find, graph, illustrate, implement, interpret, interview, investigate, locate, make, model, operate, organize, perform, plan, prepare, present, produce, prove, record, relate, schedule, show, sketch, solve, use, write

The Definitive Middle School Guide, Revised Edition
Copyright © 2014 World Book, Inc./Incentive Publications, Chicago, IL

Bloom Action Verbs for Classroom Action

Level	Related Action Verbs		
4. ANALYZING *Break down the information into its component parts.* Analyzing refers to the ability to break down material into its component parts so that its organizational structure may be better understood. This may mean the recognition of relationships between parts or the recognition of the organizational principles involved. Learning outcomes represent a higher intellectual level than understanding and applying because they require comprehension of both the content and the structural form of the material.	analyze appraise attribute categorize compare contrast criticize debate deconstruct deduce diagram differentiate discover	discriminate distinguish divide draw conclusions examine experiment find coherence focus form generalizations group implement infer integrate	organize outline point out question relate sort structure subdivide survey take apart test uncover
5. EVALUATING *Judge the information.* Evaluating is concerned with the ability to judge the worth of material for a given purpose. The judgments are to be based on definite criteria. These may be internal criteria (organization) or external criteria (relevance to the purpose), and the student may determine the criteria given to them. Learning outcomes are high in the cognitive hierarchy because they contain elements of all the other categories, as well as conscious value judgments based on clearly defined criteria.	appraise argue assess award check choose consider critique defend	detect discriminate distinguish evaluate grade hypothesize judge justify measure	rank rate recommend select support test validate value verify
6. CREATING *Put information together in new and different ways.* Creating is combining elements to form a coherent or functional whole. This involves reorganizing components into a new pattern or structure through generating, planning, or producing. Parts are synthesized into something different. Creating results in a unique form, original product, or coherent work (such as a speech, experiment, essay, or drama).	arrange assemble blend build combine compile compose construct create derive design develop	devise formulate generate hypothesize imagine integrate invent make up organize originate perform plan	prepare present produce propose rearrange reconstruct revise rewrite synthesize write

EXPLORING THE WORLD OF TECHNOLOGY

*Remembering

What is cyberbullying?

*Understanding

Explain the purpose of a blog and describe information one might find on a blog.

*Applying

Investigate social networking sites and write down three reasons why they are important to kids.

*Evaluating

Select an Internet site and judge its authenticity or quality of information.

*Analyzing

Compare and contrast two of your favorite video games.

*Creating

Create a PowerPoint presentation or podcast on a topic of your choice.

Name_____ Date_____

The Definitive Middle School Guide, Revised Edition
Copyright © 2014 World Book, Inc./Incentive Publications, Chicago, IL

Curricular Model 2
Taxonomy of Creative Thinking (Williams)

Williams' Taxonomy is an important model to use when teaching thinking skills. While Bloom's Taxonomy is used for teaching critical-thinking skills, Williams' Taxonomy is used for teaching creative-thinking skills.

Although there is a relationship between these two models, and even some overlap, it should be noted that critical thinking tends to be more reactive and vertical in nature, while creative thinking tends to be more proactive and lateral in nature. Another way of saying this is that critical thinking tends to involve tasks that are logical, rational, sequential, analytical, and convergent. Creative thinking, on the other hand, tends to involve tasks that are spatial, flexible, spontaneous, analogical, and divergent. Critical thinking is "left brain" thinking, while creative thinking is "right brain" thinking.

Williams' Taxonomy has eight levels, also arranged in a hierarchy, with certain types of student behavior associated with each level.

The first four levels of the Williams' model are cognitive in nature, while the last four levels are affective in nature.

Each level is accompanied by a few cue words to be used to trigger student responses to a given creative stimulus or challenge.

FLUENCY

FLEXIBILITY

ORIGINALITY

ELABORATION

RISK TAKING

COMPLEXITY

CURIOSITY

IMAGINATION

Suggestion to the teacher: Keep a copy of Williams' Taxonomy in your lesson plan book so that the levels and behaviors can be an integral part of most lesson plans and student assignments. The next page gives a brief overview of the levels in Williams' Taxonomy. Page 125 is a sample student assignment that challenges students to use all the levels of creative thinking related to one topic.

Source: Williams, F. E. (1970). *Classroom ideas for encouraging thinking and feeling.* Buffalo, NY: D.O.K. Publishers.

Williams' Taxonomy of Creative Thinking Levels

FLUENCY

Enables the learner to generate a great many ideas, related answers, or choices in a given situation.

Sample cue words:
generating oodles, lots, many ideas

RISK TAKING

Enables the learner to deal with the unknown by taking chances, experimenting with new ideas, or trying new challenges.

Sample cue words:
experimenting with and exploring ideas

FLEXIBILITY

Lets the learner change everyday objects to generate a variety of categories by taking detours and varying sizes, shapes, quantities, time limits, requirements, objectives, or dimensions in a given situation.

Sample cue words:
generating varied, different, alternative ideas

COMPLEXITY

Permits the learner to create structure in an unstructured setting or to build a logical order in a given situation.

Sample cue words:
improving and explaining ideas

ORIGINALITY

Causes the learner to seek new ideas by suggesting unusual twists to change content or by coming up with clever responses to a given situation.

Sample cue words:
generating unusual, unique, new ideas

CURIOSITY

Encourages the learner to follow a hunch, question alternatives, ponder outcomes, and wonder about options in a given situation.

Sample cue words:
pondering and questioning ideas

ELABORATION

Helps the learner stretch by expanding, enlarging, enriching, or embellishing possibilities that build on previous thoughts or ideas.

Sample cue words:
generating enriched, embellished, expanded ideas

IMAGINATION

Allows the learner to visualize possibilities, build images in his or her mind, picture new objects, or reach beyond the limits of the practical.

Sample cue words:
visualizing and fantasizing ideas

The Definitive Middle School Guide, Revised Edition
Copyright © 2014 World Book, Inc./Incentive Publications, Chicago, IL

Name_____ Date_____

THINK CREATIVELY ABOUT TECHNOLOGY

Complete each task.
In some cases, you will need to do
the task in another space where
you have more room.

FLUENCY

Make a list of as many terms or phrases as you can think of that deal with computers and the Internet. Write your list on the back of a copy of this page.
How many words and phrases did you write?

FLEXIBILITY

Look at your list on the back of the paper (for the "Fluency" task). Classify the terms into a few different categories. Title the categories. Then think of one NEW word or phrase to add to each category.
Circle that new term.
Name your categories.

ORIGINALITY

If you could plan to a create a new and unusual website for young teens,
what would you call it?

ELABORATION

Create a visual presentation that expands on this idea: *Computers have changed the way we live for the better, but at the same time they have also created serious problems for users.*
Describe what you did or will do to complete this task.

RISK TAKING

Ask someone to introduce you to a piece of technology or program that is not familiar to you. Experiment for at least 30 minutes to see what you can figure out about using it.
Describe something you learned.

COMPLEXITY

Some people don't make full use of computers as a life tool.
Give two reasons as to why this might be the case for an individual.

CURIOSITY

Choose a career associated with the computer industry (such as programmer or web page designer).
Write two questions you would ask someone in that occupation.

IMAGINATION

Pretend that you could go back in time 100 years and take a computer with you.
To whom would you want to show it?
How could it be helpful to them?

Curricular Model 3
Multiple Intelligences (Gardner)

The theory of multiple intelligences emphasizes a student's learning style or how one best internalizes new information and skills as part of the learning process. Howard Gardner has identified nine different intelligences. The information about these intelligences is useful to teachers when making curricular decisions and when developing a variety of instructional strategies for diverse student populations.

Source: Gardner, H. (1983). *Frames of mind: The theory of multiple intelligences.* New York: Basic Books.

Intelligence	Focus	How to Recognize This in Your Students	Sample Strategies for Learning
Verbal-Linguistic (Word Smart)	the power of the spoken and written word; the acts of reading, writing, listening, and speaking	– well-developed verbal skills and sensitivity to the sounds, meanings, and rhythms of words – excellent auditory-receptive (input) and verbal-expressive (output) skills – like to: read, write, play word and card games, solve word puzzles, journal writing	making speeches storytelling reading
Logical-Mathematical (Number Smart)	the ability to engage in scientific thinking and inductive-deductive reasoning, to interpret data, to analyze abstract patterns, to see relationships, and to solve problems	– think conceptually and abstractly – identify numeric patterns – speak with a "reasoned voice" – like to: perform mathematical calculations, play number and logic games, work with computer spreadsheets and databases, conduct science investigations, analyze and solve problems	developing outlines creating codes calculating problem solving
Visual-Spatial (Picture Smart)	eye-hand coordination; the ability to create and manipulate mental images in the visual world; the orientation of the body in space and of objects or places throughout the universe	– think and process information through pictures and images – excellent visual-receptive and fine motor skills – vivid imaginations and an unusual ability to conceptualize the world – like to: make maps or blueprints or floor plans; do jigsaw puzzles and solve mazes; build things; draw, paint, or sculpt	drawing imagining making mind maps creating charts
Body-Kinesthetic (Body Smart)	the ability to work skillfully with objects involving both fine and gross motor skills; one's sense of manual dexterity, physical agility, balance, and eye-hand coordination	– know how to control their body movements and express themselves through physical activities – are highly aware of the world through touch and movement – like to: play outdoor games and sports, perform dances, play charades or work puppets, act out scenes from plays or movies; fool around with construction materials, arts and crafts, or hands-on tools and equipment	role-playing dancing moving playing games using manipulatives

Intelligence	Focus	How to Recognize This in Your Students	Sample Strategies for Learning
Musical-Rhythmic (Music Smart)	auditory skills; the way one can hear tones, rhythms, and musical patterns—through the human voice and as part of the environment; an individual's ability to understand and express oneself through music and rhythmic movements	– understand the relationship between sound and feeling – think, feel, and process information primarily through music – like to: listen to music, play an instrument, dance, drum, review musical works, sing in a choir, create raps or poems, chant, or make up advertising jingles and commercials	singing performing writing compositions playing instruments moving to music giving choral readings setting concepts to rhythm
Interpersonal (People Smart)	the ability to get along well with others; the individual skills of being able to collaborate, socialize, compromise, interact, and care for those with whom one comes in contact	– have the capacity to detect and respond appropriately to the moods, motivations, and desires of others – like to: do group projects, take part in debates and panels, role-play, conduct interviews or surveys, tutor or coach others, play games, enjoy text messaging or instant messaging or join chat rooms on the Internet	working with mentors and tutors participating in interactive projects working cooperatively
Intrapersonal (Self Smart)	the ability to recognize and accept his or her own strengths and weaknesses; an individual's natural intuition and inner wisdom	– have a capacity to be self-aware and in tune with their inner feelings, values, beliefs, and thinking processes – have a strong sense of independence and self-confidence – like to: work and play alone, help other people, keep personal diaries or journals, learn about themselves, pursue individual hobbies	using learning centers participating in self-reflection tasks taking personal inventories relate learning to real-life experiences
Naturalist (Nature Smart)	the ability to navigate easily in the natural world and see the patterns in nature; an understanding and valuing of Earth's ecosystem	– notice the intelligence of nature; appreciate the intricacies and subtleties of the connectedness found within the environment – like to: identify and categorize rocks or plants or animals; explore and wander in the out-of-doors, predict weather based on patterns, plant and tend gardens, care for pets and animals	observing digging, planting displaying sorting uncovering comparing, relating
Existentialist (Wonder Smart)	the proclivity to pose and ponder questions about life, death, and ultimate realities; thinking about life's big issues	– curious about deep questions of human existence, life, death, and ultimate realities – like to: think of questions (sometimes unanswerable) beyond those of most children and adults; study different dimensions of life and death; examine philosophical positions and complex theories	explaining ideas analyzing big concepts summarizing questions comparing thought systems or ideas studying complex systems

A Sample Interdisciplinary Unit

(Organized Around the Multiple Intelligences)

"Historical Heroes"

Note: Multiple intelligences can serve several purposes in the classroom. They can be used as a structure for identifying learning styles; they can be used as a structure for creating interdisciplinary or thematic units; and they can be used as a structure for setting up permanent learning stations.	**MUSICAL-RHYTHMIC TASK** Suggest three different pieces of music, composers, or instruments that you think best typify the personality of this historical hero, and give reasons for your choices. Give an explanation set to the sounds of the music, a piece by the composer, or a sample of the sounds of the instrument.
VERBAL-LINGUISTIC TASK Choose a historical figure that you consider a hero, and write a description of his or her major accomplishments, including the one that you would be most proud of if you were that individual. Or, give a speech as if you were that figure, describing his or her actions and beliefs.	**INTERPERSONAL TASK** Determine what leadership qualities this historical figure demonstrated that enabled him or her to get along with people. Give specific examples to support your viewpoint. Pose as the hero, and get another person to interview you in order to communicate these qualities.
LOGICAL-MATHEMATICAL TASK Create a timeline of the important events that made up the life of your historical hero.	**INTRAPERSONAL TASK** Give a written or oral reflection that your historical hero might have written or said in completion of this starter statement: "If I have one regret about my life, it is that . . ."
VISUAL-SPATIAL TASK Draw a picture or make a model of something that you think this hero might accomplish today if he or she were alive.	**NATURALIST TASK** If this historical figure could live in one geographical part of the world today, where do you think he or she would decide to move, and why?
BODILY-KINESTHETIC TASK Act out, mime, or role-play a significant event from your historical figure's childhood. Get some friends to help you if needed.	**EXISTENTIALIST TASK** Assume the identity of this historical figure and make an inference about what she or he would believe to be the biggest mystery in life. Share your inference in a speech, or a mime, or by drawing a diagram or illustration.

The Definitive Middle School Guide, Revised Edition
Copyright © 2014 World Book, Inc./Incentive Publications, Chicago, IL

Curricular Model 4
Cooperative Learning (Johnson and Johnson)

Cooperative learning refers to work or learning that is accomplished by students working in small groups.

ELEMENTS OF COOPERATIVE LEARNING

David W. Johnson and Roger T. Johnson identify five elements that must be present in order for authentic learning to occur. These elements are:

1. Positive interdependence, which demands that students collaborate through group goals, shared resources, joint rewards, and interactive role assignments

2. Face-to-face interaction, which encourages togetherness through mutual body language, eye contact, and collaborative problem solving

3. Individual accountability, which advocates group goal achievement through individual efforts and tasks

4. Interpersonal skills, which emphasize consistent application of basic social and communication skills among group members

5. Group processing, which provides the individual members with meaningful feedback and effective input on how they functioned as a group while completing the assigned task

RANDOM WAYS TO GROUP STUDENTS

1. Draw names out of a hat.

2. Use a deck of cards with all fours in a group or all kinds in a group.

3. Use academic procedures with all cities of same state, all math problems with same solution, all characters within same story, or all synonyms with same meaning in a group.

RULES TO GUIDE STUDENT BEHAVIOR IN GROUPS

1. You are responsible for your own behavior.

2. You are accountable for contributing to the assigned task.

3. You are expected to help any group member who wants it, needs it, or asks for it.

4. You are able to ask the teacher for help only when everyone in the group has the same need.

5. You may not criticize another person in any way.

Source: Johnson, D. W., & Johnson, R. T. (1999). *Learning together and alone: Cooperative, competitive, and individualistic learning* (5th ed.). Boston: Allyn and Bacon.

SOCIAL SKILLS TO STRESS IN GROUP

1. Using quiet voices
2. Taking turns
3. Accepting and offering constructive criticism
4. Clarifying ideas
5. Expressing feelings
6. Using time wisely
7. Listening closely to others
8. Asking for help
9. Expressing honest appreciation and feedback
10. Staying on task

ALTERNATIVE WAYS TO GRADE GROUP WORK

1. Average members' individual scores; each member receives group average as grade.
2. Total members' individual scores so all members receive total score.
3. Issue group score on single product.
4. Randomly grade one member's paper or product; all group members receive that score.
5. Assign individual scores for each group member based on individual performance or contribution.

POSSIBLE ROLES FOR GROUP MEMBERS

1. Recorder
2. Checker
3. Artist
4. Reader
5. Timekeeper
6. Coordinator-Manager
7. Gopher
8. Encourager-Cheerleader

STUDENT MEASURES OF SUCCESS

1. Setting achievable goals
2. Organizing to work together
3. Defining group roles
4. Accepting individual responsibility
5. Listening with respect
6. Taking turns to speak
7. Maintaining group order
8. Completing group task
9. Evaluating group progress
10. Applying social skills

Circle of Knowledge

Use:

This activity is good for review and reinforcement of learned material or for introducing a new unit of study and eliciting questions from students as to what they want to know or learn from that study.

Benefits:

. . . Every student has an equal opportunity to respond and to participate.

. . . Each student knows in advance when it is his or her turn to contribute.

. . . The quality of a student's response is not judged.

. . . Listening skills are fostered through the rule of "no repetition of the same or similar ideas in either the brainstorming or sharing process."

How it works:

• The teacher places students in groups of four to six. A Recorder is assigned to each group. (This person does not participate in the brainstorming because he or she is busy writing down student responses.)

• The same question or prompt is given to all groups. Everyone in the group takes a turn to brainstorm and respond to the question or prompt, beginning with the person to the left of the Recorder.

• Responses should be given by individuals around the circle, in sequence, as many times as possible within a five-minute period of time or "until the well runs dry." If a student runs out of ideas before the time is up, he or she may PASS. Group Recorders are asked to record responses until the teacher notifies them that time is up.

• Group Recorders then report their group's responses to the teacher one idea at a time and one group at a time until all groups have given all of their responses to the teacher.

• The teacher reminds Group Recorders not to repeat an idea that has already been shared by another Group Recorder. Also, a Group Recorder can PASS once all of his or her responses have been shared.

• These collective responses are written on the active board or whiteboard for all to see and discuss as needed.

• Group Recorders list the names of all group members on the informal recording sheet and turn it in to the teacher at the end of the activity for a potential grade or comment as to number and quality of responses cited.

Some sample questions or prompts to use for Circle of Knowledge are:

SOCIAL STUDIES	LANGUAGE ARTS	SCIENCE	MATH
– Cite an important fact about the Revolutionary War Period. – Identify as many political issues as you can that were important to this year's election. – List some positive (or negative) things that impact our society or lifestyle today that are a direct or indirect result of our reliance on computer technology.	– Name a figure of speech and give an example. – Think of synonyms for overused words such as "said, run, mad."	– State as many facts as you can about the human body. – Name both conductors and insulators of electricity. – List as many causes of erosion as you can.	– List uses of math in everyday life. – State as many mathematical formulas as you can. – Name some math terms that are used when creating and solving word problems.

Team Learning Task

Use:
This group activity can be used to learn, explore, strengthen, or review just about any concept or skill.

Benefits:
1. Students build, critique, and edit one another's ideas.
2. Teachers have only a few papers to grade because there is only one paper per group rather than one per student.
3. Students collaborate on the work for a group grade rather than compete for an individual grade.

How it works:
- The teacher places students in groups of four.
- Each group is given a formal Recording Sheet (see example below) and asked to appoint a Recorder and to assign other group roles.
- The Recording Sheet is a "group worksheet" that contains four to six questions or tasks to be completed.
- A team must reach consensus on a group response for each question or task only after each member has provided input.
- The Recorder writes down the consensus response.
- When the work is finished, all team members review the group responses and sign the Recording Sheet to show they have read it, edited it, and agreed with it.
- These papers are collected and graded.

Springboards:
A wide variety of springboards can be used to develop Team Learning questions or tasks. You can use such things as: math manipulatives, tangrams, measurement tools, compasses, protractors, calculators, word problems or puzzles, reading resources (poems, plays, novels, short stories, editorials, speeches, or articles), science-related items or objects (charts, graphs, or tables; lab manuals or experiments; rock or shell collections; or specimens), or social studies aids (globes, maps, compasses, atlases, travel folders, or museum websites).

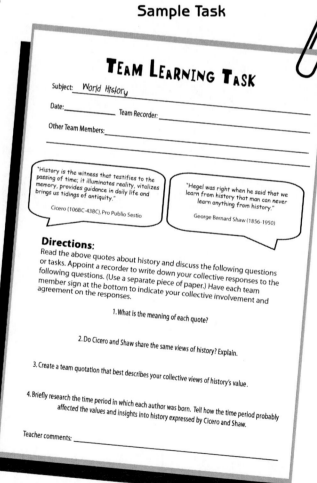

Sample Task

TEAM LEARNING TASK

Subject: World History

Date: _____ Team Recorder: _____

Other Team Members: _____

_____

"History is the witness that testifies to the passing of time; it illuminates reality, vitalizes memory, provides guidance in daily life and brings us tidings of antiquity."

Cicero (106BC-43BC), Pro Publio Sestio

"Hegel was right when he said that we learn from history that man can never learn anything from history."

George Bernard Shaw (1856-1950)

Directions:
Read the above quotes about history and discuss the following questions or tasks. Appoint a recorder to write down your collective responses to the following questions. (Use a separate piece of paper.) Have each team member sign at the bottom to indicate your collective involvement and agreement on the responses.

1. What is the meaning of each quote?

2. Do Cicero and Shaw share the same views of history? Explain.

3. Create a team quotation that best describes your collective views of history's value.

4. Briefly research the time period in which each author was born. Tell how the time period probably affected the values and insights into history expressed by Cicero and Shaw.

Teacher comments: _____

Curricular Model 5

Six Thinking Hats (de Bono)

This thinking and discussion model is based on Edward de Bono's research on lateral thinking. It is an effective tool for small discussion groups that want to solve problems, examine issues, or reflect on a series of proposed changes. Students are divided into small groups of six, and each person has a different role to play and type of thinking to portray based on the color of a hat. To dramatize the different role or thinking required, it is suggested that inexpensive plastic hats be purchased or constructed out of cardboard by students. The colored hats and their corresponding roles are as follows:

BLUE HAT THINKING
This hat is the "control hat." Blue hat thinking requires the student to present the topic, define the problem, structure the discussion, summarize comments, call on participants, stop arguments, and draw conclusions.

WHITE HAT THINKING
This hat is the "neutral and objective hat." White hat thinking requires the student to stick to the facts and figures related to the topic and not to offer interpretations or opinions. White hat thinking strives to be neutral and more objective when presenting information.

YELLOW HAT THINKING
This hat is the "positive and constructive hat." Yellow hat thinking requires the student to look at values and benefits related to the topic. Yellow hat thinking is practical, constructive, and concerned with looking at the bright side of things.

RED HAT THINKING
This hat is the "feeling and emotional hat." Red hat thinking requires the student to express fears, dislikes, hunches, feelings, strong emotions, and attitudes about the topic.

PURPLE HAT THINKING
This hat is the "negative assessment hat." Purple hat thinking requires the student to point out what thoughts are wrong, incorrect, or in error about the topic. Purple hat thinking points out mistakes in the thinking procedure and methods of the others in the group.

GREEN HAT THINKING
This hat is the "creative, fertile, and optimistic hat." Green hat thinking requires the student to generate new and alternative ideas, concepts, and perceptions related to the topic.

How it works:

- Divide students into groups of six and assign a specific hat to each student. Point out to students that there are six different colored hats and that each hat stands for one type of thinking. Review the role and thinking associated with each hat.

- Introduce a topic of discussion to students.

- Remind students that they must play the role attached to their assigned hat and use only the type of thinking indicated by that hat.

- Reinforce the roles and questions for each hat. Duplicate the reminder poster on page 134. Enlarge these to 11" x 17" and hang a few around the room. Students can color the hats. Put these in prominent places in the room to remind students who does what in the thinking groups!

Source: De Bono, E. (1999). *Six thinking hats.* Boston: Back Bay Books.

6 THINKING HATS

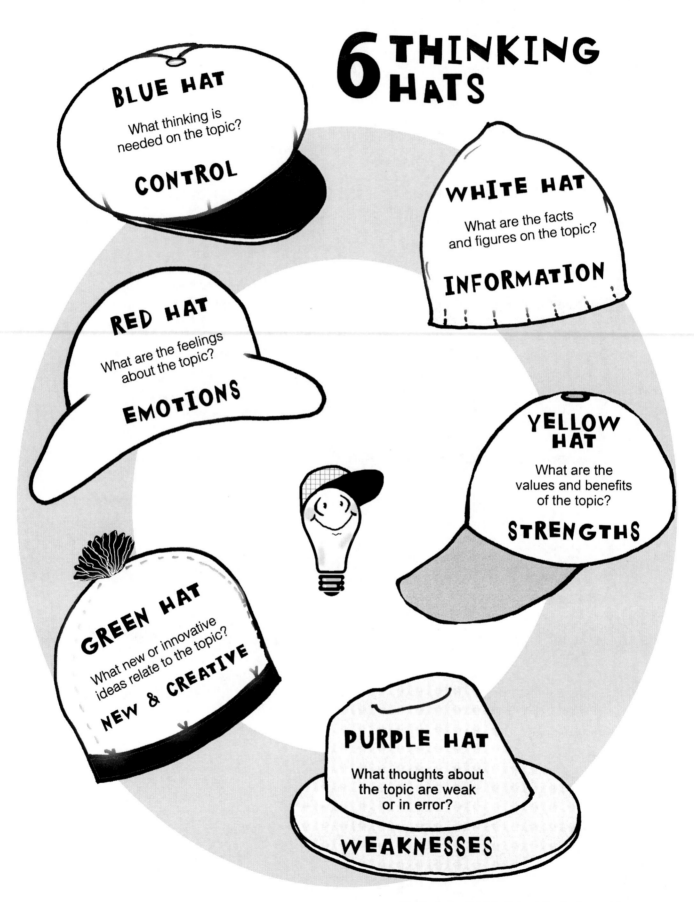

BLUE HAT

What thinking is needed on the topic?

CONTROL

WHITE HAT

What are the facts and figures on the topic?

INFORMATION

RED HAT

What are the feelings about the topic?

EMOTIONS

YELLOW HAT

What are the values and benefits of the topic?

STRENGTHS

GREEN HAT

What new or innovative ideas relate to the topic?

NEW & CREATIVE

PURPLE HAT

What thoughts about the topic are weak or in error?

WEAKNESSES

Warm Up to Six Hat Thinking

Before engaging in a formal Colored Hat Thinking Discussion activity, class time should be spent practicing the six different ways of looking at a problem from each perspective. Use the following activities for each hat as writing or thinking challenges to help students "warm up" to their various hats. Remember that students and adults do not learn only from their experience, but they also learn from processing that experience. Also, keep in mind the thinking associated with each color hat. (Use the poster on page 134.)

BLUE Hat Thinking Warm-Up Activities

1. **Outline the thinking steps you would take to plan and carry out one of the following:**
   a) A school-wide fair, book sale, or special sporting event
   b) A class where teenagers can learn money-management skills
   c) A welcoming committee for students new to your school
   d) A podcast promoting tourist attractions in your community

2. **Use your blue hat thinking to determine possible results of each of the following situations:**
   a) You received an unexpected low grade on your report card.
   b) You overslept and are late for school.
   c) You remember your best friend's birthday a week late.
   d) You have a flat tire on a bike trip and find you have no tools with which to repair it.

WHITE Hat Thinking Warm-Up Activities

1. **List as many true or important facts as you can about each of the following:**
   a) iPods or cell phones
   b) poetry
   c) bullying
   d) TV commercials
   e) Washington, D.C.
   f) junk food

2. **What are the key facts you need to know in order to begin . . .**
   a) Studying for an important test or exam
   b) Trying out for a school sport or play
   c) Getting into a college of your choice
   d) Writing a resume to apply for a job after school

YELLOW Hat Thinking Warm-Up Activities

1. **What are the benefits or value of each of the following?**
   a) Students will be required to wear school uniforms this year.
   b) Male and female students at your school will be separated for science and math instruction.
   c) At the end of eighth grade, middle school students will be assigned to an academic path in high school according to their grade point average.
   d) Students should be required to graduate from high school before they can receive a driver's license.

2. **Tell what is positive about each of these:**
   a) Banning cell phone use while driving
   b) Restaurant-style dining and quality food in school cafeterias
   c) Voice-controlled automobiles
   d) Lowering the voting age to 16

PURPLE Hat Thinking Warm-Up Activities

1. **Wearing your purple hat, examine the following situations:**
   a) Families should be allowed to own only one car in order to keep the price of oil and gas down.
   b) Every student should be required to do a community service project in order to graduate from high school.
   c) Mandatory drug testing should be required of all middle and high school students.
   d) Children should be allowed to divorce their parents.

2. **Find weaknesses in each of the following statements:**
   a) Salary is a true measure of one's worth.
   b) Responsible citizens vote in every election.
   c) Academic grades are the best way to judge what a student knows and can do in a given course.
   d) The government should provide health care for all citizens of a country.

RED Hat Thinking Warm-Up Activities

1. **Respond to each of these situations with words or phrases that express your true feelings.**
   Situation A: Your favorite sports team lost the championship on a questionable call.
   Situation B: The driving age has been raised to 18 in your state.
   Situation C: You've just learned that your best friend has spread gossip about you.
   Situation D: You unexpectedly received an A on a test you thought you had failed.

2. **Choose a date 6 years from now. List changes that you fear will happen in each of the following areas. List changes that you HOPE will happen in each of the following areas:**
   a) Teen homelessness
   b) Employment options for teens
   c) Leisure activities for teens

GREEN Hat Thinking Warm-Up Activities

1. **What creative uses can you suggest for each of the following?**
   a) Discarded and outdated computers
   b) A talking clock
   c) An inflatable bathtub
   d) Old 45, 78, or 33 phonograph records

2. **Imagine:**
   a) A dozen ways to reuse junk mail
   b) Ten ways to structure a book report
   c) Seven jobs of the future that currently don't exist
   d) Schools that hold class on weekends instead of during the week

The Definitive Middle School Guide, Revised Edition
Copyright © 2014 World Book, Inc./Incentive Publications, Chicago, IL

Sample Topics for
Six Hat Thinking Discussion Groups

- The right to privacy should prohibit the government or other institutions from collecting information about you without your permission.

- The practice of sports teams to use the names of American Indian tribes as their official title and mascot is a form of discrimination and ethnic injustice.

- Parents should receive jail time for the crimes their underage children commit.

- Tasers are too risky for police officers to use.

- Men and women in the armed forces should be treated equally in combat.

- We should allow physician-assisted suicide for persons with fatal illnesses who request it.

- Noncitizens should be allowed to vote in the United States.

- Students behave better and perform better academically when the school has strict dress code guidelines.

- A change is needed in the way we vote for President of the United States.

- Schools should ban cell phones for students.

- The Internet is a dangerous place for teenagers.

- The United States should once again begin a military draft.

- Gun makers should be made to pay the cost of gun violence.

- Student athletes should have good grades to play sports.

- Hunting should be banned as a sport.

- Television and movies have a negative influence on adolescents.

- Teen curfews are a good thing to have in today's communities.

- Students should get paid for attending and staying in school.

- Oil drilling should be allowed off the shores of Florida and Alaska.

- Teen criminals should be locked up in adult prisons for serious crimes.

- The government should be allowed to rate music as it does other forms of entertainment.

- Today's teenagers grow up too fast.

Curricular Model 6

SCAMPER Model of Creative Thought
(Osborn and Eberle)

The SCAMPER process, introduced by Alex Osborn and Bob Eberle (1996), allows students to use their imaginations while brainstorming. They can find new ideas, interpret symbols, and offer unique solutions to problems. This model has seven different levels of a creative problem-solving technique, represented by the acronym SCAMPER.

SUBSTITUTE
What could be substituted?
Who else could do this instead?
What other place or time could this happen?
What other ingredients might be used?

COMBINE
What things could be brought together?

Always take time to discuss the changes that would result. What difference is made by the substitution, combination, adaptation, modification, putting to other uses, elimination, rearrangement, or reversal?

ADAPT
What else is like this?
What other purpose could this fit?
What could you change?
How can I adjust to this?

MODIFY, MAGNIFY, MINIFY
What would happen if I changed the meaning, form, shape, texture, size, frequency, or pace?

PUT TO OTHER USES
In what other ways could you use it?
How many ways could you use it?

ELIMINATE
What could I do without?

REARRANGE, REVERSE
What would happen if you turned it around
or inside out or upside down?
What would happen if you changed its order or pattern?
What would happen if components were interchanged?

Source: Eberle, B. (1996). *Scamper on: Games for imagination development*. Waco, TX: Prufrock Press.

SCAMPER Stuff!

Examples of Scampering

SUBSTITUTE . . .

Substitute a better system to elect a United States president than the present Electoral College process.

What would happen if there were three Fridays in a week instead of one?

What would Einstein be doing if he lived in the 21st century?

If you put only egg yolks into the cake mix instead of the whole egg, how will the cake be different?

COMBINE . . .

Combine the function of a camera with some other piece of equipment to make a new invention.

How could a poem help you learn division facts?

What topic or event might bring loggers and anti-logging groups together?

ADAPT . . .

If money came in liquid form, what changes would have to be made?

If the wind blew at 40 mph all the time, what would you do differently?

How would you change your schedule to add ten hours of work a week?

What could be done to your room to increase your privacy?

MODIFY, MAGNIFY, or MINIFY . . .

What could an octopus do (that it can't do now) if it had sixteen arms?

What could an octopus do (that it can't do now) if it were much larger?

What could an octopus do (that it can't do now) if it were much smaller?

PUT TO OTHER USES . . .

What other use can you think of for old, worn out television sets?

What could a garbage lid be used for (other than its obvious use)?

How many ways can you think of to use empty soda cans?

ELIMINATE

If you had to take out one amendment from the Constitution, which one would it be and why?

What benefits might you experience if you got rid of your cell phone?

What would happen if you could not use any vowels in writing a paragraph?

What do you spend money on currently that you could do without?

How would your day change if you eliminate watching TV?

REARRANGE, REVERSE . . .

What use could you make of an umbrella if you turned it upside down or inside out?

What would the Statue of Liberty look like if its parts were rearranged?

Rearrange the rooms of the White House and give your reasons for doing so.

Rearrange the numbers and variables in an equation. How does the solution change?

What would you do differently if the order of events in your day were reversed?

Source: Eberle, B. (1996). *Scamper on: Games for imagination development*. Waco, TX: Prufrock Press.

More SCAMPER Stuff!

Examples of Scampering

Directions: Apply some or all of the SCAMPER levels to any topic or idea. Read the ideas below and then add others to the list. Try SCAMPERING common objects, historical events, or anything else you want to study or examine! Always take time to discuss the change. What difference is made by substitution, combination, adaptation, modification, putting to other uses, elimination, rearrangement, or reversal?

Let's SCAMPER a Picture of a Sea Star

SUBSTITUTE . . .
Substitute rubber and it becomes a rubber stamp, a throw toy, or a teething ring. Substitute metal and it becomes a jello mold or cookie cutter.

COMBINE . . .
Combine with flowers or shells and it becomes a wall decoration, or add a light bulb and it becomes a wall switch or ceiling fan.

ADAPT . . .
Cut a hole in the center and make it into a candleholder, or add parts to make it into a wind chime.

MINIFY . . .
Minimize to make a beautiful jeweled pin or an interesting belt buckle.

MAGNIFY . . .
Magnify to make a giant inner tube for the beach or a floating chair for the pool.

PUT TO OTHER USES . . .
Put to use by adding a stick and use as a back scratcher or pinwheel.

REVERSE . . .
Reverse and turn into an interesting table or footstool for the house.

REARRANGE THE PIECES . . .
Rearrange and create a jigsaw puzzle or game board.

Let's SCAMPER the American Revolutionary War

SUBSTITUTE . . .
Substitute General Eisenhower for General Washington.

COMBINE . . .
Combine knowledge of Civil War and html language to create a historical web page.

ADD . . .
Add television coverage of Thomas Paine to create a show called "Common Sense."

MAGNIFY . . .
What if the revolution had lasted twenty years instead of eight?

ELIMINATE . . .
Eliminate the Boston Massacre or the Boston Tea Party as causes for the rebellion.

REVERSE . . .
What if the British had won the war?

PUT TO OTHER USES . . .
Apply the Bill of Rights to a different cause to identify the Bill of Wrongs.

LET'S SCAMPER!

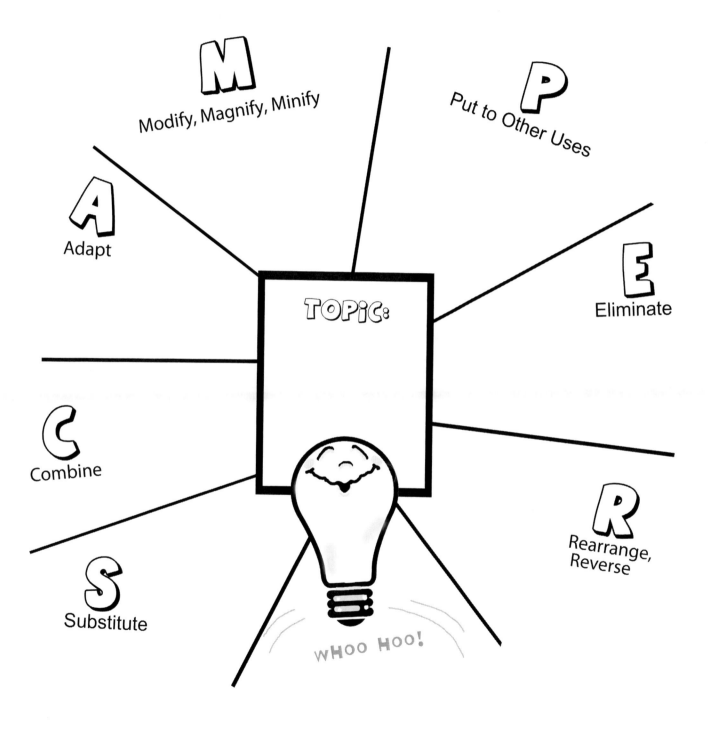

M Modify, Magnify, Minify

P Put to Other Uses

A Adapt

E Eliminate

C Combine

R Rearrange, Reverse

S Substitute

TOPIC:

WHOO HOO!

Name_____ Date_____

Curricular Model 7
Q-Matrix Questioning Model (Wiederhold)

The Q-Matrix, designed by Chuck Weiderhold, is an excellent model for developing a series of varied and high-quality questions for discussions, curriculum guides, interdisciplinary units, independent student work, and quizzes or tests. It is a great device for getting students to think through a problem or an issue. This template interfaces well with Bloom's Taxonomy and offers the teacher two different options for asking questions during a discussion.

1. It can be used to create a number of preset questions in advance, or it can be used to select questions at random to keep the dialogue less formal and more spontaneous.

2. The matrix can help the teacher balance the questions asked of students by checking the appropriate box once a question has been addressed.

Successful Questioning with the Q-Matrix
Introductory Activities for the Teachers

Activity 1: Before using the Q-Matrix as an instructional model, work together with fellow teachers to discuss the following questions as they relate to your various subject areas:
   a. Who needs to understand the art and science of asking good questions?
   b. What makes a good question and what is inquisitiveness?
   c. When do we ask questions in the teaching of our subject area?
   d. Where in the curriculum can we logically teach questioning skills?
   e. Why do we need good questioning skills?
   f. How do good questioning skills benefit students? Benefit teachers?

Activity 2: Next, study the Q-Matrix and note how the 36 question prompts are arranged. Notice how the matrix arrangement connects to Bloom's Taxonomy of Cognitive Development. Note also that the remembering question prompts are in the upper left-hand corner of the Q-Matrix and that, as you move out from that corner, the prompts encourage movement toward higher-order questions.

Activity 3: Use this list to review each of the 36 question prompts. Think about which types of questions tend to . . .
   1) stimulate one's curiosity.
   2) encourage one to make predictions.
   3) challenge one to examine probabilities.
   4) prompt one to analyze own findings.
   5) lead one to reflect on one's past.
   6) keep one focused on the present.
   7) spark one's imagination.
   8) clarify one's choices.
   9) apply one's reasoning skills.
   10) examine the concept of "means to an end."

Activity 4: Refer to the Q-Matrix-based graphic organizer on page 144 as an instructional model when designing questions for a planned discussion guide, test, study unit, or textbook survey to be used with students in the classroom.

Source: Wiederhold, C. W., & Kagan, S. (1998). *Cooperative learning & higher-level thinking: The Q-Matrix.* San Clemente, CA: Kagan Cooperative Learning.

GREAT IDEA

THE Q-MATRIX

	Event	Situation	Choice	Person	Reason	Means
Present	What is?	Where or when is?	Which is?	Who is?	Why is?	How is?
Past	What did?	Where or when did?	Which did?	Who was?	Why did?	How did?
Possibility	What can?	Where or when can?	Which can?	Who can?	Why can?	How can?
Probability	What would?	Where or when would?	Which would?	Who would?	Why would?	How would?
Prediction	What will?	Where or when will?	Which will?	Who will?	Why will?	How will?
Imagination	What might?	Where or when might?	Which might?	Who might?	Why might?	How might?

The Definitive Middle School Guide, Revised Edition
Copyright © 2014 World Book, Inc./Incentive Publications, Chicago, IL

CREATE YOUR OWN QUESTIONS FROM THE Q-MATRIX

Directions:
Write your idea, topic, concept, process, or idea in the IDEA bubble. This can be related to any subject area you are studying or investigating. Use this organizer to develop one or more questions at some or all levels of the Q-Matrix. (Keep your Q-Matrix handy!) Consider questions that focus on events, situations, choices, persons, reasons, and means, as well as those that reflect on the present, past, possibilities, probabilities, predictions, and imagination.

IDEA

GOOD QUESTIONS!

WHO? *(is, are, was, were, did, does, can, could, would, should, will, might)*

Your question: _____

WHAT? *(is, are, was, were, did, does, can, could, would, should, will, might)*

Your question: _____

WHEN? *(is, are, was, were, did, does, can, could, would, should, will, might)*

Your question: _____

WHERE? *(is, are, was, were, did, does, can, could, would, should, will, might)*

Your question: _____

WHICH? *(is, are, was, were, did, does, can, could, would, should, will, might)*

Your question: _____

HOW? *(is, are, was, were, did, does, can, could, would, should, will, might)*

Your question: _____

WHY? *(is, are, was, were, did, does, can, could, would, should, will, might)*

Your question: _____

Name:_____ Date:_____

Curricular Model 8
RAFT (Santa)

RAFT (Santa, 1988) stands for Role, Audience, Format, and Topic. RAFT is a tool that guides students in writing to learn. Students respond to a writing assignment that spurs them to think from various perspectives. The RAFT keeps them afloat and helps them to improvise, write, think, and create a unique product. The teacher prepares a RAFT based on a concept or topic for learning. This is given to students as a prompt. Or the teacher may provide a menu of choices for each of these four categories and ask students to choose one from each of the columns as the basis for completing a unique task. This curriculum model can be adapted to any subject area, topic, and skill level. It is particularly effective for content-area writing. Students appreciate the flexibility of this model that gives them both choices and guidelines.

R = ROLE .... a role or perspective from which to do the writing. The role may be one's self, any other person, a fictitious character, an animal, or an inanimate object.

A = AUDIENCE .... an audience for whom the writing is intended. The audiences for student writing may cover a wide range—from self to small groups to parents or peers to specific organizations to the general public. Encourage students to vary the audience targets.

F = FORMAT .... a format in which to write. Encourage students to experiment with a variety of formats, including many real-life formats and the usual school writing formats (such as essays).

T = TOPIC .... a topic about which to write. Help students explore the idea that they should choose a role and audience that relates to the topic.

Many teachers and writing programs that make use of the RAFT model expand it to RAFTS, adding an S to help students think about the purpose of the writing.

S = STRONG VERB .... a strong verb that relates to the purpose of the writing. Students ask themselves, "What do I want to happen as a result of this writing?" or "What is the action I am putting into it or hoping for from the reader?" This verb helps students choose a tone for the piece of writing.

Here are some examples of an individual RAFT:

R Euclid A middle school students F poem T uses of geometry	R citizen of your state A State Representative F letter T school funding	R astronaut A inhabitant of Mars F warning poster T dangers of space travel

R firefighter A community of San Francisco F editorial T effects of earthquakes	R alimentary canal A surgeon F limerick T health of the digestive system

Source: Santa, C. M. (1988). *Content reading including study systems: Reading, writing and studying across the curriculum.* Dubuque, IA: Kendall/Hunt Pub. Co.

Using the RAFT Model

Step 1: Think about the big ideas that you want your students to learn from the subject matter information presented in class through textbook readings, group discussions, teacher lectures, or audio, visual, video, or podcast presentations. Use this information to build a RAFT prompt.

Step 2: Explain to students how all writers have to consider various aspects before every writing assignment, including role, audience, format, and topic. Review what is meant by the acronym *RAFT*.

> **R** stands for the Role of the writer. It asks, *"Who are you as a writer?"*
> **A** stands for Audience. It asks, *"Who will be reading the writing?"*
> **F** stands for Format. It asks, *"What is the best way to present the writing?"*
> **T** stands for Topic. It asks, *"What is the subject of this writing?"*

Tell students that they are going to structure their writing around these elements.

Step 3: Display a completed RAFT example on the overhead projector, bulletin board, whiteboard, or other projection tool and discuss the key elements with the class.

Step 4: Give students their RAFT prompt, and answer questions. Encourage them to use their textbooks, class notes, study guides, or other references and resources as they write. Remember, they are writing to LEARN, not writing to show that they have it all figured out already. Unless you are using the RAFT as an assessment, students should have access to learning resources.

Step 5: After students have written, give them time to gather in small groups and share their writing.

Step 6: Once students are comfortable with the RAFT method, give them choices by providing a grid for the RAFT assignment. Prepare a list of possible roles, varied audiences, optional formats, and alternative topics for students to consider using in their assigned writing. Encourage each individual or small group of individuals to select a role, audience, format, and topic from the lists provided to complete and share with others in the class.

Example:

ROLE	AUDIENCE	FORMAT	TOPIC	STRONG VERB
Lewis & Clark	Frontiersmen	Journal entries	Details of the expedition	Captivate
Wagon train family	School students	Series of annotated cartoons	Pioneer life	Amuse
Pony Express rider	Teenagers	Advertisement for job	Job description of the rider	Attract
Davy Crockett	Settlers	Song	Remember the Alamo	Commemorate

Step 7: After students become even more proficient in developing this style of writing, have them generate RAFT or RAFTS assignments with the group or on their own, based on current topics studied in class.

Sample RAFTS Assignments

ROLE	AUDIENCE	FORMAT	TOPIC	STRONG VERB
Write as though you are . . .	*Write something to be heard or read by . . .*	*The writing will take the form of . . .*	*The writing will be about . . .*	*The purpose of the writing will be to . . .*
sun	plant	invitation to a date	how I can help you	entice
young dancer	Mozart	series of phrases	style of Mozart's music	praise
Jewish male	his family	journal entries	life in concentration camp in World War II	console
rapper	peers	rap	wasteful energy consumption	denounce
fish	Congress	protest sign	water pollution	plead
equation	math students	sonnet	uses of algebra	inspire
overused credit card	credit card owners	advertisement	credit card debt	persuade
Bermuda Triangle	sailing vessel	mystery story	disappearances in the area	baffle
stalactite	cave visitors	manual	chemical weathering processes	instruct
elementary school child	Robert Frost	list of questions	poem: "Stopping by Woods on a Snowy Evening"	wonder
equilateral triangle	acute triangle	poem	different kinds of triangles	explain
hamburger	young children	picture book	workings of the digestive system	amaze, inform
essay	fable	dialogue	the relative merits of each genre	argue
heart	red blood cell	thank-you note	workings of the circulatory system	appreciate
zero	other whole numbers	news report	talents of the zero	brag
Dear Abby	ruthless dictators	advice column	how to treat your citizens humanely	challenge
Loch Ness Monster	visitors seeking to find "Nessie"	series of jokes	advice for finding me	amuse
hurricane	Atlantic Ocean	weather report	my characteristics and activities	awe
Adolf Hitler	the Allies	personal monologue	causes of the war	justify
Scout Finch	Maycomb County residents	eulogy for Tom Robinson	discrimination	admonish
Ulysses	his wife, Penelope	letter	unexpected turns in his journey	apologize
comma	general public	how-to guide	stopping misuses of the comma	correct
Suez Canal	self	diary entries	conflicts I have seen in my lifetime	regret
red sock	other socks in drawer	recipe	determining probability	instruct

Curricular Model 9
Brain-Based Learning

Brain-based learning theory (also referred to as brain-compatible learning or brain-based learning theory) is based on the structure and function of the brain. The foundation of the theory is this: As long as the brain is not prohibited from fulfilling its normal processes, learning will occur. A curriculum modeled on brain-based learning theory is one with curriculum choices and instructional strategies designed to be compatible with the brain's propensities for seeking, processing, and organizing information in order to maximize learning. Educators and neuroscientists have been working together to apply information from clinical to practical classroom situations. Teachers do not have to be neuroscientists, but some basic understandings about brain-based learning will offer real possibilities for improving teaching practices. When teachers know how the brain perceives, senses, processes, stores, and retrieves information, they can plan learning experiences that take advantage of (rather than inhibit) the brain's natural processes. That way, students WILL learn!

Core principles of brain-based learning are:

Uniqueness – Every human brain is organized in its own unique way.

Mind-body connections – The WHOLE physiology is involved in all learning.

Challenge – Learning is enhanced by challenging, complex experiences.

Stress-threat – Stress or threat can inhibit learning, sometimes significantly.

Emotions – Emotions drive learning, memory, attention, patterning, and understanding.

Social need – The brain likes company. Brains work best in connection and cooperation with other brains.

Innate need for meaning – The brain is naturally driven to find and make meaning.

Novelty – The brain seeks novelty. New stimuli engage the brain to learn.

Patterns – The brain seeks to find and construct meaningful patterns.

Complexity – The brain is an awesome, complex system. The deepest learning makes use of the whole system.

Parts and whole – The brain processes parts and wholes at the same time.

Attention – Brain attention is NOT continually high-level. The brain needs rest and time to process meaning. Learning comes through peripheral attention as well as focused attention.

Feedback – Brains need feedback.

Multi-talents – Information is learned, stored, retrieved through many different neural pathways. The brain can perform several activities at once.

Types of memory – We have two types of memory: rote and spatial-contextual-dynamic memory. The brain understands best when facts are embedded in natural, spatial memory.

Conscious and unconscious – Learning is both conscious and unconscious.

Developmental – All learning is developmental.

The Definitive Middle School Guide, Revised Edition
Copyright © 2014 World Book, Inc./Incentive Publications, Chicago, IL

Brain-Based Learning

Brain-Based Fundamentals of Effective Teaching and Learning

Based on the core principles of brain-based learning, there are three conditions that must be present in order to optimize the use of the brain's capacity for making connections. Teachers must strive to set these conditions:

1. **Relaxed alertness:** Eliminate fear and stress for students, while maintaining a learning environment that is highly challenging and stimulating.

2. **Orchestrated immersion:** Create learning environments that fully immerse students in complex, authentic learning experiences.

3. **Active processing:** Give students time and ways to internalize and consolidate concepts by processing them actively.

Brain-Compatible Practices

Provide students with activities that include:

- physical and psychological safety
- use of the whole body
- a variety of challenging activities
- a level of novelty
- patterns, rhythms, and cycles
- learning designed around their interests
- learning set in meaningful contexts
- choice
- meaningful content
- chunking of concepts, material, and activities
- active processing of ideas
- self-directed learning
- many opportunities for mastery
- personally meaningful challenges
- opportunities to learn in pairs and groups
- learning built around real problems
- strong emotional connections
- humor and laughter
- art, visuals, cartoons, graphics, color
- auditory experiences
- kinesthetic experiences
- music and movement
- plenty of immediate feedback
- details connected to the big picture
- chances to customize their own learning
- authentic, real-life assessment
- adequate time to think, interact, and complete tasks
- connecting of new concepts to their knowledge backgrounds
- learning in settings outside the classroom and the school building
- involving students in planning their own learning and assessment

Brain-Smart Learning in My Classroom
(Teacher Self-Inventory)

Directions:
Consider each brain-compatible learning practice. For each one, note an example that you HAVE included in your classroom. Or, note an example that you WOULD LIKE TO include. Or, note examples of both.

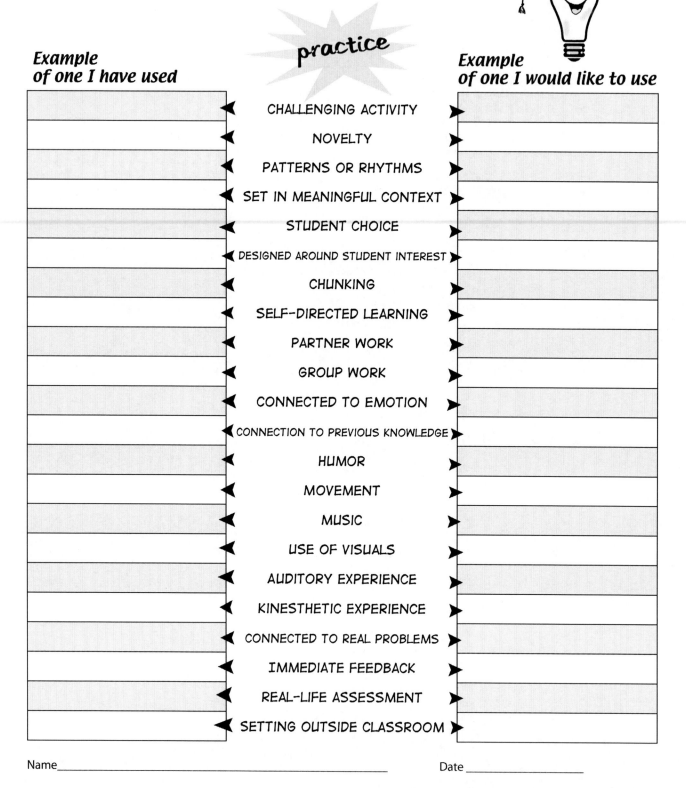

practice

Example of one I have used	CHALLENGING ACTIVITY	*Example of one I would like to use*
	NOVELTY	
	PATTERNS OR RHYTHMS	
	SET IN MEANINGFUL CONTEXT	
	STUDENT CHOICE	
	DESIGNED AROUND STUDENT INTEREST	
	CHUNKING	
	SELF-DIRECTED LEARNING	
	PARTNER WORK	
	GROUP WORK	
	CONNECTED TO EMOTION	
	CONNECTION TO PREVIOUS KNOWLEDGE	
	HUMOR	
	MOVEMENT	
	MUSIC	
	USE OF VISUALS	
	AUDITORY EXPERIENCE	
	KINESTHETIC EXPERIENCE	
	CONNECTED TO REAL PROBLEMS	
	IMMEDIATE FEEDBACK	
	REAL-LIFE ASSESSMENT	
	SETTING OUTSIDE CLASSROOM	

Name_____   Date _____

Teaching with the Brain in Mind

A Lesson, Mini-Unit, or Unit Plan

Directions:
Choose several brain-compatible strategies that you will use in the lesson, mini-unit, or unit.
For each one, write a brief description of what you will do with the students.

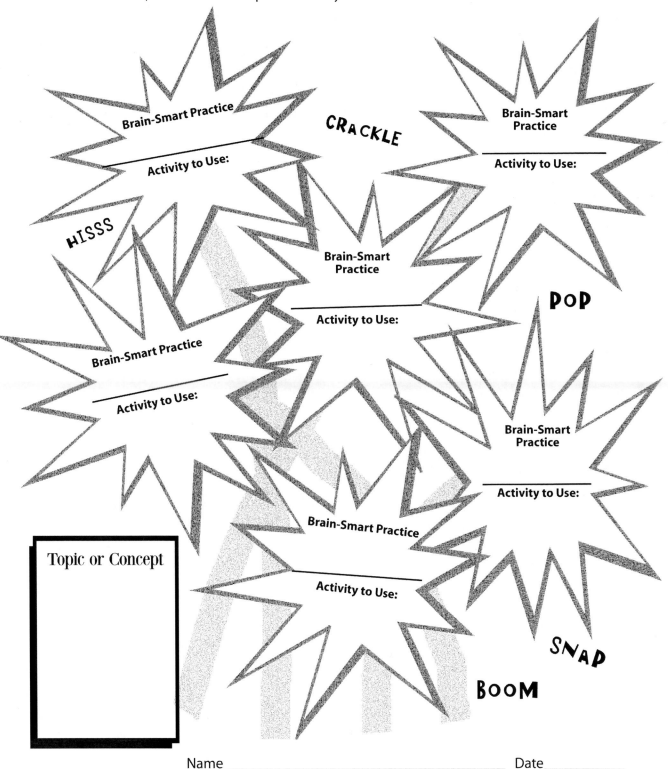

Name _____ Date_____

Guidelines to Consider When Planning Instruction for Students

1 Familiarize yourself with the nine curricular models described on pages 118–151, as well as with other models important to your subject area and grade level.

2 Determine the preferred learning styles, personal interests, special needs, and academic proficiencies of the students in your classes. Use an instrument such as the Student Profile and Differentiation Data Sheet (pages 153 and 154) to record your information. It is important that this information be kept confidential to protect the student's legal rights for privacy.

3 Review multiple tools and techniques that help you determine student learning styles, personal interests, and special needs, which are available through your school district, online, in school or community libraries, and/or included in this book.

4 Consider multiple ways to differentiate instruction and to manage a differentiated classroom by compiling a personal collection of ideas and examples that can be applied in your own subject area and classroom setting. Experiment with several of the instructional strategies and methods suggested in this section of the book (pages 152–203).

5 Use team meetings and teacher in-service days to discuss and share key materials and methods for planning instruction with team members and other colleagues in your school.

6 If possible, visit other classrooms within your school or district that serve as positive role models for effective classroom management and instruction.

7 Maintain a daily or weekly journal that records, reflects, and critiques, both for lesson plans that were successful and those that were not as effective as you had hoped.

8 Use instruments such as those found on pages 204–207 to evaluate your teaching in the classroom. Use this feedback to assess your classroom delivery system for students.

9 Periodically, review your lesson plans to determine whether or not they reflect diversity of classroom practices, differentiation for varied learning styles, adaptations for students with special needs, and inclusion of ample student-generated interests and choices.

10 Develop a personal plan for ways to seek professional development options that can help you be more effective in meeting the academic and personal needs of students that you serve.

The Definitive Middle School Guide, Revised Edition
Copyright © 2014 World Book, Inc./Incentive Publications, Chicago, IL

Student Profile and Differentiation Data Sheet

To be completed by teachers of an interdisciplinary team.
(Confidential)

Student name_____

Date of birth _____

Teacher_____   Date begun _____

Socioeconomic status:

_____free or reduced lunch
          and/or breakfast

_____**no** free or reduced lunch
          and/or breakfast

Family background information:
(Check all that apply.)

_____living with both parents

_____living with single parent

_____living with step parents

Other _____

_____

Names and ages of siblings:

_____

_____

_____

Exceptionalities: _____

_____

Special learning needs or modifications: _____

_____

Special interests or hobbies: _____

_____

Other factors to note: _____

_____

continued on page 154

Learning Style Preferences:

Auditory _____ Visual _____ Kinesthetic _____

Learning environment preferences:
(Check all that apply. Ask students about preferences where needed.)

Sound: Noise_____ Quiet_____

Light: Bright_____ Low_____

Room temperature: Warmer_____ Cooler_____

Group or classroom work preferences:

Work with partner_____ Work alone_____ Work in group_____

Flexible groupings_____

Formal classroom structure_____ Informal classroom structure_____

Time:

Likes unlimited time to work on a task _____

Likes time limits for tasks_____

Works best in the morning_____ Works best in the afternoon_____

Movement: Likes to learn moving and doing_____ Likes to learn sitting at a desk_____

Reading level: _____Below grade level _____On grade level _____Above grade level

Note:

Auditory learners are often:
Verbal-Linguistic,
Logical-Mathematical,
Interpersonal, Intrapersonal,
or Naturalist learners.

Visual learners are often:
Visual-Spatial,
Logical-Mathematical,
Intrapersonal,
or Naturalist learners.

Kinesthetic learners are often:
Visual-Spatial, Musical-Rhythmic,
or Naturalist learners.

Notes

Characteristics of
Five Varied Learning Styles

Characteristics of Auditory Learners

1 Auditory learners like someone to read to them.

2 Auditory learners sit where they can hear.

3 Auditory learners are most likely to read aloud or sub-vocalize when they read.

4 Auditory learners enjoy music.

5 Auditory learners acquire information primarily through sound.

6 Auditory learners are easily distracted by noises.

7 Auditory learners may not coordinate colors or clothes, but can explain what they are wearing and why.

8 Auditory learners enjoy listening activities.

9 Auditory learners enjoy talking.

10 Auditory learners hum or talk to themselves or others when bored.

Characteristics of Visual Learners

1 Visual learners like to read.

2 Visual learners take copious notes.

3 Visual learners often close their eyes to visualize or remember.

4 Visual learners are usually good spellers.

5 Visual learners learn best from things they can see.

6 Visual learners tend to value planning and organization.

7 Visual learners are often meticulous and neat in appearance.

8 Visual learners notice details.

9 Visual learners find something to watch when bored.

10 Visual learners find quiet, passive surroundings ideal.

Characteristics of Kinesthetic Learners

1 Kinesthetic learners enjoy using manipulatives.

2 Kinesthetic learners speak with their hands and with gestures.

3 Kinesthetic learners remember what was done but have difficulty recalling what was said or seen.

4 Kinesthetic learners will try new things.

5 Kinesthetic learners rely on what they can directly experience, do, or perform.

6 Kinesthetic learners are outgoing and expressive by nature.

7 Kinesthetic learners tend to be messy in habits and dress.

8 Kinesthetic learners are uncomfortable in classrooms where they lack hands-on experience.

9 Kinesthetic learners like physical rewards.

10 Kinesthetic learners need to be active and in motion.

Characteristics of Right-Brain Learners

1 Right-brain learners think intuitively and respond well to open-ended activities.

2 Right-brain learners have a common-sense approach to problems.

3 Right-brain learners remember faces.

4 Right-brain learners make subjective statements.

5 Right-brain learners are spontaneous, impulsive, flexible, and creative.

6 Right-brain learners solve problems through synthesis.

7 Right-brain learners are free with feelings.

8 Right-brain learners prefer essay tests.

9 Right-brain learners lack a strong sense of time and structure.

10 Right-brain learners "see the forest."

Characteristics of Left-Brain Learners

1 Left-brain learners are rational, logical, and verbal.

2 Left-brain learners like facts and knowledge.

3 Left-brain learners remember names.

4 Left-brain learners make objective judgments.

5 Left-brain learners respond to structure, order, and rules.

6 Left-brain learners solve problems through analysis.

7 Left-brain learners control feelings, emotions.

8 Left-brain learners prefer multiple-choice tests.

9 Left-brain learners like schedules and lists and have a well-developed sense of time.

10 Left-brain learners "see the trees."

The Definitive Middle School Guide, Revised Edition
Copyright © 2014 World Book, Inc./Incentive Publications, Chicago, IL

Characteristics of Instruction Within a Differentiated Curriculum

1 Provide students with legitimate choices and decision-making options that are meaningful and manageable within a lesson, unit, or course.

2 Offer alternative learning activities and tasks that cater to predetermined individual learning styles or preferences.

3 Arrange for students to have many encounters with varied learning materials and resources.

4 Enable students to pace their own learning with input and assistance from the teacher.

5 Select and develop both common (group) and individual objectives or student performance standards based on both assessment and diagnostic data about students.

6 Provide some flexibility in scheduling "time on task" so that students have some choice in the way their time is spent on any given day or assignment.

7 Vary group size and individual study. Base the variance upon instructional purposes to be served.

8 Consider alternative assessment and evaluation measures for students and involve them in the process according to their abilities to participate.

9 Increasingly involve students in curriculum and instruction planning according to their abilities to participate.

10 Incorporate commercial, teacher-made, and student-generated materials as part of the delivery system to teaching content.

11 Base instruction on a combination of elements including interest, ability, achievement, and performance levels.

12 Consider the following criteria when proposing and selecting learning alternatives for students:

. . . Are the alternatives designed for individual students with varying interests, learning styles, and levels of ability?

. . . Are the alternatives likely to help students accomplish the group and individual objectives for which they were designed?

. . . Are the alternatives explained fully and concretely so that students can use them and so that teachers can assess the results?

. . . Are there alternatives available for small group activity, individual activity, collaborative activity, and competitive activity?

. . . Are the alternatives appropriate for teaching the required curricular content and skills for the subject area?

. . . Are the alternatives written in such a way so as to include all essential information for students, including what they are to do, where they can find information and resources, and what student products or evidence are expected from the alternative?

Instructional Components to Differentiate and Examples of Each

Differentiate . . .

1 . . . assessment data.

   a. interest surveys
   b. learning style inventories
   c. left- or right-brain indicators
   d. skill competency checklists
   e. pre-test and post-test results

2 . . . the content level of the material.

   a. different levels of textbooks
   b. different levels of resource materials
   c. textbook(s) in podcast from
   d. manipulatives
   e. audiovisual presentations

3 . . . the complexity of learning tasks.

   a. Bloom's Cognitive Taxonomy
   b. Williams' Creative Taxonomy
   c. Krathwohl's Affective Taxonomy
   d. Kohlberg's Stages of Moral Development
   e. Maslow's Hierarchy of Needs

4 . . . the kinds of resources.

   a. peer and volunteer resources
   b. library books and reference materials
   c. audiovisuals
   d. computers and computer software
   e. Internet technologies

5 . . . the instructional delivery systems.

   a. games and simulations
   b. learning-interest centers
   c. cooperative learning activities
   d. individual inquiry and study packages
   e. investigation cards

The Definitive Middle School Guide, Revised Edition
Copyright © 2014 World Book, Inc./Incentive Publications, Chicago, IL

Differentiate . . .

6 . . . the duration of learning activities.

    a. division of task into two or more sessions
    b. allowing students time to infuse personal interests
    c. reteaching as needed
    d. allowing for student choice
    e. providing enrichment

7 . . . the degree of student involvement in planning.

    a. development of organizational skills
    b. development of time-management strategies
    c. establishment of goal-setting methods
    d. creation of feeling of ownership
    e. maintaining motivation

8 . . . the expected outcomes.

    a. gearing standards to individual abilities
    b. gearing standards to individual interests
    c. gearing standards to group norms
    d. setting criteria for quality of work
    e. setting criteria for quantity of work

9 . . . the evaluation process.

    a. self-evaluation
    b. portfolio evaluation
    c. product evaluation
    d. performance evaluation
    e. paper-pencil evaluation

10 . . . the types of recognition used in the classroom.

    a. a quiet pat on the shoulder
    b. papers displayed
    c. a rousing cheer and round of applause
    d. a happy-gram
    e. a personal note, e-mail, or text message

Strategies for Differentiating Instruction

1 **Acceleration:** This strategy focuses on the identification of students who are ready for advanced concepts in a given area of study. The teacher develops a hierarchy of these key concepts ranging from the most basic to the most advanced and designates which concepts will be required for each group of students to learn.

2 **Curriculum compacting:** This strategy requires the teacher to examine a particular subject area or topic and identify content or skills that could be accelerated, eliminated, or pre-assessed. Curriculum compacting

   a) eliminates repetitions of mastered content or skills;

   b) increases the challenge level of the existing curriculum; and

   c) provides the student with time to investigate a topic that is beyond the scope of the established curriculum.

3 **Scaffolding:** This strategy provides whatever assistance and support is needed for a student to move from prior knowledge and skill to the next level of knowledge and skill. Some types of assistance to consider are:

   a) text survey strategies;

   b) matching resource and reading materials to student reading level;

   c) teaching through varied learning modes and intelligences; and

   d) re-teaching using alternative strategies.

4 **Tiered assignments:** This strategy focuses on varied assignments that are intended to provide a better instructional match between students and their individual needs or skills. For instance, assignments can be tiered:

   a) by challenge level, using a model such as Bloom's Taxonomy or Williams' Taxonomy;

   b) by complexity, addressing the needs of students who are at introductory levels of learning as well as those who are ready for more abstract or advanced work;

   c) by resources, basing instruction on the varied reading abilities of students as well as on the complexity of content to be taught;

   d) by desired outcome, varying the set of tasks or activities required of students to complete;

   e) by process (which is the opposite of outcome), varying the complexity of the behavioral processes used by students to get from one place to another; and

   f) by product, giving students a learning preference based on Gardner's multiple intelligences.

The Definitive Middle School Guide, Revised Edition
Copyright © 2014 World Book, Inc./Incentive Publications, Chicago, IL

5 **Study guides of varying difficulty:** This strategy requires the students to answer questions or clarify statements in a teacher-prepared guide as they read assigned textbook selections. Students look for passages that either answer the questions asked or verify the validity of the statements given. They must correct all statements that are false and designate where they have found the answers to the questions.

6 **Graphic organizers of varying difficulty:** This strategy provides students with a wide variety of graphic organizers ranging in complexity from the very simple KWL (what I Know, what I Want to learn, what I did Learn) strategy to the more complex strategies, such as multiple Cause-and-Effect Ladders.

7 **Differentiated study or interest groups:** This strategy assigns students to small groups based on their distinct interests and aptitudes. All groups are given the same basic academic question to answer or topic to study. However, each group is free to choose both the sources and the resources for locating and assembling their information. Finally, each group decides on how to share the results of the inquiry with others in the class.

8 **Independent learning contracts:** This strategy provides for an individual student to design a learning plan based on his or her own interest, ability, or learning style. With the teacher acting as consultant or guide, the student creates a plan, process, and timeline for a study of some topic or idea. The contract includes goals, resources to be used, expected outcomes, and processes. It is best constructed as a written agreement which the student signs to show the shape and intent of the study. The contract can be created for a short assignment or a long project.

9 **Computer programs:** This is a strategy that draws on the rich variety of available computer programs that support differentiated learning. The teacher selects programs that fit the learning level, interest, topic, and learning style of individual students or small groups. Many topics and concepts appropriate for the middle level classroom can be introduced, taught, or reinforced in a different mode through use of a computer.

10 **Tic-Tac-Toe menus:** This strategy is based on the popular Tic-Tac-Toe game. The teacher prepares one or more different tic-tac-toe matrices at three different levels of difficulty. Students are then assigned to one of these and instructed to complete any three activities from the tic-tac-toe design—across a row, down a row, or on the diagonal row.

Strategies for Managing a Differentiated Classroom

Differentiation expert Carol Ann Tomlinson (2001, pp. 32–38) offers educators these seventeen key strategies that they can use to successfully meet the challenges of designing and managing differentiated instruction for middle school learners.

1 Have a strong rationale for differentiating instruction based on student readiness, interest, and learning profile.

2 Begin differentiating at a pace that is comfortable for you.

3 Time the differentiated activities to support student success. (Allot a time period for an activity that is somewhat shorter than that student's attention span.)

4 Use an "anchor activity" (option for students after assigned work is completed at a high level of quality) to free you up to focus your attention on your students.

5 Create and deliver instructions carefully.

6 Assign students into groups or seating areas smoothly.

7 Have a "home base" (assigned seats) for students.

8 Be sure that students have a plan for getting help when you're busy with another student or group.

9 Minimize noise.

10 Make a plan for students to turn in work.

11 Teach students to rearrange the furniture to maximize flexibility with room arrangements.

12 Minimize "stray" movement.

13 Promote on-task behavior.

14 Have a plan for "quick finishers." (Be prepared for those students who get everything done fast.)

15 Make a plan for "calling a halt" and bring closure to a lesson sequence or unit even though there may be students who are not yet finished.

16 Give your students as much responsibility for their learning as possible.

17 Engage your students in talking about classroom procedures and group processes.

Source: Tomlinson, C. A. (2001). The role of the teacher in a differentiated classroom. In *How to differentiate instruction in mixed-ability classrooms*. Alexandria, VA: Association for Supervision and Curriculum Development.

Suggestions for Flexible In-Class Grouping

1 Use whole group instruction for introducing new content, concepts, and skills to students.

2 Use whole group instruction for showing movies, videos, or other audiovisual images.

3 Use whole group instruction for conducting demonstrations or experiments.

4 Form smaller, short-term groups to follow up these whole group instruction tasks and to reinforce learning through practice and application tasks.

5 Provide in-class instruction for low-achieving or at-risk students whenever possible to do so in lieu of pullout classes and programs. Reduce in-class instructional tasks for those students who miss class for pullout options.

6 When grouping students of lower ability or achievement levels, make certain to deliver the same high-quality level of instruction as you do for those in higher performing groups. Include varied learning materials and methods as well as infuse higher-order thinking skills. Keep in mind that all students can perform at all levels of Bloom's Taxonomy. One varies the sophistication of the content, not the level of the taxonomy.

7 Review and adjust groups as often as possible, moving students as interest, ability, and performance levels change from week to week and subject to subject.

8 Use cooperative learning groups for approximately one-third of instructional time so as to balance it with both individualized learning and competitive learning. Keep in mind that high-achieving students love competition, whereas low-achieving students prefer collaborative learning situations.

9 When grouping students for instruction, include tasks that require both group rewards and individual accountability.

10 Use small groups for peer tutoring and peer evaluation purposes to provide student feedback and support on their work. Keep in mind that students often learn better from their peers than from their teachers.

11 When organizing small group work, allow students to select the students they want to work with from time to time, as long as they can stay "on task."

12 Do not hesitate to form a small group, with the teacher as facilitator, for those students who cannot or will not perform in peer group settings.

Questions for Teachers to Ask When Planning a Lesson

1 Are my objectives relevant and realistic in terms of intent and number?

2 Have I planned a varied delivery system to accommodate different learning modalities?

3 Have I organized my lesson into the quartile system (one-fourth of the class period each for direct instruction, class discussion, cooperative group work, and independent time)?

4 Are my directions clear and to the point?

5 Have I selected questions and activities representative of different levels of the cognitive and creative taxonomies?

6 What method of assessment best suits this lesson?

7 How and what will I need to differentiate (content level, learning tasks, resources, delivery systems) to meet my students' needs?

8 Have I provided alternatives to the textbook (posters, learning centers, audiovisuals, technology, etc.)?

9 Does the pacing fit into the planned time frame?

10 What materials, supplies, manipulatives, technology, and other resources do I need?

11 How will I start the lesson off in a way that grabs attention and engages students?

12 How will I wrap up the lesson in a memorable way?

Ways to Respond to Incorrect Student Answers

1 If the answer is incomplete, provide a hint or clue.

2 Rephrase the question, in case it was not understood.

3 Supply the correct answer and discuss it with the student.

4 Give examples of possible answers in a positive way.

5 Tell the student where the answer may be found.

6 Ask the student to determine the question that he or she actually answered.

7 Ask a classmate to determine the question that the student actually answered.

8 Next time, after questioning, be sure to allow "wait time" for all students to think.

9 State reasons that the answer seemed logical.

10 Ask the student to explain his or her reasoning.

Note: Make sure that your repertoire of questions includes many that have a variety of "right" answers, so that students are not always faced with a "right or wrong" situation.

Potential Strengths of Textbooks

1 They are written by professional writers, and not teachers.

2 They are kept up to date with frequent revisions.

3 They come with supplemental materials (workbooks, transparencies, blackline masters, tests, etc.).

4 They come with comprehensive Teachers' Manuals that include classroom discussion questions and other suggestions for activities.

5 They contain alternative suggestions for meeting needs of special students such as gifted students, handicapped students, and ELL students.

6 They are appropriate for designated grade level because readability formulas are used.

7 They are written for national distribution and therefore are designed to please all different geographical and cultural locations.

8 They include some information on just about every topic a teacher might want to teach in a given content area.

9 They make extensive use of colorful and attractive graphics, illustrations, maps, charts, graphs, and tables to increase student motivation and comprehension.

10 Race, sex, and other biases have been greatly reduced or limited.

11 Content is appropriate for the designated grade level.

The Definitive Middle School Guide, Revised Edition
Copyright © 2014 World Book, Inc./Incentive Publications, Chicago, IL

Potential Weaknesses of Textbooks

1 Textbook programs are rarely field-tested or validated before publication.

2 Revisions are not necessarily based on feedback from teachers, and revisions are minimal involving less than 10% change.

3 In many cases, supplemental materials are drill-and-practice tools with little emphasis on higher-order thinking or problem-solving skills.

4 All students are required to read the same book for school year regardless of ability or background.

5 Readability standards have often resulted in shortened sentences and reduced vocabulary that sometimes obscures meaning.

6 Mass-distributed books lack flexibility to meet the unique and specific needs of each state, district, or classroom.

7 A common criticism is that minimal information is presented on any one topic. Thus the textbook may lack the depth of coverage necessary for meaningful instruction.

8 Sometimes the wealth of graphics can overwhelm the text and distract students from content.

9 In many cases, definitions of concepts are common dictionary definitions rather than statements of defining attributes.

10 Many textbook revisions or changes are cosmetic and superficial rather than academic.

11 There is little improvement on standardized test scores as the result of textbook instruction.

Guidelines for Developing Simulation Games to Strengthen Thinking Skills

Educational games play an important role in the middle-level classroom because students have an inherent passion for games. When playing games, students can constructively interact with one another, apply their communication and decision-making skills in a nonthreatening environment, and participate regardless of their ability level. They are evaluated by the outcome of the game and not by grades. Games will be most useful in inspiring students to high-level thinking if these guidelines are followed:

1 Determine the overall purpose of the simulation game for the students.

2 Determine the specific content (concepts) and skill (competency) objectives to be addressed as part of the gaming process.

3 Determine the major players whose collective decisions will have an impact on the game's actions.

4 Determine the outcomes (influence, knowledge, etc.) desired most by the major players.

5 Determine the resources that the major players will have at their disposal throughout the game.

6 Determine the sequence of events and the information outlets that will occur among the major players.

7 Determine the key guidelines, rules, and decision opportunities that will have an impact on the major players.

8 Determine the external barriers or roadblocks that will limit the actions of the major players.

9 Determine the rules and criteria by which winners will be selected from the major players, making certain to accommodate the application of skills and content mentioned in Guideline 2 above.

10 Determine the format and props for implementation of the game.

11 Determine the type of follow-up debriefing session you will have with the major players.

One interesting way to get students to apply thinking skills from any of the models is to assign them the task of constructing a game as the culmination of a unit of study. If you try this, be sure to provide students with an outline of what should be included in this gaming project. Make certain that students know that they must use one of the thinking skill models as the basis for designing all game questions, events, tasks, or challenges. Encourage them to include an outline of the thinking skill model as part of the game's directions.

Guidelines for Making the Mini-Lecture a Thinking and Learning Tool for Students

A mini-lecture is a short period of time where the teacher is directly presenting material to students. This may be any length of time up to twenty minutes. Some student involvement or response should be a goal of a mini-lecture.

1 Limit the goal of the mini-lecture to one of the following: introducing or summarizing a unit of study, presenting or describing a problem, providing information otherwise inaccessible to students, sharing personal experiences of the teacher, clarifying important concepts associated with a unit of study, or reviewing ideas necessary for student retention.

2 Develop a set of specific content and process objectives for the mini-lecture.

3 Prepare and use an outline or set of notes for the mini-lecture.

4 Rehearse the delivery of the mini-lecture.

5 Enhance the content of the mini-lecture with audiovisuals and multi-sensory stimulation.

6 Talk for ten minutes and then pause between two and five minutes, allowing time for students to reflect on their notes or discuss their notes with partners.

7 Use vocabulary and examples in the mini-lecture that are familiar to the students and appropriate for their age and ability levels.

8 Provide students with a written outline or study guide of the mini-lecture to serve as advanced organizers of the content to be covered.

9 Make modifications in the mini-lecture for students with special needs.

10 Maintain positive eye contact, body language, and voice pitch during the mini-lecture.

Varieties of Interactive Lectures

Interactive lectures (often referred to as informal or mini-lectures) break down the delivery of important information into manageable chunks for the students to remember. In contrast to formal lectures, which are teacher talks where student involvement is limited or nonexistent, these informal lecture activities require some student participation in the form of questions, comments, or feedback.

1 The Feedback Lecture

Students are given a pre-lecture reading assignment and an outline of the lecture notes prior to the lecture. The teacher talks for ten minutes and then divides the students into small study groups for twenty minutes. Each study group is given a question to answer, a point to ponder, or a problem to solve related to the content of the lecture itself. The teacher then reconvenes the students for another ten-minute lecture segment and addresses the assigned question, point, or problem in the lecture.

2 The Guided Lecture

Students are given a list of three to five objectives for the lecture. They are then told to put their pencils down and listen to the lecture for fifteen minutes without taking notes. At the end of this time segment, students are given five minutes to write down all the information they can recall individually. Students then work with a partner and together they combine their notes to reconstruct the lecture content. The teacher then fills in any gaps through a whole group recall and sharing session.

3 The Responsive Lecture

Once a week, structure the lecture period so that its content reflects only questions the students have generated on a given topic. To prepare for this lecture method, give individuals or small groups of students a 3" x 5" file card and ask them to write an important question they have on a current topic or unit of study. Ask the class to order the questions in terms of general interest. The teacher then proceeds to answer as many questions as time allows.

The Definitive Middle School Guide, Revised Edition
Copyright © 2014 World Book, Inc./Incentive Publications, Chicago, IL

4 The Demonstration Lecture

In this lecture format, the teacher prepares a fifteen- or twenty-minute mini-lecture that involves an active demonstration, experiment, or hands-on application related to the topic. Students respond by writing a conclusion, summary, or brief explanation of what happened and what they observed.

5 The Pause-and-Think Lecture

Deliver a fifteen- or twenty-minute mini-lecture and ask students to take notes on the content. After each five-minute segment, the teacher pauses and gives the student two minutes to share his or her notes with a peer. It is sometimes helpful to give the students an outline that has a series of starter statements on the content which they must complete as the lecture is given.

6 The Think-Write-Discuss Lecture

The teacher prepares three questions to ask students throughout the lecture.

- The first question is a motivational question that is given before the lecture begins.
- The second question is given during the middle of the lecture and requires the student to write a short response to clarify a point or concept presented in the lecture.
- The third question is given at the end of the lecture and is a feedback type question about something learned, something that needs further clarification, or something misunderstood.

7 The Bingo Lecture

Prepare a Bingo grid (or use the grid supplied on the next page). In each cell, write a key concept that will be included in the lecture. As students hear the concept explained during the lecture, they cover the appropriate space with a marker. The first person to get the cells completed across, down, or on a diagonal shouts "Bingo" and wins that round. Students may work alone or in pairs.

BINGO LECTURE

Directions to the student:

This BINGO board contains key ideas about a topic. It will be a learning tool to help you get the most out of a lesson that the teacher will present. As the teacher talks, listen and watch for these ideas. Each time you hear an idea, place a marker on that square on the board. When you have a row completed (across, down, or diagonal), shout **"Bingo!"**

B	I	N	G	O
		THINK BINGO!		

Name_____ Date_____

Essential Elements of an Interdisciplinary Unit

1 **Theme**

Make it broad enough to:

   a. include objectives from
       several subject areas.

   b. motivate and interest
       students and teachers.

   c. include several
       creative activities.

   d. accommodate small
       and large group
       instructional strategies.

   e. last from 3 to 5 days.

2 **Title**

Make it creative and fun!

3 **Objectives**

List at least two objectives
for each subject area:

      Language Arts
      Social Studies
      Math
      Science
      Industrial Arts
      Art
      Music
      Physical Education

4 **Background information on
the topic for students**

Write a one-page overview of
the subject area concepts that
gives students the appropriate
background or springboard
information to effectively
launch the unit.

5 **Glossary**

Prepare a glossary of key terms,
vocabulary words or phrases, and
concepts that are important to
the mastery of the material.

6 **Student record sheets**

Design and maintain record
sheets to keep track of student
progress, or that guide
students in keeping track of
their own progress.

7 **Activities in each discipline**

Use the same format in preparing
your activities, including:

      a. title
      b. objective
      c. materials needed
      d. procedure
      e. evaluation

8 **Homework and enrichment ideas**

Create a list of tasks that could
be assigned as homework or
enrichment for students.

9 **Post-test or project preparation**

Include a post-test or directions
for a final project to serve as
the evaluation for the unit in
addition to those used as part
of the activities.

10 **Bibliography**

List resources and references
for follow-up or for use during
the unit.

Steps for
Beginning to Integrate the Disciplines

Interdisciplinary units contain two or more different disciplines as their focus, with a curriculum theme that should, according to James A. Beane, "emerge from the natural overlaps between the personal concerns of early adolescents and the larger issues that face our world." Thematic units are effective for these reasons:

1) The real world is integrated.

2) Students do best when learning is connected to more than one discipline.

3) Integrated programs are useful in tracking other areas of concern.

4) It is difficult to teach subjects and skills in isolation during an instructional day, even with the flexible block schedule in place.

Step 1: Each teacher on a team should develop a workable definition of interdisciplinary instruction as he or she understands it. All team members compare and discuss individual interpretations of interdisciplinary instruction. Finally, the team synthesizes the best ideas from all team members and comes up with a workable definition for the group.

Step 2: Each team member brainstorms a wide variety of possible topics for interdisciplinary instruction that would most easily incorporate their core subject areas. Team members meet to share their respective lists, to eliminate duplicates or overlaps, and to compile a master list that appeals to all team members.

Step 3: Each team schedules a formal meeting to select any one of the designated themes for future implementation. Team members brainstorm related topics for each of the core subject areas. Next, teams locate resource materials on the topic and look for activities that lend themselves to science, social studies, math, or language arts.

Step 4: The fourth step involves a series of team meetings that require team members to complete an outline for teaching the interdisciplinary topic agreed upon in Step 3. Each teacher determines the key skills or concepts that are important parts of the interdisciplinary process.

The Definitive Middle School Guide, Revised Edition
Copyright © 2014 World Book, Inc./Incentive Publications, Chicago, IL

Step 5: Team members exchange classes for at least one period, teaching one another's subject areas according to prepared lesson plans. For example, the science and math team members teach each other's classes for a session while the social studies and language arts team members do the same.

Step 6: Next, team members set aside the textbook in their subject area for a minimum of three consecutive days. Emphasis is placed on the use of other resources and delivery systems for teaching required basic skills and concepts. This requires team members either to practice using other types of reproducible materials for instruction with students or to develop individual activities of their own using varied tools and techniques to differentiate instruction.

Step 7: Team members spend at least three days practicing the art of "creative questioning" within their disciplines. This approach encourages students to tease their minds and stretch their imaginations. Using the same types of higher-order questions in different subject areas can help the early adolescent to see the connectedness of both content and thinking skills.

Step 8: Team members decide upon an individual skill such as drawing conclusions or the concept of measurement and develop a short lesson in science, math, social studies, and language arts to present to their students for one week. This activity will provide each team with a chance to approach a skill or concept from several interdisciplinary points of view.

Step 9: The team composes a letter to parents or guardians outlining plans for the interdisciplinary unit and the involvement of the family. The content of the letter includes specific information about theme, purpose, length, objectives, varied activities, and projected outcomes. In addition, the letter invites parents to become involved in a variety of ways. The team members should also prepare their homeroom or group of assigned students for this interdisciplinary adventure, making certain that all stakeholders understand its purposes.

Step 10: Finally, the interdisciplinary unit is field tested by team members with their students. The team designs a simple student evaluation form for assessing the unit's effectiveness. The evaluation form includes questions about all aspects of the interdisciplinary unit, including appropriateness of the subject matter, activities, time span, team teaching, and learning resources.

Building an Interdisciplinary Planning Matrix

Directions:
As a team, list all the major concepts, units, skills, or topics each of you will be covering during the school year.
Try to record by subject area and by month. Look for overlaps or changes that could easily be worked into interdisciplinary units.

	SEPT	OCT	NOV	DEC	JAN	FEB	MAR	APR	MAY
Science									
Math									
Social Studies									
Language Arts									
Exploratory									
P.E.									

Reasons to Use Learning Stations

A learning station is a space in the classroom where students can go to participate in a wide variety of activities to learn or practice a new skill or to extend their knowledge on a given topic or concept.

Learning stations come in many different sizes and shapes.

They can be located on walls, easels, bulletin boards, tables, clotheslines, display boards, or countertops, just to name a few possibilities. The entire classroom can be set up for learning stations, which would contain clusters of tables or desks. On the other hand, a single area of the classroom could house a single learning station or two for enrichment or reinforcement tasks.

Learning station tasks can be organized around Bloom's Taxonomy, Williams' Taxonomy, Multiple Intelligences, or any combination of these models to ensure higher-order thinking skill tasks and to integrate a variety of learning styles.

Learning centers . . .

1 offer choices to students.

2 empower students to assume responsibility for their own learning.

3 motivate students because the stations are rich in diverse materials and resources.

4 cater to the unique needs and characteristics of the early adolescent.

5 enable learners to work in various groups of mixed abilities.

6 encourage active participation and interaction among learners.

7 teach learners how to follow directions, make decisions, and work independently.

8 facilitate both individualized and differentiated learning tasks.

9 give students an opportunity to assume responsibility for their own learning.

10 free teachers up to work with small skill groups.

11 provide for different student interests and learning styles.

12 provide a manageable structure for integrating subject areas.

13 make better use and organization of learning resources.

14 simultaneously foster individual and small-group instruction.

15 give teachers more information about student work habits, attitudes, interests, and abilities.

Name _____ Date _____

Questions to Answer
When Creating a Learning Station

Directions: *Answer these questions before putting the station to use. Check off each one when it is answered.*

Type and purpose

____ 1. What major purpose or umbrella theme will the station serve?

____ 2. Will the station be an enrichment station, a skill station, or an interest station?

Objectives

____ 3. What student performance standards can best be met at this station?

____ 4. How do the performance standards relate to the abilities and interests of the students?

Design of the space

____ 5. How much and what type of space can be allocated to this station?

____ 6. What kinds of furniture and equipment are needed for this station?

____ 7. How will the location of the station affect other classroom activities?

Material needs

____ 8. What instructional materials are needed for the station?

____ 9. How will the materials be housed, stored, displayed at the station?

Activities

____ 10. Are there varied activities available at the station?

____ 11. Are the activities compatible with the purpose or objectives of the station?

____ 12. Are the activities able to accommodate varying abilities, learning styles, and interests of students?

____ 13. Are the activities explained in such a way that the student knows what to do and how to do it?

____ 14. Do the activities require higher-order thinking skills and active rather than passive tasks?

Guidelines for student use

____ 15. How many students can use the station at the same time, and how are they scheduled?

____ 16. What can students do at the station?

____ 17. What assessment, evaluation, or accountability measures are in place for assessing student work?

____ 18. What do students do with incomplete and finished work?

Management of the process

____ 19. Is there a management system in place for the station?

____ 20. Is the management system appropriate for age and ability levels of students?

____ 21. Does the management system maximize student self-management and recordkeeping?

____ 22. What arrangements are needed for teacher-student consultation on student progress and evaluation?

Orientation of students

____ 23. Do students understand the purposes, procedures, and management of the station?

____ 24. Do students understand the relation of the station to other instructional activities in the classroom?

____ 25. Do students understand what behavior and academic standards are expected of them at the station?

A Laughing Matter
Sample Learning Station, Topic: Humor

The learning station design is based on Gardner's Multiple Intelligences. Students coming to the station can choose from among several activities.

Verbal-Linguistic Intelligence

1 Write a descriptive paragraph based on one of these starter statements:

A funny thing that happened to me was . . .

People are funny who . . .

I had to laugh at myself when . . .

2 Write a classroom newsletter strictly on the lighter side.

3 Find, practice, and read something humorous to the class.

Logical-Mathematical Intelligence

1 Research to find information about the history and science of humor.

2 Analyze humorous literature or modern (or classical) art for types of humor.

3 Construct a chart to show your funniest choices when it comes to movies, television shows, classmates or friends, books, songs, recordings, jokes, riddles, and cartoons or comic strips.

4 Design a display that shows examples of figural humor, verbal humor, visual humor, and auditory humor.

Visual-Spatial Intelligence

1 Do a humor collage of words, smiles, and faces.

2 Plan a silly hat day, funny T-shirt day, or a clever button day for your class.

3 Use a digital camera to take candid and spontaneous photos of a school event.

Body-Kinesthetic Intelligence

1 Learn signing of humor words as used by hearing impaired (words like *smile, laugh, giggle*).

2 Study the "art and science of clowns" and perform a simple clown act for classmates.

3 Stock a toy box for the classroom full of fun games and props that anyone can use whenever things get tense or they have some free time.

4 Plan and perform a mime to share a joke.

Musical-Rhythmic Intelligence

1 Listen to humorous podcasts or watch humorous videotapes. Write reviews of each podcast or tape.

2 Start a people chain with a joke and have others whisper or sing it to one another around the room. Summarize the funny things that happen.

3 Collect lyrics to humorous songs and post them for others to read and enjoy.

Interpersonal Intelligence

1 Establish a Humor-Joy-Fun committee for the class and rotate membership and responsibilities.

2 Organize a joke festival or marathon. Have a joke dropbox that students can read from when other work is complete. Have students rate submitted or performed jokes to determine their funniest rating. Does the rating scale have benchmarks for a grin, smile, grimace, loud laugh, or guffaw?

3 Start a class collection of humorous quotations to which students can add. Keep them in a file box or post on a bulletin board.

Intrapersonal Intelligence

1 Maintain a "Laughter Log" that records your "humorous moments" during a given day, week, or month. Keep track of when and why you laugh.

2 Develop a personal plan for you and your family to celebrate Humor Week or National Humor Day on April 15th.

3 Think of something that would cause you to express yourself through each of these types of laughter: smirk, smile, grin, snicker, giggle, laugh, howl, shriek, roar, and die laughing.

Naturalist Intelligence

1 Locate a series of jokes and riddles that tease or make fun of nature in some way, shape, or form. Share them with a friend.

2 Go online and search for websites that are related to Mother Nature. Locate humorous photos, anecdotes, or news stories that appeal to your sense of humor. Bookmark these websites so that others can visit them as well.

Existentialist Intelligence

1 Answer this big question: Is one's sense of humor inherited, learned from someone else, a gift from God, or the result of an accident?

2 Make up puns about some of the great serious theories in history.

Portable Learning Stations for Middle Level Students

These six learning station formats work well for middle school students and teachers because they are practical to store, set up, move about the room, fit in small spaces, and develop.

1 Desktop Station: This is a three-sided, free-standing cardboard station constructed out of storage boxes. The boxes may be of a size that fits on top of a student desk or one that sits on top of a table or bookcase. The station's title, directions, assigned tasks, and colorful graphics are glued on the inside of the folding cardboard structure.

2 Pocket Packet Station: This is a king-size brown or manila envelope with graphics on the front and a clasp or tie on the back. Individual task and direction cards are placed inside the envelope.

3 File Folder Station: This is a regular or king-size manila or colored file folder with a storage envelope attached to the back of the folder. The title goes on the front of the folder. Directions and tasks are written on the insides of the folder. Reference materials are in the envelope on the back.

4 Poster Station: This is a king-size piece of poster board that has the title at the top and mini-task or direction cards glued on the front. Graphics should be used to add color and interest where appropriate.

5 Shopping Bag Station: This is a large, colorful shopping bag with handles that can be purchased at most gift and drugstores. The title goes on the front of the bag and both task and direction cards go inside the bag along with assorted reference books, pamphlets, and handouts.

6 Pizza Box Station: This is a standard pizza box which can be obtained at most fast-food outlets. The title goes on the top of the box. Task and direction cards and assorted resources or props are housed within the box itself.

Suggestions and Instructions for Stations

1 Each learning station should focus on a central theme and a curricular model. Consider Bloom's Taxonomy, Williams' Taxonomy, or the Multiple Intelligences.

2 Prepare sets of task cards for the model chosen. These can be made of card stock or heavy duty paper and laminated for durability. Be sure to include at least one task card for each level of Bloom, for each level of Williams, or for each of the multiple intelligences, depending upon the focus of your learning station. Try making the cards in a specific shape to reflect the theme of the station. For example, if the theme is geometry, make the task cards in different geometric shapes. If the theme is literature, make the task cards in the shape of a book. If the theme is patriotism, make the task cards in the shape of different patriotic symbols. If the theme is oceanography, make the task cards in the shape of different sea creatures.

3 Prepare a "Direction Card" so students know what to do and how to do it. Also, prepare an "Objectives Card" that outlines the content to be covered, as well as a "Prop-Resource Card" that lists the reference materials or websites to be used for research and information.

4 Try to make the learning station interdisciplinary so that students are applying many different skills and producing many different types of outcomes or products.

5 Think about developing a written quiz or other assessment task that students can take independently once they have completed the learning station tasks successfully.

Creative Student Options for Products and Performances

1. Present a mock trial based on a popular fairy tale.

2. Design a web page.

3. Prepare a travelogue from an explorer's point of view.

4. Create a rainbow of textures.

5. Burn a data disk.

6. Design a Rube Goldberg-type invention.

7. Plan a campaign for a cause or issue you feel strongly about.

8. Conduct a how-to or training session.

9. Maintain a Class Chronicle of daily activities, events, and anecdotes.

10. Investigate how something works.

11. Compile an annotated bibliography of Internet websites.

12. Plan a walking tour for your neighborhood or community.

13. Create a subject glossary or dictionary.

14. Construct a model.

15. Write and produce a commercial.

16. Design a series of greeting cards.

17. Plan an academic-based scavenger hunt for your school.

18. Make a storyboard.

19. Create and present a photo-essay.

20. Invent a code and use it to write something.

21. Create a series of bumper stickers on an important topic.

22. Design an interactive notebook between you and other classmates.

23. Role-play a press conference with a celebrity.

24. Write an encyclopedia entry.

25. Develop and use a questionnaire.

26. Record a video.

27. Do a demonstration.

28. Design a computer game.

29. Write a set of "Cliff Notes" for books you have read.

30. Choreograph native dances or exercise routines.

31. Plan a podcast.

32. Assemble an e-portfolio.

The Definitive Middle School Guide, Revised Edition
Copyright © 2014 World Book, Inc./Incentive Publications, Chicago, IL

Benefits and Challenges of Group Discussions

Both large and small group discussions should be common instructional practices in every classroom. All discussions should focus on the use of higher-order questioning skills.

Benefits of group discussions:

1 They provide the teacher with feedback about student learning.

2 They lend themselves to higher-order thinking skills.

3 They help students develop interests and values and attitudes.

4 They allow students to become more active participants in their learning.

5 They enable students to hear and offer alternative points of view and to explore complex issues.

There are complexities and challenges to be aware of before beginning group discussions. Attend to these and devise strategies to meet the challenges, because the benefits of discussion are too great to be missed by your students!

Challenges of group discussions:

1 It is sometimes difficult to get students to participate freely, as discussions may be threatening to students for many reasons (e.g., peer pressure, fear of ridicule, self-consciousness).

2 It takes time to conduct a proper, meaningful discussion.

3 Discussions are not always well suited to covering significant amounts of content.

4 Significant forethought and planning on the part of the teacher are required.

5 Discussions may sometimes be threatening to the teacher, because the process can seem to be less controlled than other means of instruction.

Questions to Ponder When Setting Up a Classroom Discussion

Classroom discussions, when planned and carried out well, can do wonders toward deepening thinking skills.

Answer these questions before you begin your discussion:

1 Why is a classroom discussion important to the teaching of this topic or subject?

2 What specific content and process objectives do I have for this discussion?

3 How do I want to physically arrange the room and student seating for this discussion?

4 What ground rules should I establish for student participants before starting this discussion?

5 What plans do I have for dealing with students who dominate the discussion or who will not participate in the discussion?

6 What preparations should the students make before the discussion?

7 What roles will I play throughout the discussion?

8 How can I actively involve all students in the discussion?

9 What classroom activities would be appropriate as a follow-up to this discussion?

10 How long should the discussion last?

11 Should students be graded for their participation in the class discussion? If so, how?

12 What kinds of questions nudge students toward critical thinking?

13 What kinds of questions do little to promote critical thinking?

14 What, then, are the key questions that I should prepare for leading this discussion?

The Definitive Middle School Guide, Revised Edition
Copyright © 2014 World Book, Inc./Incentive Publications, Chicago, IL

Steps for Improving Classroom Discussions

Step 1: Decide on a topic or theme.

Step 2: Prepare a simple outline of major and minor points to cover during the discussion. This could include terms defined, concepts described, problems to address, points to make, and events or situations to be explained.

Step 3: Write down a series of questions to be asked during the discussion. Code each as a lower-order and closed question or a higher-order and open-ended question. Make sure there is a balance between the two types.

Step 4: Initiate a discussion by having students write out questions they have about the topic on individual file cards. Collect the cards and use these student-generated questions as part of the discussion dialogue.

Step 5: Stop the large group discussion at several points and instruct students to discuss this "last major point" with a partner.

Step 6: Use this list of SIX strategies for students to respond to a series of discussion statements, facts, opinions, or decisions. The student responds to the idea by doing one of the following:

    a) Raise hand as fist to indicate "do not agree with idea and will block idea"

    b) Raise one finger to indicate "do not agree with idea but will not block idea"

    c) Raise two fingers to indicate "am neutral on idea"

    d) Raise three fingers to indicate "agree with this idea"

    e) Raise four fingers to indicate "agree with this idea and will actively support it"

    f) Raise five fingers to indicate "agree with this idea and will lead the charge, action, or discussion on this idea"

Step 7: Apply the above strategies during the session to help facilitate the dialogue among and between participants.

Step 8: Write down each student's name on a separate file card. As a student volunteers or is called upon, his or her card is set aside until all have made contributions.

Step 9: Post a list of discussion guidelines that students under your direction have developed. Post these prominently so they can be observed during discussion dialogues. Guidelines to consider are:

    a) Try to make at least one contribution to every discussion.

    b) Address remarks to any or all group members, not just the leader.

    c) Speak loudly and clearly so everyone can hear what you have to say.

    d) Get to the point and make your point.

    e) Stick to the discussion and don't introduce irrelevancies.

    f) Respect all opinions and contributions and disagree agreeably.

Step 10: Keep students on their toes with a beachball-toss strategy. Toss the ball to a student after a question has been asked. Whoever catches the ball must respond to the question. This also involves students in the discussion who otherwise might not participate.

Tips for More Effective Discussions

1 Ask for opinions and feelings.

> **Example:** What is your reaction to . . .?
> **or** How do you feel about . . .?

2 Paraphrase back to the speaker.

> **Example:** Are you saying that . . . ?
> **or** What I think I am hearing is . . .

3 Encourage participation.

> **Example:** Sasha, how would you answer that question?
> **or** Jason, why do you agree or disagree with Sasha's idea?

4 Ask for summary.

> **Example:** Will someone please summarize what has been said?
> **or** Summarize your major objections.

5 Ask for clarification.

> **Example:** Explain your last comment further . . .
> **or** Tell us how your idea would apply to. . .

6 Ask for examples.

> **Example:** Will you give us some examples of what you mean?
> **or** Tell us one example of this in the real world.

7 Test for consensus.

> **Example:** Does everyone accept the idea that . . .?
> **or** Before we go on, can we agree that . . .?

8 Initiate action.

> **Example:** How do you think we should . . . ?
> **or** How would you suggest we proceed on this . . .?

9 Explore an idea in more detail.

> **Example:** What are some more things we could consider . . . ?
> **or** What would you add to what has been said . . .?

10 Conduct a quick survey.

> **Example:** How many agree with this idea . . . ?
> **or** How does everyone feel about this . . . ?

11 Suggest a procedure.

> **Example:** Would it help if we put the items in order of importance . . .?
> **or** Let's go around the room to see how others would feel . . .

12 Reinforce a good point.

> **Example:** That's a good point . . .
> **or** I wish I had thought of that!

13 Mediate differences of opinions.

> **Example:** I think you aren't really disagreeing with each other, but rather expressing yourselves differently.
> **or** Let's see how your views are alike.

14 Change the group process.

> **Example:** Let's break into smaller groups and . . .
> **or** Let's stop the discussion for a moment and . . .

The Definitive Middle School Guide, Revised Edition
Copyright © 2014 World Book, Inc./Incentive Publications, Chicago, IL

Ways to Integrate Thinking Skills into the Curriculum

Teachers can integrate thinking skills into the curriculum by:

1 Keeping visual reminders (poster or bulletin board displays) and class discussions about thinking skills as a regular part of the classroom environment.

2 Regularly asking students to . . .

    a. elaborate on a statement made by another student.

    b. "agree" or "disagree" with an idea expressed by another student in the class.

    c. challenge responses and ideas (with reasons for the response).

    d. paraphrase, summarize, or respond to another student's ideas before adding to the discussion.

3 Asking open-ended and extension questions rather than closed and single-response questions.

4 Refraining from offering personal opinions, value judgments, or comments on the topic.

5 Giving a grade, reward, or extra credit mark for demonstration of good thinking.

6 Developing wait time with students through such strategies as . . .

    a. counting to twenty before calling on a student.

    b. giving students a short writing assignment to answer a series of questions before calling on them.

    c. waiting until at least half the class members have their hands up to respond before calling on anyone.

7 Keeping a tally of student responses to encourage widespread participation.

8 Organizing students into cooperative learning "think tanks" when doing complex-level thinking activities.

9 Using Bloom's Taxonomy or Six Hat Thinking when structuring discussion questions, worksheets, tests, or assignments so that students are using all levels of thinking skills.

10 Using Williams' levels of creative thinking or the SCAMPER model when structuring discussions, assignments, and assessments to stretch student's creative-thinking opportunities.

11 Taking time for a short recap of the issues, the major themes, the prevalent viewpoints, and the remaining questions.

12 Complimenting all students at the end of a group discussion for the quality of their thinking and their contributions.

A wide range of thinking skills is crucial and beneficial to students in career and in life. Many of these can be developed during the teaching of all disciplines through encouragement and rewards, effectively structured questions, the employment of higher-level thinking taxonomies, and the use of simple teaching strategies.

Ways to Use Questions to Develop Higher-Level Thinking Skills

1 **Knowledge Questions: Who, what, when, where, why, and how**

Recite, recall, record, or reproduce _____.

Locate, label, or list _____.

2 **Comprehension Questions: Retell** _____ **in your own words.**

Describe, summarize, discuss, or explain the main idea of_____.

Give examples of _____.

Explain _____.

3 **Application Questions: How is _____ an example of or related to _____?**

Distinguish between _____ and _____.

Illustrate the workings of a _____.

4 **Analysis Questions: What are the parts or features of** _____?

Compare and contrast _____ and _____.

Outline, diagram, or web _____.

Draw conclusions or make inferences about _____.

5 **Synthesis Questions: What would you predict or propose about** _____?

What might happen if you combined _____ and _____?

How would you improve a _____?

What creative solutions would you suggest for _____?

6 **Evaluation Questions: Rank order according to** _____.

What criteria would you use to assess or evaluate _____?

Defend or validate this idea or statement: _____.

7 **Personal Questions: How do you feel about** _____?

Do you think _____?

Where do you stand on the issue of _____?

8 **Observation Questions: What seems to be happening in this picture** _____?

What might you infer from your observations of _____?

9 **Cause-Effect Questions: Why did** _____?

What would happen if _____?

10 **Viewpoint Questions: How would this look to a** _____?

What would a _____ mean from the viewpoint of a _____?

How would _____ view this?

Essential Components of Independent Learning Contracts

A learning contract is a written agreement between a student and a teacher. In the contract, the student commits to completing a series of learning activities on a particular topic within a specified time. The contract concept is highly flexible. The student may commit to a short assignment or a long independent project. With a contract that is specifically labeled "independent," the student takes the major responsibility for initiating, developing, and implementing the contract.

Contracts empower the student because they can be completed independently with a minimum of teacher direction and because they emphasize shared decision making between the teacher and student when setting up the terms of the contract itself. Contracts are wonderful differentiation tools, because they are custom-designed.

The essential components of the contract process are:

1 **Topic:** The student chooses the specific topic.

2 **Teacher role:** The teacher serves as a consultant, guide, or mentor at all stages of the study.

3 **Major responsibility:** The student has the main responsibility for initiating, planning, carrying out, and evaluating his or her own learning. As much as is possible, the student takes the lead in learning.

4 **Goals:** The contract sets specific goals.

5 **Resources:** The contract identifies resources to be used.

6 **Steps:** The contract outlines the steps the student will take, describing precisely what will be done.

7 **Evaluation:** The contract offers specific criteria against which the project or assignment is to be judged and specifies tools for doing the evaluation.

8 **Timeline:** The contract includes a timeline outlining when parts and the whole of the assignment will be completed.

9 **Time:** Adequate time is allotted for a study to the depth and application needed.

Other advice:

- There are no specific rules about the kinds of contracts, the length or complexity of the study, or the kinds of activities involved. Be open to many varieties and designs of independent learning contracts to fit the needs, abilities, interests, and learning styles of many students.

- Start with short-term projects. Once students have success with short projects, they can expand and experiment with longer projects.

- Thoroughly explain the role and function of contracts to both students and parents.

- Do not expect all students to be able to use the same kinds of contracts effectively.

- Do not assume that all instruction can take place through activities in the contracts without some supplementary teaching and monitoring sessions with the teacher.

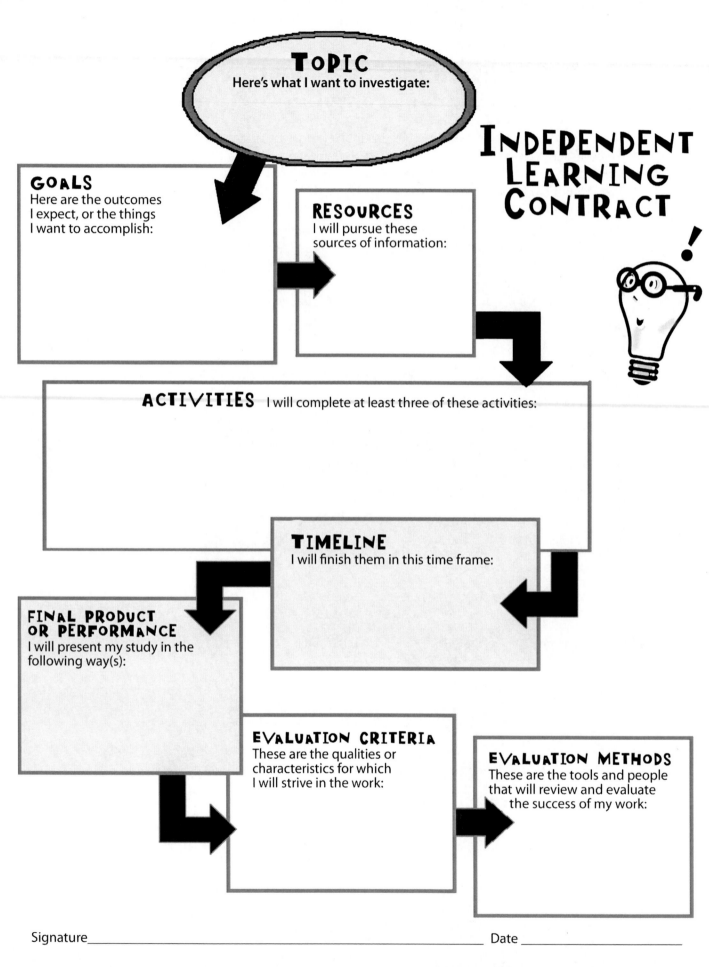

TOPIC
Here's what I want to investigate:

INDEPENDENT LEARNING CONTRACT

GOALS
Here are the outcomes I expect, or the things I want to accomplish:

RESOURCES
I will pursue these sources of information:

ACTIVITIES I will complete at least three of these activities:

TIMELINE
I will finish them in this time frame:

FINAL PRODUCT OR PERFORMANCE
I will present my study in the following way(s):

EVALUATION CRITERIA
These are the qualities or characteristics for which I will strive in the work:

EVALUATION METHODS
These are the tools and people that will review and evaluate the success of my work:

Signature_____ Date _____

STEPS TO LEARNING - INDEPENDENT STUDY PLAN

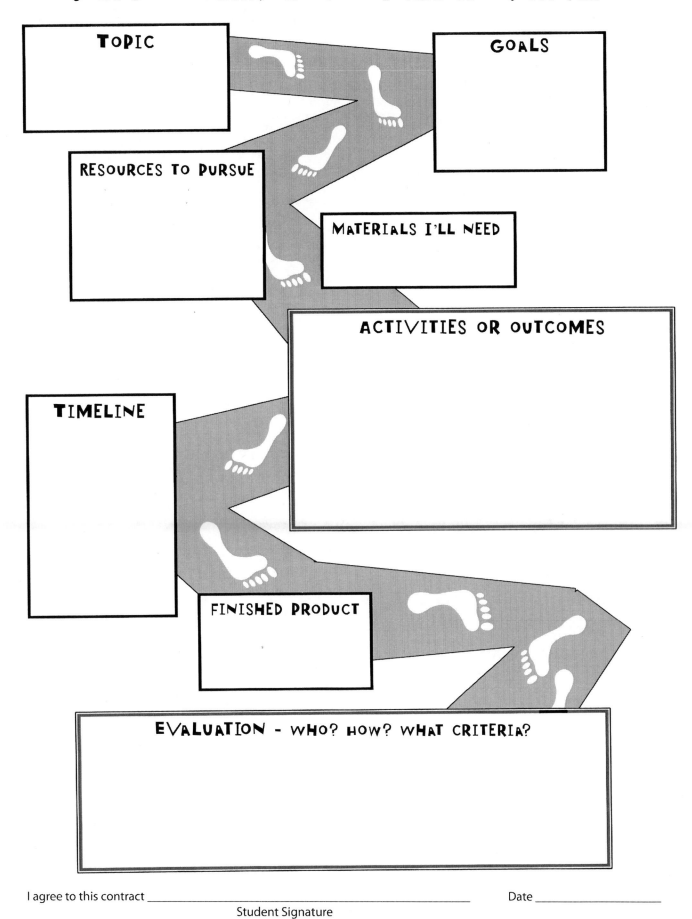

TOPIC

GOALS

RESOURCES TO PURSUE

MATERIALS I'LL NEED

ACTIVITIES OR OUTCOMES

TIMELINE

FINISHED PRODUCT

EVALUATION - WHO? HOW? WHAT CRITERIA?

I agree to this contract _____ Date _____
Student Signature

How DID I Do? Self-Evaluation of Independent Study

Name_____

Topic_____ Date_____

Directions: For each task, color the word that tells how you did.

TOPIC
I chose a topic that was interesting and manageable.

YES   NO   SOMEWHAT

GOALS
I set reasonable goals for my study.

YES   NO   SOMEWHAT

I was committed to this study.

YES   NO   SOMEWHAT

PLANNING
I developed a clear and workable plan.

YES   NO   SOMEWHAT

I chose activities that led me to my goals.

YES   NO   SOMEWHAT

I set a reasonable timeline for the work needed.

YES   NO   SOMEWHAT

I identified and used appropriate resources.

YES   NO   SOMEWHAT

I chose useful criteria and tools for evaluation.

YES   NO   SOMEWHAT

CARRYING THROUGH
I completed the tasks that were in my plan..........................YES   NO   SOMEWHAT

I made good use of my work time..YES   NO   SOMEWHAT

I made good use of people, information, and other resources....YES   NO   SOMEWHAT

I asked for help when I needed it.......................................YES   NO   SOMEWHAT

I was able to adapt the plan when it became necessary..............YES   NO   SOMEWHAT

COMMUNICATING
I chose a satisfactory method for sharing what I learned.

YES   NO   SOMEWHAT

I was able to communicate what I learned to others.

YES   NO   SOMEWHAT

EVALUATION
The evaluation criteria and tools proved to be helpful to me.........................YES   NO   SOMEWHAT

I can explain what I learned from this study......................................YES   NO   SOMEWHAT

I can explain what I did well and the problems I encountered.......................YES   NO   SOMEWHAT

I know what I will do to improve my next independent study plan...............YES   NO   SOMEWHAT

The Definitive Middle School Guide, Revised Edition
Copyright © 2014 World Book, Inc./Incentive Publications, Chicago, IL

Technology Applications for the Classroom

1 **Blogs:** A blog is a website on the Internet, usually created by an individual or company, with regular commentary, descriptions of events, or such other content as photos, videos, music, or artwork. Many blogs provide commentary or news on a particular subject, while others function more as personal online diaries. Blogs designed for educators provide a forum for the exchange of ideas. Teachers can also create their own classroom blogs with passwords where students can exchange ideas about a topic with one another as well as with the teacher.

2 **Bulletin board discussions:** These web-based forums (sometimes called newsgroups, message boards, or discussion boards) connect students and teachers from around the world. This form of communication provides users with an opportunity to discuss and share mutual issues, concerns, ideas, and problems.

3 **Collaborative software:** This tool (also known as groupware or workgroup support systems) is designed to help groups of people achieve a common goal by working together. The software has the ability to manage collaborative groups in action.

4 **E-portfolio:** An e-portfolio is a collection of electronic evidence assembled and managed by a user. Evidence might include text files, images, multimedia, blog entries, and hyperlinks. This type of learning record provides actual evidence to document the user's abilities and self-reflections.

5 **M-Learning:** Mobile learning is related to e-learning and distance learning. The focus of m-learning is on learning through portable technologies, such as tablet computers, smartphones, and mp3 players. For example, podcasts or curriculum reviews can be downloaded to student mp3 players for easy access and extended follow-up.

6 **Podcasts:** This tool distributes audio and visual files over the Internet for use on portable media players such as iPods as well as on a computer. Teachers or students can download lessons, museum tours, how-to videos, or tutorials for students to access at any time and from most remote locations. It can also be a tool for teachers to communicate curriculum, assignments, and other academic information.

7 **Social networking services:** These online communities of people share personal interests and activities. YouTube and Facebook are sites popular with young people today. However, they also raise concerns from parents and teachers because students give out personal information that should be kept private. This can be a dangerous practice for those involved. New educational social networking initiatives are hoping to tap into the popularity of such sites for educational purposes.

8 **Virtual classroom:** This type of classroom is a learning environment delivered through the Internet. Such classrooms are used to improve access to learning experiences not available locally. Students can do everything from taking field trips to famous museums and historical sites to online courses and self-taught classes.

9 **Web cam:** These images from small cameras can be accessed using the Internet through instant messaging or via computer videoconferencing applications.

10 **Wiki:** A wiki is a web page or collection of web pages that allow anyone to contribute to or edit its content. This is a great resource for fostering group collaboration. With this tool students can build the perfect set of class notes, develop a research project, or author a comprehensive essay.

11 **Web Quests:** Web Quests are used to integrate the power of the Internet into the classroom by transforming or scaffolding information into newly constructed meaning. They also integrate into the classroom sound learning practices, such as motivation theory, questioning theory, differentiated learning practices, thematic instruction options, authentic assessment measures, and metacognitive dimensions.

Steps to Integrate Internet Sources into Lesson Plans

1 Choose the topic or subject area to be reinforced or enriched with the Internet.

2 Divide the subject area into manageable sections according to an outline and timeline that will be followed by the students.

3 Determine the specific objectives and learning activities for each section.

4 Identify which instructional activities could best be supported with the Internet. Also, consider new interactive and special communication tools for student projects beyond PowerPoint, such as digital storytelling, podcasts, and wikis.

5 Use search engines and consult with your librarian to locate websites that are best suited for your specific instructional and curricular needs. Also, explore ways to bring experts and writers into your classroom using telecommunication tools like SKYPE and Internet2.

6 Evaluate each website for its appropriateness. Consider content, ability levels of students, authenticity, currency, and credibility.

7 Bookmark the selected sites for student use. In other words, you organize the Internet resources for your learners. Make sure your learners can access developmental and curricular databases, portals, and websites.

8 Prepare a student recording sheet that students can use as they research the assigned questions on the Internet. (See sample below.)

Internet QUESTION & ANSWER Search Record

Topic for Internet research: _____

Questions to Answer	Web Address	Answers
1.		
2.		
3.		
4.		
5.		
6.		
7.		
8.		
9.		
10.		

Name_____ Date_____

The Definitive Middle School Guide, Revised Edition
Copyright © 2014 World Book, Inc./Incentive Publications, Chicago, IL

Ways for Teachers to Become Internet-Smart

1 Explore your own personal and academic passions online. Read ed tech journals and ed tech blogs and visit the webcast archives of conferences related to your field. Use these interests and hobbies as entrees to the Internet.

2 Develop an acceptable use policy (AUP) for your students. Be sure to teach basic Internet safety rules and enforce them consistently. It is important for you to share your AUP with parents and post it near the classroom computers for students to review. You may even want the students to sign a contract committing them to these guidelines.

3 Develop a list of quality, safe websites available for your subject area as well as for the age and ability levels of your students. Ask for help from the school librarian or local public librarian.

4 Know your search engines and experiment with those designed specifically for middle school students. Bookmark the ones you like best and organize them into a "search engine folder" on your web browser. Limit these options as much as possible to specific topics you have researched in advance.

5 Consider using a filter if possible, as filtering software can accomplish three things:

    a) It blocks access to undesirable content.

    b) It keeps a log that tracks where students have been on the Internet.

    c) It puts controls on what students can do online.

6 Use the Internet to help you with subject area research, creative lesson plans, assessment checklists, and reproducible activities. Many educational companies publish free sites for teachers and students alike.

7 Teach students to navigate a website effectively. An LCD panel or other projection device can help you with this task. Also, be sure to show students the correct way to document media in all formats and explore the many copyright-friendly portals available to them.

8 Use the Internet as a professional development tool through online chat rooms, blogs, podcasts, and social networking services, which can provide you with opportunities to communicate and interact with other teachers and professional organizations.

Technology-Based Student Research, Product, and Performance Challenges

1 Research to find out how computer technology has changed over the years since you were born and what changes will likely occur during your generation.

2 Research to determine how databases have affected our lives both negatively and positively over time. Give specific examples to support your findings.

3 Research to discover just how many adults and businesses work out of "electronic cottages" or "home offices." Find out what types of people and work lend themselves to this type of workplace organizational structure.

4 Research to find out what types of software in today's marketplace are the best learning tools for students your age. Establish a rating scale for judging software based on your readings.

5 Research to uncover why some people are computer addicts while others harbor computer phobias. Try to construct a personality profile for each one.

6 Research to find out how technology has influenced the world of advertising and marketing for consumer products. Use some specific data to support your findings.

7 Research to find out how technology has influenced the home and family environment for better or worse. Gather and "publish" evidence or cautions you might pass on to your family and others.

8 Design a kid's website for the Internet on a topic of your choice.

9 Create a plan for weaning members of your family from their overdependence on the technology found in your home (computers, iPods, cell phones, text messaging, podcasts, computer games, etc.).

10 Compile a scrapbook or e-portfolio of relevant articles, hyperlinks, media, blogs, etc.

11 Prepare a consumer guide for "young technology buffs" in your school who want to get the most for their money when purchasing new technology-related products.

12 Compile a directory of computer-related careers that might be of interest to you and your peers.

13 Plan and create a weekly or monthly online newsletter centered on the theme of technology. Include factual or statistical information, charts or graphs, jokes or riddles, reviews or interviews, and bibliographies or summaries of software or publications.

14 Organize a computer or technology club for your school or neighborhood.

15 Conduct and record an interview with a "computer nerd" in your school or community.

16 Write and deliver a "mini-lecture" on an active board for your classroom.

17 Give a speech on the pros and cons of social networking services. Discuss YouTube and Facebook in your presentation.

18 Create a set of puppets and a skit to teach young children more about the wonders of technology.

19 Be prepared to criticize or defend this statement: "Electronic computer games inhibit the development of interactive communication skills between and among students."

20 Prepare a demonstration and photo show using a digital camera.

Ways to Evaluate Internet Resources

Evaluate the sites and materials with these questions. Direct students to a source ONLY once you have satisfactory answers to these questions about the source:

1 Accuracy

- Do information sources appear clearly on the page?
- Can you verify any of the information from your own knowledge?
- Can you verify any of the information from other sources?
- Is the information free of grammatical, spelling, and typographical errors?

2 Authority

- Is the name of the author or creator on the page?
- Do the author's credentials (occupation or education) appear on the page?
- Is the author qualified to write on the given topic? Why? How do you know?
- Is there contact information (such as an e-mail address) somewhere on the page?
- Is there a link to a homepage?
- What does the domain name or URL reveal about the source of the information, if anything?

3 Objectivity

- Who is the intended audience—experts or the general public?
- What do you think is the purpose of the site (to inform, explain, persuade, or sell a product)?
- Is the information mostly fact, opinion, or propaganda?
- Is the author's point of view objective?
- Is the language free of emotion-rousing words?

4 Currency

- Is the information up to date?
- When was the site last updated?

5 Credibility

- Why should anyone believe information from this site?
- Is there evidence to support the information?
- Do quotes appear with their source?
- If there is a link to a homepage, is it for an individual or for an organization?
- If the author is with an organization, does the organization sponsor the page?
- Is there a non-Web equivalent of this material?

> *Note: One good way to document information taken from the Internet is:*
> - *name of person or group who provides the information;*
> - *title of page(s) you are viewing written in quotation marks;*
> - *Internet address; date page was posted, updated, or read.*
> **Example:** *Adapted from: Boston Public Library. "Using the Internet for School Reports." http://www.bpl.org/KIDS/Evaluate.htm. July 2001.*

Source: Urquhart, V., & McIver, M. (2005). *Teaching writing in the content areas.*
Alexandria, VA: Association for Supervision and Curriculum Development.

Big Steps to Planning a School-wide Technology Fair

Step 1:

Decide on a date, time, and place for the fair.

Consider

- an evening time to accommodate working parents.

- tying it in with a regularly scheduled meeting, such as an open house, parent-teacher association meeting, or a parent conference week.

- using all key areas of your school facility, including indoor spaces such as classrooms, hallways, media center, and cafeteria, as well as outdoor spaces such as sports fields and parking lots.

- a popular time of the year for the fair, such as early fall to establish a community learning climate, a holiday season to establish a festive mood, or a late spring evening to commemorate the ending of a school year.

Step 2:

Choose a Fair Steering Committee to plan and coordinate the activities.

Include student, teacher, administrative, and parent representatives on your committee. Include parents or community members who are in the technology or media market in order to enlist their support, expertise, and resources.

Several subcommittees might also be formed to include such responsibilities as:

- **Invitation and Public Relations Committee** to determine the invitation design and the methods for advertising the fair throughout the school community

- **Booth and Exhibit Committee** to determine the structure, theme, and organizational plan for the various functions and activities of the fair

- **Refreshment Committee** to determine what food and beverages will be served and at what cost

- **Set-up Committee** to determine the people power and methods required to get the fair up and running on the appointed day and at the designated time

- **Clean-up Committee** to determine the people power and methods required to take down the fair booths and exhibits, as well as to clean up the entire affected area

- **Host and Hostess Committee** to determine who will greet the guests and serve as guides for the fair's special events and attractions

- **Budget Committee** to determine the funding sources for the fair and to monitor all costs, expenses, and/or profits

- **Evaluation Committee** to determine what assessment measures will be used to obtain feedback on the fair's success and problem areas

The Definitive Middle School Guide, Revised Edition
Copyright © 2014 World Book, Inc./Incentive Publications, Chicago, IL

Step 3:

Decide on a format and program for the fair.

Consider such options as:

- Student, teacher, and business exhibits of technology and media projects
- Student, teacher, and business demonstrations of technology and media tools, concepts, and applications
- Opportunities for guests to experiment with various technology and media-related equipment and software
- Ongoing panels of students, teachers, and business people discussing topics and issues related to the changing world of technology and media
- Public forums to exchange the mutual concerns, questions, and areas of expertise as they relate to technology and media
- Special events such as technology- and media-related skits, shows, role-plays, case studies, and contests

Step 4:

Decide on any follow-up steps or procedures to be conducted after the fair, as well as ways to record or document the entire fair planning and implementation process for future reference.

Ways to Investigate Computer Lingo

Students may choose some or all of these activities from the Bloom levels to complete:

1 REMEMBERING

Write down twenty different computer terms with their definitions that you know and could define for someone else.

2 UNDERSTANDING

In your own words, explain what it means to be "computer literate."

3 APPLYING

Use the computer to construct a crossword puzzle or other word puzzle for the twenty computer terms listed for the REMEMBERING level.

4 ANALYZING

Compare and contrast the concept of a computer "virus" and a virus that causes humans to be sick.

5 EVALUATING

Give three benefits and three negative consequences of virtual realities available through the Internet.

6 CREATING

Use five to ten of the words from the REMEMBERING level in an original poster, advertisement, joke, anecdote, news announcement, story, or fable about computers.

The Definitive Middle School Guide, Revised Edition
Copyright © 2014 World Book, Inc./Incentive Publications, Chicago, IL

Things to Do with a Computer Graphics Software Program

Students may choose some or all of these activities from the Bloom levels to complete:

1 REMEMBERING

Graphics can be in the form of letters, numbers, pictures, lines, boxes, graphs, borders, patterns, icons, and many other types of decorative tools found on graphics software programs. Draw a symbol, sample item, or an example to represent each of these forms.

2 UNDERSTANDING

Graphics programs come with their own pictures called "clip art." Most programs today will let you draw your own artwork and save it on the computer. Describe one of these programs and how it works or operates.

3 APPLYING

Use an updated "paint and draw" graphics computer software program to create a basic picture on your computer screen. Then practice using each of the following tools to embellish your picture: fill, spray, magnify, erase, and line draw. Try some others as well.

4 ANALYZING

Compare and contrast several different graphics programs on the computer, outlining the advantages and disadvantages of each.

5 EVALUATING

Some artists feel that computer graphics are an inferior art form because they are generated by artificial, software-programmed tools and not by a human artist. Develop a set of arguments to support or negate this position.

6 CREATING

Use a computer graphics program to create an original greeting card, poster, stationery, award, certificate, or banner.

Ways to Learn More About Databases

Choose some or all of these activities from Williams' creative-thinking levels to offer as tasks for students:

1 FLUENCY

A database is a collection of data, facts, statistics, or information. Sports scores in newspapers, words in dictionaries, and listings in address books are databases. Write down at least ten more personal or school-based databases that you know about or have used.

2 FLEXIBILITY

A database program is just a computer version of the examples you listed above. But because computers work so fast, they can make the information very easy to find and update. Add types of database programs that you would like to access on your school or home computer if they were available.

3 ORIGINALITY

Each fact in a database is a piece of information called a field. All the information about one item in a database is called a record. Imagine the most unusual and unique database idea for the principal to have in your school. Justify your choice.

4 ELABORATION

Databases take a great deal of time and energy to develop and make operational. Compose a short essay defending this process, entitled "The Means Justify the End." Give personal examples to support your position.

5 RISK TAKING

Think of database ideas that do not benefit you personally.

6 COMPLEXITY

It has been noted that databases are often a threat to our privacy. Explain how this could be true.

7 CURIOSITY

Databases are used in lots of ways in the business world. Interview someone you know who owns or runs a business and ask him or her about the uses and misuses of their database information.

8 IMAGINATION

Pretend you are in charge of creating a database for the next generation of students. Write down possible things you would want to keep track of for these yet-to-be-born students.

Ways to Investigate the World of Video and Computer-Based Games

Choose some or all of these activities from Bloom's cognitive levels to offer as tasks for students:

REMEMBERING

1 Record the name and publisher of your favorite game.

2 Make a list of the major characters and the physical descriptions for each in this game.

3 Write down the different obstacles and challenges for the player to overcome.

UNDERSTANDING

4 In your own words, summarize the major goals to accomplish in this game.

5 Describe how you feel when you play this game.

6 Explain what special skills are required for being successful in this game.

APPLYING

7 Compose a letter to the manufacturer of this game telling why you like it so well.

8 Time yourself and a group of friends during the play of this game. How time consuming is it? Does it take too much of your time? Could your time be better spent on something else?

9 Construct a model or sketch a drawing to show a favorite excerpt, setting, or scenario from this game.

ANALYZING

10 Conclude reasons why people like you enjoy playing these games.

11 Deduce how publishers dream up the challenges and obstacles for these games.

12 Compare and contrast two of your favorite games. How are they alike and how are they different?

EVALUATING

13 Critique people's obsession with these games and comment on their addiction to them.

14 Write a list of alternative activities that someone like you could do instead of playing these games in his or her spare time. Rank them in order of importance to you.

15 Defend this position: "Computer-based games teach players many different skills including hand-eye coordination, problem solving, and decision making." Give examples to support your defense.

CREATING

16 Design a mini-poster or advertisement promoting the purchase of this game by other students in your class.

17 Think up an unusual title and a set of challenges for a new or revised game like this one.

18 Create a postage stamp commemorating the video game craze.

Tools to Assess Instructional Effectiveness
Overview

TOOL 1: Questions for a Student Focus Group on Classroom Instruction

This tool is designed to obtain student input on the teacher's effectiveness in a given classroom or series of classroom settings. It requires an outside observer who is trained both in effective classroom practices at the middle grade level and in conducting focus group sessions. Building administrators, team leaders, district level staff, and outside consultants may be used successfully for this purpose. Focus groups should consist of a randomly selected group of no more than ten students at the same grade level and in the same subject area discipline. The best way to do this is to take an alphabetized grade level list of all seventh-grade students taking English from the same teacher and divide that list into equal segments. For example, if the total number of students for that teacher is 130, then divide that number by 10 and select every 13th name for your focus group. Each person conducting the focus group should plan to record the session, which should be limited to about 50 minutes (approximately the length of a class period). Students should be given name tags so that focus group leaders can refer to each boy or girl by name, and the purpose of the focus group should be explained to students prior to the inquiry session. It is also important that each student contribute to the discussion and that no one monopolize the discussion. Responses to the focus group questions should be compiled by the observer and shared openly with the teacher involved.

TOOL 2: Classroom Observation Form

The focus of this tool is a formal classroom observation of a teacher actively engaged in a learning situation with students. The observation should be completed by an educator who is knowledgeable about both the content and best practices of the grade level and the content area under scrutiny. The observation should cover a typical instructional period that is mutually agreed upon by both the observer and the teacher involved. The purpose of this observation tool is formative in nature, because the teacher willingly volunteers for the observation and can prepare a typical classroom lesson plan for the critique. The inventory provides an outline of what to expect and assess by both the observer and the teacher being observed.

TOOL 3: Teacher's Classroom Practices Self-Inventory

This self-assessment tool is used by any teacher who is interested in having some way to measure what and how he or she is doing as an instructional leader in a particular classroom setting. It can be effective with either a beginning teacher who wants to monitor progress over a short period of time or a veteran teacher who wants to monitor progress as a semi-annual benchmark over an extended career. The labels on the continuum can be used as shown or they can be refigured into numbers on a 1 to 10 scale for a more definitive assessment. It is important that the teacher be able to justify any designated score on any line item with specific examples and documentation to maximize growth (or lack of it) over time.

TOOL 1: Questions for Student Focus Group on Classroom Instruction

Name of person conducting focus group

_____

Role_____

Date_____ Time_____

Place_____

Number of participants_____

Grade level(s)_____

Directions:
Plan to record this focus group session so that responses can be noted and edited at a later date. Limit the discussion to these questions as much as possible, and encourage equitable input from all participants. Use this page as a guide to asking questions and as a place to take notes as you listen to the recording.

1. Does your teacher share information about goals or content standards that are important for you to learn and practice as part of every teaching activity?

2. Does your teacher vary teaching methods in the classroom? What types of activities are used most often? Least often?

3. Does your teacher use a variety of learning materials and resources other than the textbook to teach you what you need to know? If so, what are they?

4. Does your teacher use the multiple intelligences as a way of designing classroom and homework activities for you to do? What intelligence areas are your strengths or preferences?

5. How does your teacher account for different learning styles and ability levels in your classroom?

6. How does your teacher give you feedback during a classroom lesson?

7. After your teacher presents you with new information or skills, are you given enough practice time to learn them? How is this accomplished?

8. How does your teacher know when you have learned the material or skills being taught during a given lesson?

9. Do you know the difference between higher-order and lower-order thinking skills? How does your teacher encourage different types of thinking?

10. How does your teacher tie in what you are learning today with what you learned yesterday or last week on the same topic or the same skill?

11. How does your teacher make learning fun or interesting?

12. If you could give your teacher one word of advice for doing his or her job better, what would it be?

TOOL 2: Classroom Observation Form

Name of person conducting observation

_____

Job title or role_____

Date and time of observation period

_____

Directions:
This form is to be completed by a staff member or consultant who is actively observing a typical teaching-learning situation with students. Indicate the degree to which you observe implementation of that factor or behavior. Use this number rating system.

**5 = Consistently   4 = Frequently
3 = About half the time   2 = Occasionally
1 = Rarely**

_____ 1. Objectives or standards were written down for lesson.

_____ 2. The instructional time for the lesson was appropriate.

_____ 3. The method of instruction was changed as needed.

_____ 4. Instruction began promptly and continued until end of designated period.

_____ 5. Students were informed of purpose, goals, or standards for lesson.

_____ 6. New ideas were related to earlier content taught.

_____ 7. Clear directions were given to student.

_____ 8. More than one modality or learning style was addressed.

_____ 9. More than one learning resource or material was used in delivery of lesson.

_____ 10. More than one instructional strategy was used.

_____ 11. All or most students were actively involved in the lesson.

_____ 12. There was evidence of differentiated instructional strategies.

_____ 13. The teacher circulated among students during the lesson.

_____ 14. Questions at all or most levels of Bloom's Taxonomy (or other questioning model) were evident.

_____ 15. Activities or tasks from at least three of the multiple intelligences were incorporated.

_____ 16. The lesson provided practice in application of the skills and concepts taught.

_____ 17. A procedure for evaluating outcomes (as related to the goals) was evident.

_____ 18. Constructive feedback was given to students.

_____ 19. The teacher used noticeable motivational techniques to engage the students.

_____ 20. Individual rewards and reinforcements were used with students.

_____ 21. Acceptable level of discipline was evident during the lesson.

_____ 22. A positive learning environment was fostered during the lesson.

TOOL 3: Teacher's Classroom Practices Self-Inventory

Name of teacher
conducting inventory _____

Job title or role _____

Date and time
period of inventory _____

Directions:
Use this inventory to look at what you are already doing in your classroom to differentiate instruction and vary teaching-learning approaches.

Mark an X on each line to show where your current teaching practices and strategies lie on the continuum. Be prepared to explain your results.

very little   *somewhat*   *most of the time*

1. I emphasize student learning needs over content coverage.

2. I strive for adjustable learning goals based on individual needs.

3. I place emphasis on thinking skills and problem solving.

4. I consistently use many and varied learning resources.

5. I favor multiple group formats over whole class instruction.

6. I include brain-compatible strategies in lessons.

7. I favor a combination of lecture, large group, and small group sessions.

8. I set time limits and pace of instruction based on student needs.

9. I give students options on most tasks and assignments.

10. I arrange for students to collaborate more than compete.

11. I employ varied authentic assessment measures whenever possible.

12. I use differentiated strategies (scaffolding, compacting, tiering) often.

Findings from the Published Literature
Related to Curricular Models and Instructional Methods

FINDING #1:

Barbara Brodhagen and Susan Gorud write:

Technology can be a useful tool in many student- or teacher-designed projects and appeals to today's early adolescents' learning preferences. Most students are able to access more information when using technology. It allows them to get more up-to-date facts (such as weather and economic status reports), to correspond more quickly with other adolescents both at home and abroad, and to access a wider range of databases. And of course, using a word-processing program allows for corrections and revisions in a less labor-intensive manner, making it especially appealing to students for whom writing does not come easily.

Source: Brodhagen, B., & Gorud, S. (2005). Multiple learning and teaching approaches that respond to their diversity. In Erb, T. O. (Ed.), *This we believe in action: Implementing successful middle schools.* Westerville, OH: National Middle School Association.

FINDING #2:

Carol Ann Tomlinson points out:

Teachers who differentiate instruction focus on their role as coach or mentor, give students as much responsibility for learning as they can handle, and teach them to handle a little more. These teachers grow in their ability to

1) assess student readiness through a variety of means;
2) "read" and interpret student clues about interests and learning preferences;
3) create a variety of ways students can gather information and ideas;
4) develop varied ways students can explore and "own" ideas; and
5) present varied channels through which students can express and expand understandings.

"Covering information" takes a back seat to making meaning out of important ideas.

Source: Tomlinson, C. A. (2001). The role of the teacher in a differentiated classroom. In *How to differentiate instruction in mixed-ability classrooms.* Alexandria, VA: Association for Supervision and Curriculum Development.

FINDING #3:

Brian J. Caldwell outlines ten strategic intentions that contribute to a gestalt, or vision, of the new school in action. Of those ten, several apply directly to curricular and instructional choices:

1) Subject boundaries will be broken and learning will be integrated across the curriculum as the new learning technologies become universal, challenging rigidity in curriculum and standards for frameworks.

2) Teachers will have access to the best resources to support their work, with many of these resources accessed from CDs, DVDs, and the Internet.

3) Students, teachers, and other professionals will increasingly work in teams.

4) Schools will expand their policies and practices for students to include cyber-policy addressing student interaction with virtual learning via the Internet or other means.

5) Issues of access and equity will be addressed in school cyber-policy, with a range of strategies including the sharing of resources among schools, partnerships with the private sector for donations and subsidies, and the creation of community-based learning centers.

6) Virtual schooling will be a reality at every stage of schooling, but there will be a place called school, with approaches to virtual schooling including the neighborhood educational houses.

7) New cultures for learning will take hold in schools for the knowledge society. There will be "lifelong learning" and "just-in-time-learning" that allows state-of-the-art approaches to learning and teaching to be designed and delivered on short notice in any setting for all learners.

Source: Caldwell, B. J. (1999). Education for the public good: Strategic intentions for the 21st century. In Marsh, D. D. (Ed.), *Preparing our schools for the 21st century.* Alexandria, VA: Association for Supervision and Curriculum Development.

Review and Reflect
on Curricular Models and Instructional Methods

Level 1: Remembering

Task

Locate at least one quality website on the Internet for each of the curricular models discussed in this section. Record the address and share with a peer.

1. **Taxonomy of Cognitive Development**

2. **Taxonomy of Creative Thinking**

3. **Multiple Intelligences**

4. **Cooperative Learning**

5. **Six Thinking Hats**

6. **SCAMPER**

7. **Q-Matrix**

8. **RAFTS**

9. **Brain-Based Learning**

Level 2: Understanding

Your Reflections

Task

Identify the strategies that you use successfully with your students to differentiate instruction and the reactions of your students to them.

Write a phrase to identify each one.

Level 3: Applying

Your Reflections

Task

Complete a Student Profile Sheet (pages 153–154) for each student. Use these sheets to help plan more effective instructional strategies and grouping patterns. Make some notes here about how this process was helpful to you.

Notes:

continued on page 210

continued
Review and Reflect
on Curricular Models and Instructional Methods

Level 4: Analyzing	Your Reflections

Task	
Examine each of the nine curricular models presented in this section. List one strength and one weakness of each model (from your perspective as a teacher).	1. **Taxonomy of Cognitive Development** 2. **Taxonomy of Creative Thinking** 3. **Multiple Intelligences** 4. **Cooperative Learning** 5. **Six Thinking Hats** 6. **SCAMPER** 7. **Q-Matrix** 8. **RAFTS** 9. **Brain-Based Learning**

Level 5: Evaluating	Your Reflections

Task	
How technologically savvy are you? On a 1 to 10 scale with 1 indicating very little know-how and 10 indicating great skills, rate yourself on the ways you now use this tool in the classroom with your students. Explain your rating.	**Rating:** **Why?**

Level 6: Creating	Your Reflections

Task	
Choose one of the six portable desktop learning station formats (page 181). Create one to field test with your students. Or, design a learning contract for one of your students and try it out.	**Describe what you did.**

Module IV

Classroom Management

and

Discipline

Contents of Module IV

Overview of
Classroom Management and Discipline

Effective classroom management and discipline depends on . . .

- the establishment of a trusting, respectful relationship between the teacher(s) and all students (individually and as a group).

- a set of meaningful classroom rules and procedures that are developed collaboratively by a team of teachers with input and support from students.

- a team discipline policy that is compatible with school and district guidelines.

- a set of disciplinary practices that promote harmony in the classroom and minimize student behavior problems.

- a teacher who knows how to head off discipline problems before they become major disruptions.

- adequate planning of classroom lessons and activities that are based on the unique traits and characteristics of the early adolescent.

- a process for promoting and ensuring group work success.

- a well-thought-out allocation of space in the classroom that facilitates student movement, student interaction, and student learning.

- a set of practical study tips and tidbits for students to know and use.

- a series of interactive strategies that maximize student participation.

- the elimination of teacher behaviors that turn students off to the learning process.

- a teacher's understanding and practical use of the behavior-discipline contract to improve an individual's attitude and performance in the classroom.

- a teacher's ability to create and apply a realistic discipline hierarchy.

- a teacher's ability to establish and facilitate possible classroom meetings as a tool that can address important student concerns and issues.

- an arsenal of disciplinary practices for teachers to consider when promoting positive classroom management practices.

- the teacher's ability to understand and apply the principles of conflict mediation.

- the elimination of homework hassles and hazards for students.

- the opportunity for students to make up or redo selected classroom assignments.

Terms Important for Understanding Classroom Management and Discipline

Assertive discipline: giving a firm, clear, and non-hostile response to student misbehavior

Behavior contract: a formal agreement regarding behavior, which is negotiated between a child and a school staff member, parent, or other individual. The contract should include:

   a) a clear definition of the behavior the child is expected to exhibit;

   b) the positive and negative consequences for performing and not performing the desired behavior;

   c) what the student (and each adult involved) is expected to do; and

   d) a plan for maintaining the desired behavior.

Behavior modification: systematic application of antecedents and consequences to change behavior

Benefits & rewards: the natural outcomes of positive behavior, attitudes, and communication

Cheating: giving or receiving assistance (answers) on tests or other independent assignments or forms of assessment

Classroom management: the process of ensuring lessons run smoothly without disruptive behavior by students

Consequences: the natural results or outcomes of poor behavior, attitudes, and communication

Discipline: training that enables students to make appropriate choices in a climate of warmth and support, which includes limitations with both positive and negative consequences (Discipline in school has two main goals: to ensure safety of staff and students and to create an environment conducive to learning.)

Dishonesty or lying: making false accusations against staff or other students; giving false information that may be harmful to others or interfere with the duties of staff

Disrespectful behavior: behaviors or actions that show a lack of respect to others, to include but not limited to: refusal to listen to teacher, name-calling, making fun of others, teasing, spreading rumors or gossiping, eye-rolling, and verbal disagreements

Disruption: any willful behavior or action that upsets orderly operation of the classroom or school

Engaged time: time on task or time students spend actually learning

Feedback: information on results of one's efforts or behavior

Fighting: any behavior that involves hitting, kicking, punching, poking, pushing, biting, or pinching with intent to harm

Gender bias: different views of males and females often favoring one over another

The Definitive Middle School Guide, Revised Edition
Copyright © 2014 World Book, Inc./Incentive Publications, Chicago, IL

Horseplay: Inappropriate physical contact, without anger or physical harm, such as hitting, kicking, punching, poking, pushing, pinching with the intent to annoy, bother, or tease others

Inappropriate language: language or gestures that are not acceptable in the school environment

Interpretation: a point of view that may add a slant or spin to the facts

Intimidation: posturing or threatening to cause harm or abusive and threatening language

Major and minor infractions: behaviors that may result in the destruction of property, severe disruption of the learning environment, physical harm, or serious disrespect toward others

Moral dilemmas: hypothetical situations that require a person to consider values of right and wrong

Motivation: an internal state that activates behavior and gives it direction

Nonverbal clues: eye contact, gestures, physical proximity, or touching used to communicate without interrupting verbal discourse

Punishment: using unpleasant consequences to weaken a behavior

Reinforcer: a pleasurable consequence that maintains or increases a behavior

Removal punishment: decreasing the chances that a behavior will occur again by removing a pleasant stimulus following the behavior

School discipline: refers to students complying with a code of behavior known as school rules (These rules may set out expected standards for clothing, timekeeping, social behavior, and work ethic. The term may also be applied to the punishment for a transgression of the code of behavior.)

Self-efficacy: the belief that one has the capabilities to execute the courses of action required to manage prospective situations

Self-esteem: a person's subjective appraisal of himself as intrinsically positive or negative to some degree

Self-regulation: rewarding or punishing one's own behavior

Sex-role behavior: behavior associated with one's sex as opposed to the other

Shaping: using small steps combined with feedback to help learners reach goals

Taking responsibility: accurately assessing any and all accountability that you may have in a situation

Tardy: situation where student is not in class at the designated time

Theft or stealing: taking or attempting to take, without permission, school property or the personal property of others

Time-out: removing student from situation in which misbehavior was reinforced

"With-it"ness: the degree to which the teacher is aware of and responsive to student performance

Guiding Questions for Classroom Management and Discipline

1 Why is it important to set classroom rules and procedures?

2 Should students be involved in establishing rules and procedures? Why or why not?

3 How do you, the teacher, decide on a given set of rules or procedures for your students to follow?

4 What are some effective ways to help students remember and follow classroom rules and procedures?

5 What indirect and direct consequences do you use for inappropriate student behavior?

6 How do you reward positive behavior in your classroom?

7 When do you involve parents or guardians in preventing or dealing with disciplinary situations with their teenagers?

8 How can or does developing effective relationships with students impact classroom management practices?

9 How would you characterize your teaching and communication style with students?

10 What strategies do you use to maintain order in the classroom?

11 What strategies do you use to head off potential discipline problems?

12 How do you help students be more responsible for themselves and their own behavior?

13 What procedures or structures do you currently use in the classroom to prevent and resolve conflicts? How effective are these approaches with students?

14 What do you do during the opening weeks of school to build strong relationships with students and to establish rules and procedures to be followed?

15 How do you reinforce students for following rules and procedures in your classroom?

16 How well do your classroom rules, procedures, and consequences fit in with the school's expectations for good behavior?

17 What kind of discipline hierarchy does your school follow and how well is it enforced?

18 When you disagree with the way a team member is handling a discipline issue in the classroom, how do you handle this?

19 What interactive strategies do you use to encourage widespread student participation?

20 How does the physical layout and arrangement of your classroom positively and negatively affect the management of your instructional program?

21 How do you foster group work success in your classroom?

22 How effectively do students deal with the homework assignments you require them to do?

23 What procedures do you have in place for students to make up or redo their work?

24 What types of things can occur in the classroom that might turn off students to learning?

The Definitive Middle School Guide, Revised Edition
Copyright © 2014 World Book, Inc./Incentive Publications, Chicago, IL

Negative Teacher Behaviors That Turn Students Off to the Learning Process

Students are discouraged, rather than encouraged, to learn by a teacher who

1. nags, threatens, shouts, or shows disrespect to students he or she serves.

2. is too quick to lose his or her temper or patience with students who are having difficulty.

3. is not well prepared for the day's lesson or fails to return graded work on time.

4. is poorly equipped to differentiate instruction or to address the special needs of diverse students.

5. is perceived as unfair or biased.

6. is incompetent or lazy.

7. singles out certain students for punishment or allows certain negative behaviors from one student and not another.

8. singles out certain students for praise or affirmation.

9. dominates the conversation in the classroom and allows little time for student-generated questions and interaction.

10. fails to contact parents in a timely fashion when a student misbehaves badly or is doing poorly academically.

11. consistently focuses on the negative rather than the positive behaviors and outcomes of students in their classroom time together.

12. fails to recognize the signs of student boredom, frustration, or misbehavior evident in the classroom due to lesson plans or instructional activities that are not effective or appropriate.

Note: When students are turned off to the learning process, management and discipline problems are sure to ensue!

Behaviors or Characteristics
Students Admire Most in a Teacher

Students grow and flourish academically when paired with a teacher they respect and admire. Students respect and admire a teacher who

1 treats all students in a friendly and fair manner.

2 believes that students are capable of doing quality work.

3 has a passion for his or her subject area.

4 comes prepared to teach on a daily basis.

5 enjoys working with students at the middle school level.

6 knows how to differentiate instruction and cater to a variety of student learning styles.

7 recognizes and values diversity in the student body.

8 can admit when he or she is wrong or made a mistake.

9 always listens to both sides of an argument or alternative positions on a controversial subject or topic.

10 is friendly, enthusiastic, and open-minded.

11 keeps promises and commitments to students.

12 is organized, disciplined, and not too strict or impersonal.

13 is a good problem solver and decision maker.

14 is respectful of student needs and concerns.

15 has a good sense of humor and can laugh at herself or himself.

16 helps students with self-monitoring and control strategies.

17 is aware of the unique needs and characteristics of ESOL, at-risk, and special-needs students.

18 maintains an optimal teacher-student relationship that consists of equal parts dominance and cooperation.

19 is patient, calm, and does not get easily upset or stressed.

20 tells students what they are going to learn and helps them to achieve those learning goals.

21 treats all students equally well and does not have favorites.

22 knows each student personally, listens to students, is interested in students, and cares about them.

Planning Strategies
for Classroom Success

1 Buy and use the best lesson plan book available.

2 Make long-range plans (well in advance) that lend themselves to constant revision and transition to manageable short-range plans.

3 Divide large projects into classroom-relevant smaller sections.

4 Delegate tasks to students, parents, or aides when appropriate and possible.

5 Consult other people for answers, help, or input.

6 Make use of classroom-ready commercial materials when they fit into learning goals and developmental objectives.

7 Upgrade and downgrade priorities as needed.

8 Set out daily goals in order of priority.

9 Make a list of "TO DOs" every day.

10 Unless absolutely necessary, refuse to make decisions under stress.

11 Carefully select a time and place free of interruptions for completing paperwork.

12 Allow a reasonable amount of time for interaction on a one-on-one basis with students and do not allow less important tasks to take precedence over this important time.

13 Keep a list and copy of class work and homework in a notebook for reference for students who have been absent.

14 Have presentation materials ready and accessible beforehand. Organize in folders by topic or instructional objective.

15 Capitalize on the use of student "experts" in the classroom whenever possible.

16 Utilize color as a classroom organizer. Color-code instructional areas with materials and supplies for easy access and return.

17 Color-code subject area notebooks (e.g., green for math, red for science, etc.) for quick reference and easy identification.

18 Color-code your grade book using different colors for daily, test, or failing grades so it is easy to spot problems and average grades.

19 Keep a small pad of paper and a pen in your school mailbox for instant replies and on-the-spot notes.

20 Show a scheduled video or film only once, to the entire team, at the same time freeing the remaining class periods for instruction instead of viewing.

21 Utilize uniform team timesaving procedures: conference form, substitute form, and team meeting agenda form.

22 Share and exchange teaching ideas, lesson plans, and creative activities with peers.

Classroom Management Tips for Teachers

Below is a collection of assorted "tips and tidbits" for teachers who would like new ideas for improving their classroom management and instructional efforts. They are not organized in any significant way, but are recorded as "random ideas" from which teachers can select ones that may work for them.

1 Prepare more material than you think you will need for any given lesson plan. This not only ensures that you will have adequate material for the time allowed, but that you will have options within the time frame to pick and choose what activities or experiences seem most appropriate as the lesson progresses.

2 Divide the chalkboard (or other visual board) into sections with colored rubber tape according to your lesson plans. Use one section for schedule and date, another for the day's assignments, a third section for notes and reminders, and a fourth section for homework assignments.

3 Maintain an "IN BOX" and an "OUT BOX" on or near your desk for students to hand in their work as it is completed and for corrected papers that are ready to be handed back. Assign a student to check the OUT BOX each day and to take responsibility for distributing papers, placing those papers without names with the "NO NAME CLIP" suggested below.

4 Use a large magnetic clip to hold all student work that does not have a name. Attach it to your desk or the chalkboard so students know where to look if they do not get an assignment back.

5 When handing out new worksheets or assignments, put the name of each absent student at the top of any of the papers and place in a strategic location (or the "OUT BOX" if you have one) to be distributed upon their return.

6 When collecting assignments and papers from the entire class, call for them in alphabetical order to save time during the grading and recording processes.

7 Speed up the attendance process by having students check off their names on a standard attendance sheet when entering the classroom.

8 Use special school letterhead (if school will allow you to do so) or classroom letterhead (design your own) for all official communications to the home. This immediately signals to parents or guardians the communication's importance.

9 Prepare a Team Homework Sheet for each day of the week that lists the homework assignments for each class period or teacher. The last teacher of the day distributes and briefly reviews this with the students. Use this strategy also as a planning tool so that students do not have to study for more than one test on any given day.

10 Arrange student desks in islands of two, three, or four as opposed to straight rows. This makes walking around the room easier for the teacher, and when the teacher is working with a student at one of the islands, he or she is also influencing the others close by. This idea also encourages peers to help one another in their small group and to be less influenced by others working outside their group.

The Definitive Middle School Guide, Revised Edition
Copyright © 2014 World Book, Inc./Incentive Publications, Chicago, IL

11 Create a Student Participation Log to keep track of student interaction during a class discussion. List the names of students in the class and check off a space every time you call on a student. This is a good way to note who has or has not been called upon to participate in a group discussion. It would look something like this:

> Class or Course _____ Date from _____ to _____.
>
> Student's Name _____
>
> Called upon ( ) ( ) ( ) ( ) ( ) ( ) ( ) ( ) ( ) ( ) ( ) ( ) ( ) ( ) ( ) ( ) ( ) ( )

12 Another strategy for keeping track of student participation in a group discussion or activity is to write each student's name on a file card, and as you call on a student, put aside her or his card until all names have been used.

13 Yet another strategy to consider for keeping track of student participation is a Stick Jar. Print students' names on Popsicle sticks or tongue depressors and place the sticks in a glass jar. Remove names from the jar as each student is called upon or volunteers a response.

14 Establish a reward program that focuses on the idea of catching someone doing something good, kind, appropriate, or helpful. A teacher, staff member, or other adult in the setting can give out a certificate such as this at any time:

> This is to certify that _____ performed
>
> a kind act on _____ as observed or witnessed by
>
> _____ .

15 When establishing due dates for assignments, consider giving students a requirement that is not limited to just one day, but one of three days such as Monday, Tuesday, or Wednesday. This allows for individual student differences, reduces the number of late hand-ins, and spreads the teacher's time for grading papers.

16 Use students as facilitators and presenters at the annual Open House to share their experiences and perceptions of the assigned work and classroom expectations. They can serve as assistants to the teacher and can make the time as student-centered as it is teacher-centered.

17 Prepare a special "Follow-Up Activity Book" for students to do when their regular classroom work is completed. This activity book should contain related puzzles, riddles, games, and other fun tasks related to content or subject matter being taught. This can be used as an incentive to finish early or for extra credit.

18 When students work in cooperative learning groups or on one-group projects, have each one initial those parts or pages that they worked on and were responsible for to ensure equal participation and contributions.

Interactive Strategies
That Encourage
Student Participation

1 Always attribute ideas and comments to those students who offered or presented them.

2 Encourage everyone's classroom participation and don't focus on a select few.

3 Don't indicate to students that they should have known the answer to a question and don't make subjective comments about incorrect answers.

4 Don't allow negative comments or criticisms from some students about another student's contribution.

5 Do provide correctives to student answers when needed and always state the question that the incorrect response addressed.

6 Encourage collaboration between and among students by allowing individuals to seek help from their peers.

7 Restate questions as needed and give guiding hints and cues when appropriate to do so.

8 Let students opt out when they are truly embarrassed or confused in teacher-directed question and answer sessions, as well as when they are confronted with a question they don't understand or have no clue to answer.

9 Provide the answer to a given question and then ask the student to add his or her personal thoughts and details to it in some small way.

10 Always acknowledge the students' participation even if ideas are incorrect.

11 Try rephrasing a question from more than one perspective in an attempt to increase the student's understanding of the question.

12 Provide the answer to a question the student is unable to answer and then have the student repeat the response as a memory aid for future reference.

The Definitive Middle School Guide, Revised Edition
Copyright © 2014 World Book, Inc./Incentive Publications, Chicago, IL

Ways to Ensure Group Work Success

1 Start with small groups of two or three and never form groups larger than five. Keep in mind that if you expect every student in the group to participate equally, then the smaller the group the more participation there will be per group member.

2 Pay special attention when placing students in a group. Determine in advance whether you want homogeneous or heterogeneous groups. Consider the advantages of putting students randomly in a group whenever possible to do so. First, students consider this fair. Secondly, students whom you wouldn't think function well together often do. Third, in random groupings, students don't tend to label themselves as the token ELL student in the group, the low achieving student in the group, or the smartest kid in the group. Finally, keep in mind that it is not a good idea to let students choose their own group members except in special circumstances.

3 Post and stress rules for functioning in the group. Some good rules to consider are these: Every person in the group must pull his or her own weight; Every person in the group must support and help one another as needed; No "put-downs" of individual group members will be tolerated; and Don't ask the teacher for help until all members of the group cannot proceed further without teacher assistance.

4 Set very clear objectives and timelines for the group task or assignment. Make sure that each group member understands this information by having one of the members explain it to the others in her or his own words.

5 Make certain that each group member is assigned a specific job or role for the group's assignment and understands its purpose. Some roles to consider are: Timekeeper, Recorder, Reader, Gopher Person, Chairperson, or Artist.

6 Provide each group with important resources and materials they will need to complete the task, as well as periodic checklists and deadlines to help them stay on task.

7 Be certain that the interpersonal skills important to the group's functioning are well taught in advance, and re-teach or review these as needed during the group process. Some skills to consider are: criticizing ideas and not people, speaking in quiet voices, clarifying ideas, praising contributions of others, listening to the speaker, and using time wisely.

8 Make sure that most of the group work is done during class time and not outside of class, so you can actively keep students engaged and provide ongoing supervision.

9 Create a setting that is conducive for group work, such as round tables and suitable chairs so that students can sit together and eyeball one another comfortably.

10 Make certain that each group spends some quality time reflecting back over their assigned task and discussing what they did well and what they would do differently next time.

11 Remember that the teacher's role in this small group process is to serve as guide, facilitating the group effort by coaching and monitoring, providing deadlines and feedback, solving problems and organizing resources, and teaching the group skills necessary for success.

12 When a student is having difficulty working well within the group, you can consider removing him or her from the group to work alone, or to work with you and any other students needing to be away from their group until the task or project is completed.

13 Establish a fair grading system for group work. If possible, give group members both a group grade for a collective contribution or completed task and an individual grade through an individual paper-pencil quiz or test.

The Definitive Middle School Guide, Revised Edition
Copyright © 2014 World Book, Inc./Incentive Publications, Chicago, IL

Considerations for the Physical Arrangement of a Classroom

Ask yourself these questions as you plan the arrangement of the classroom:

1 How many students will be in each class?

2 Where will whole or large group instruction take place?

3 Where will small group instruction take place?

4 What configuration of desks or tables and chairs works best for my teaching style, subject area, and the productive interaction of students?

5 What overall layout of seating makes it easy for me to see the students and for the students to see my presentations and demonstrations?

6 Where are the chalkboards, whiteboards, or active boards located?

7 Where should the teacher's desk be located in the room?

8 What are the primary patterns of movement in and about the classroom?

9 What pathways best facilitate the traffic flow?

10 What is the best placement for technology equipment to be used by me and the students? (Consider computers, printers, overhead projectors, screens, cameras, or video productions.)

11 What spaces in the classroom would be good locations for setting up learning stations?

12 What placements or spaces may invite students to bother other students or may contribute to discipline problems? (You'll want to avoid these!)

13 How can bookshelves and storage units be located most effectively so that frequently used materials are easily accessible to students?

14 What is the best placement for bulletin boards, displays of student work, assignment calendars and timelines, and student announcements or reminders?

15 What do the students see first when they enter the room? Is it something pleasing to the eye, interesting to view, or informative and important to the day's business?

The Definitive Middle School Guide, Revised Edition
Copyright © 2014 World Book, Inc./Incentive Publications, Chicago, IL

Name _____ Date _____

Guidelines to Consider
When Establishing Classroom Rules

Directions: Rules, much like laws, define acceptable and unacceptable behavior in a community setting. Although possible, it is undesirable to establish hundreds of rules in order to cover every anticipated behavior problem; therefore, the teacher should define only those rules that are most important to running a safe environment that is conducive to learning. Some guidelines to consider when establishing rules for a classroom of students are listed below. Review them and record the reactions you have to each point.

1 Guidelines must be clear and specific. That is, they must be short and simple in syntax.

Your reaction: _____

_____

2 One must always be able to determine if the rule is broken or followed; rules must not be ambiguous.

Your reaction: _____

_____

3 Rules must make sense to the people who enforce and follow them; they are best agreed upon by both student and teacher alike.

Your reaction: _____

_____

4 They must state what is allowed as well as what is not allowed. Rules should be explainable through both examples of what is acceptable and what is unacceptable.

Your reaction: _____

_____

5 Rules must be stated simply and demonstrated so that all can understand; they should be taught, discussed, or role-played before implementation.

Your reaction: _____

_____

6 Guidelines should state positive expectations rather than focus on unacceptable behaviors.

Your reaction: _____

_____

7 Guidelines should be fundamental and nonnegotiable.

Your reaction: _____

_____

Rules to Consider for a Successful Middle Level Classroom

Read through these classroom student rules carefully and evaluate each one in terms of the guidelines for establishing rules in a successful middle school setting (see page 225). It should be noted that all of these rules have been taken from existing classrooms throughout the country.

1 Always strive to be on time for classes or other engagements.

2 Keep your hands and feet to yourself.

3 Use appropriate voices when inside.

4 Treat everyone with respect.

5 Be prepared with books, pencils, and papers.

6 Respect other people and their property.

7 Be prepared to participate in activities, projects, and group projects.

8 Make sure to bring all learning materials with you to class.

9 You may tell others when you are angry, and you may give yourself time to calm down, but you may not hit, yell, act out, or use profanity.

10 Wait to talk until you are called upon.

11 Complete all assignments in a timely manner.

12 Use common sense—if you think there's a chance you or someone else might get hurt, do not do it.

13 Use only kind words when speaking of others.

14 Strive to do your best work at all times.

15 Come to class prepared to succeed.

16 Support others when they need it; let others support you.

17 When others are speaking, listen.

18 Walk, do not run, in halls and classroom.

19 If it is not yours, do not touch it.

20 Refrain from eating or chewing gum in class.

21 Clean up your own workspaces.

22 Avoid profanity, teasing, or disrespectful behavior at all times.

23 Sit in your seat, ready for class, when the bell rings.

24 Raise your hand for permission to speak.

25 Ask for restroom passes during instruction time only in cases of emergency.

26 Treat others as you would like to be treated.

27 Use friendly laughter to reduce stress, but never laugh to hurt or make fun of someone.

28 Assume responsibility for your own learning.

29 Avoid behavior that would disturb people who are working.

30 Prepare and hand in assignments on time.

Classroom Rules and Procedures That Teachers Must Clarify for Effective Classroom Management

> *Directions: Educational leaders and experts in the field of classroom management have identified these classroom procedures and rules that must be in place before any teacher and group of students can function together successfully in a productive educational setting. Spend some time thinking and writing about how you would answer each question, and plan for each of the following situations.*

1 How do you plan to seat your students? Will it be by assigned seats, open to student choice, cooperative group seating, or a combination of flexible seating patterns?

2 What constitutes being late in the room or seat? What do you do with students who are tardy or late to class? How and when will absentee slips be handled?

3 What expectations and options do you have for students when the bell rings and how they spend their time during the first five to ten minutes of class? How will you get students' attention to start class?

4 How do you want students to spend their time during the last five or ten minutes of class? How are they to be dismissed from class?

5 How do students get permission to leave the room during class, and what do they do upon returning to class? What kinds of things can they leave the classroom for?

6 How do you handle student absences from class? What is your policy for turning in their missed class work or make-up work? What is your policy for their getting information about their missed class work and homework assignments? How and when will students make up quizzes and tests missed?

7 How will students' make-up work and late projects, such as research papers, portfolios, or special assignments, be graded?

8 What are your procedures for distributing materials and equipment, collecting materials and equipment, and storage of these items?

9 What is your policy for students caught cheating in class?

10 What is your policy on chewing gum or eating food in class?

11 What happens when students come to class unprepared, without textbooks, pencils or pens, paper, and other essentials? How do students get supplies they are missing?

12 When are students free to move about in class?

13 How will students get recognized to talk, and how will they get help from you?

14 What are acceptable noise levels for discussion, seatwork, and group work?

15 What are your expectations for student attention and participation during teacher lectures and direct instruction, as well as during teacher or student presentations and demonstrations?

16 How are students made aware of your course objectives, course requirements, methods of assessment, and grading scale?

17 What is generally acceptable as out-of-seat behavior?

18 What do students do during fire and disaster drills?

19 What procedures do you have in place for whole-class activities and instruction, as well as seatwork?

20 What procedures do you have in place for small group work?

STUDENT SELF-ASSESSMENT
OF CLASSROOM BEHAVIORS

Directions:
Please read and assign a number from 1 to 4 (with 1 being *All the Time*, 2 being *Much of the Time*, 3 being *Some of the Time,* and 4 being *Little of the Time*) for each of the items listed below. Be honest in your self-assessment.

A. I DO MY HOMEWORK. _____

B. I GET TO CLASS ON TIME. _____

C. I HAVE MY CLASS MATERIALS WITH ME AND COME PREPARED TO LEARN. _____

D. I TURN IN MY ASSIGNMENTS TO MEET THE DEADLINES. _____

E. I PARTICIPATE IN CLASS DISCUSSIONS AND ACTIVITIES. _____

F. I LISTEN TO THE TEACHER DURING LESSONS. _____

G. I LISTEN TO MY PEERS DURING LESSONS. _____

H. I ASK QUESTIONS WHEN I DO NOT UNDERSTAND SOMETHING. _____

I. I FOLLOW INSTRUCTIONS WELL. _____

J. I MAKE GOOD USE OF CLASS TIME FOR WORKING ON ASSIGNED TASKS. _____

Choose one item for which you gave a score of 3 or 4. Write three things you could do to improve this behavior.

1._____

_____

_____

_____

_____

_____

2._____

_____

_____

_____

_____

_____

3._____

_____

_____

_____

_____

_____

_____

Name_____

The Definitive Middle School Guide, Revised Edition
Copyright © 2014 World Book, Inc./Incentive Publications, Chicago, IL

Name _____ Date _____

Things to Consider When Establishing Classroom Homework Policies

Directions: Homework issues continue to be a "headache" for many students, teachers, and parents alike. It is critical that a set of Homework Procedures be established and communicated to all stakeholder groups early in the school year. To begin this process, a group of teachers (and even a student and parent or two) should sit down and develop some guidelines for each of these homework-related situations. After each item, write down a tentative rule or strategy that your group agrees might work in a classroom setting.

1 Planning student homework tasks

_____

2 Assigning student homework

_____

3 Making up homework after student absence

_____

4 Collecting student homework

_____

5 Dealing with the missing homework paper

_____

6 Providing incentives for completing homework

_____

7 Copying other student's homework

_____

8 Refusing to do or hand in homework

_____

9 Grading of student homework

_____

10 Dealing with students unable to do homework

_____

11 Giving back student homework

_____

12 Contacting the home about homework

_____

13 Checking student progress in homework

_____

The Definitive Middle School Guide, Revised Edition
Copyright © 2014 World Book, Inc./Incentive Publications, Chicago, IL

Ways to Clear
Homework-Assigning Hurdles

1 Always assign homework that does one of four things:

    a) Provides practice of a skill learned in class;

    b) Reviews previously taught material or information;

    c) Focuses on enrichment or extension of previously learned material; and

    d) Emphasizes student choice, creativity, and approach to previously learned material.

2 Make certain that all homework assignments meet district or school criteria in terms of time required per day, week, or year.

3 Remember that the ideal homework assignment is one that taps student creativity, energy, interests, skill levels, and, when possible, caters to their learning style.

4 Plan homework assignments that relate directly to what is currently being taught in class, that will enhance student understanding of what is being taught, that does not require use of special resources or materials not readily available to the student, and that can be completed in a reasonable period of time.

5 Make certain that the homework assignment is given orally, is written out for students to see, and is reviewed more than once during the class period.

6 If possible, give students at least five minutes or more of class time to get started on their homework each day. Use a preplanned system to assign homework, such as the use of an assignment notebook or planner.

7 Never give homework as a punishment to students or an entire class, and never let students believe that homework is assigned just to keep them busy.

8 Be willing to modify homework assignments if students are really uncomfortable with the assigned task or the required time for completing the task. Don't use homework to lower student grades, but as partial credit for an out-of-class assignment.

9 Inform parents of your homework policy through the course syllabus, through parent open houses, through parent conferences, or through parent newsletters whenever possible to do so. Also, don't develop the habit of sending notes home to parents explaining homework a student is expected to do except in special circumstances or if dealing with a student with special needs.

10 Use the suggested tasks on page 232 to survey the students on their personal views, feelings, and opinions about the role of homework in their classroom settings. Take time to read and review the results.

HOMEWORK SURVEY TASKS

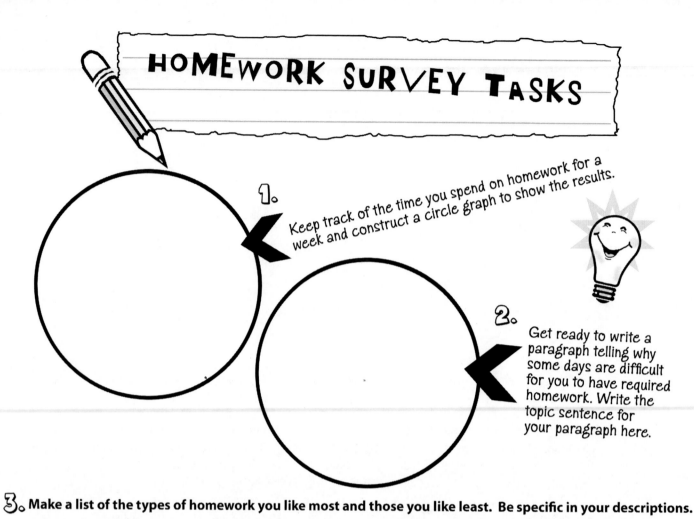

1. Keep track of the time you spend on homework for a week and construct a circle graph to show the results.

2. Get ready to write a paragraph telling why some days are difficult for you to have required homework. Write the topic sentence for your paragraph here.

3. Make a list of the types of homework you like most and those you like least. Be specific in your descriptions.

Like most:

Like least:

4. Complete this statement:
The most important reason for having homework in a given class should be . . .

_____

_____

_____

_____

_____

5. Get ready to argue for or against this statement: *Homework is an important part of the learning process.*
List three details to support your position.

_____

_____

_____

_____

Name_____ Date_____

The Definitive Middle School Guide, Revised Edition
Copyright © 2014 World Book, Inc./Incentive Publications, Chicago, IL

Suggestions to Consider
When Allowing Students
to Make Up or Redo Their Work

1 Establish a firm policy for students to follow when making up their work after an absence from class. Consider all types of absences including those due to illness, participation in school-sponsored activities (band, sports, cheerleading, debate, etc.), doctor's appointments, extra vacation time, and family emergencies. Try to enforce this policy with no (or very few) exceptions to avoid abuses of the policy in place.

2 Make certain that this policy is clearly stated in your course syllabus and in the student-parent handbook at the beginning of the school semester or year.

3 Encourage students to turn in their work as quickly as possible after their absence for maximum credit. Inform students that they are responsible for finding out what assignments they missed and for getting them from the teacher immediately upon return to class.

4 Keep extra copies of all classroom and homework assignments in a set of special folders that are filed according to the dates they were distributed.

5 Maintain an ongoing list of missed work on a classroom bulletin board or section of whiteboard or active board so that students are reminded daily of work that needs to be done due to absences.

6 Consider having students pair up with a "study buddy" the first week of class and encourage each pair to work as a team throughout the semester by taking notes for each other when one is absent, as well as informing one another about missed assignments during that absence.

7 Allow students to redo selected key assignments and tests throughout the school year as long as they follow an established set of rules.

8 Consider these options for "redo" assignments:

    a) Establish a maximum number of "redo" assignments or tests allowed for the grading period.

    b) Establish a reasonable time period for turning in the "redo" assignments or taking the "redo" tests as long as it is done at least two weeks before the end of the grading period.

    c) Insist that the old assignment or test be handed in with the "redo" for credit.

    d) In some cases, you may want to take an average of the two grades rather than totally replace the old grade with the new grade.

Levels of Offenses in a Discipline Hierarchy

Why create a discipline hierarchy?

It is important that schools or classrooms develop a discipline hierarchy to help students, teachers, and parents identify, understand, and effectively handle the different levels of negative behaviors or offenses that commonly occur in a middle or high school setting. This is important for safe operation of the school because

    a) it outlines and defines all of the offenses that are most likely to occur in typical school settings.

    b) it groups these offenses into levels: those violations of rules and procedures established by classroom teachers, those addressed outside the classroom by school administrators, and those that require mandatory suspension or expulsion because of their seriousness and threat to others on the school campus.

Every school needs a clear and comprehensive discipline policy so that all members of the school know what behaviors are acceptable and unacceptable, and what the consequences are for each unacceptable behavior.

R. Marzano, J. Marzano, and D. Pickering (2005) have identified three levels of offenses when creating a discipline hierarchy for the classroom. These are defined as follows:

LEVEL 1 OFFENSES: These offenses occur when students violate the rules and procedures that have been established by individual classroom teachers. Such violations lead to consequences that may involve the following: verbal warning, time-out, meeting with parents, visit to principal's office, or written or verbal apology.

LEVEL 2 OFFENSES: School administrators address these offenses outside of the classroom. Level 2 behavioral offenses are above and beyond violations of classroom rules and procedures and are typically viewed as "serious misconduct" offenses. They are behaviors that are causing a major disruption in the classroom, and they are chronic and continuous. These may include fighting; serious horseplay; possession of weapon or facsimile of one; throwing objects resulting in injury; possession or use of controlled substance; sexual harassment; racial or ethnic harassment; religious harassment; abusive, obscene, profane, or disrespectful language or gestures; insubordinate refusal to follow a reasonable directive or request; theft or vandalism; and general behavior detrimental to welfare, safety, or morals of students in the school. Records of Level 2 offenses are kept in a database by infraction, and a discipline file is created for students involved in such incidents. The file includes a record of infractions by year, written and telephone communications with parents, suspension letters, and copies of behavior plans as they are developed and amended. They always involve parental contact, and infractions range from detention to in-school or out-of-school suspension.

LEVEL 3 OFFENSES: These offenses are of such magnitude that suspension or expulsion is mandatory. They involve situations in which students need to be immediately removed from class or separated from fights that have a high likelihood of injury, credible threats against life or of serious bodily injury, and all types of weapons violations. For Level 3 offenses, parents are always contacted, and documentation is always prepared. Level 3 offenses often involve the local police and, in these situations, the school obtains arrest records. All Level 3 records follow a student from grade to grade and school to school.

Source: Marzano, R. J., Marzano, J. S., & Pickering, D. (2003). *Classroom management that works: Research-based strategies for every teacher.* Alexandria, VA: Association for Supervision and Curriculum Development.

The Definitive Middle School Guide, Revised Edition
Copyright © 2014 World Book, Inc./Incentive Publications, Chicago, IL

Questions to Help Determine
the Discipline Level in Your Class

1 Do you have a predetermined set of classroom rules that were not imposed on students but rather developed collaboratively by both you and the students?

2 When you are not in your classroom or arrive late to your classroom, how do the students respond or behave? Do they follow the established classroom rules and routines?

3 How do students behave during public address (PA) announcements?

4 When you have to leave the classroom during class time, how do the students react? Do you appoint someone to be in charge during your absence?

5 When you have a substitute teacher, what type of feedback do you receive from both students and the substitute?

6 Are the students comfortable asking you for assistance when they are having a problem with an assignment?

7 How do students conduct themselves during presentations by other students?

8 Do the students feel comfortable helping one another with assigned tasks and responsibilities? Is there a genuine sense of community present?

9 Do students generally treat one another in the classroom with respect and politeness? Are they courteous in their interactions?

10 Do student conversations during time in class generally focus on relevant assignments and what you have asked them to do?

11 Are students able to complete their work with minimal distractions from and among one another?

12 Do students perceive you as someone they can count on to be both fair and firm in dealing with their problems, questions, concerns, and issues?

13 When someone visits your classroom, will they generally observe a group of students who are on task and comfortable with the environment in which they reside?

14 When someone visits your classroom, will they see a group of students who are involved and excited about what they are doing?

Behavior Problems That Occur
Most Often in the Classroom

◄ *Directions: Check those that are most problematic in your classroom. Then set some goals to find solutions for those problems.* ►

_____ **1** Arguments among students who quarrel with each other or the teacher

_____ **2** Assignments not turned in by students who cannot do them, will not do them, or refuse to do them as a means of control

_____ **3** Students who bother their classmates, disrupting learning for the entire classroom

_____ **4** Behavior on a bus that is negative because of disrespect for others or because of a need to draw attention to oneself

_____ **5** Cheating among students who care either too much or too little

_____ **6** Tardiness in students who fail to appreciate time on task opportunities and responsibilities

_____ **7** Disorganization that can have an impact on a student's performance

_____ **8** Disrespectful behavior by a student who has little self-respect or few positive role models to imitate

_____ **9** Lack of enthusiasm due to a sense of powerlessness in today's world

_____ **10** Misdirected energy, manifested by the student seeking negative reinforcement rather than positive feedback for behaviors displayed

_____ **11** Profanity that has become a "way of life" for even the best students due to social norms and influences

_____ **12** Friendship problems and peer pressures which all too often impact a student's attitude toward the schooling process

_____ **13** Gangs that fill a student's need to belong to a group in order to avoid isolation

_____ **14** Gum chewing that interferes with oral communication tasks; gum that finds itself attached to desks, sidewalks, and other inappropriate places

_____ **15** Holidays causing students to be absent from class or to become distracted from academics

_____ **16** Hurrying through assigned tasks, often leading to poor-quality work and wasted time

_____ **17** Interruptions by students who are poor listeners, are egocentric learners, or are lacking in social skills

The Definitive Middle School Guide, Revised Edition
Copyright © 2014 World Book, Inc./Incentive Publications, Chicago, IL

____ **18** Isolation or withdrawal by students who lack confidence in their ability to learn

____ **19** Jurisdiction disputes and disparities that lead students to play one adult against another

____ **20** Jealousy among students who compete for attention from peers, parents, and persons in charge

____ **21** Thrills that come from the wrong sources such as tobacco, drugs, or breaking school rules

____ **22** Kissing or other forms of sexual expression or promiscuity

____ **23** Lying by students who are confronted with discrepancies between what they say and do

____ **24** Limits which students refuse to acknowledge or honor in their daily activities

____ **25** Manipulation of impressionable students who are discouraged or disillusioned about the world in which they learn and live

____ **26** Low motivation levels demonstrated by many students who approach the school setting without goals, skills, resources, or family support

____ **27** Note writing between students, which often takes priority over attention to classroom instruction

____ **28** Nonsense fads, fashions, or behaviors among students that are self-initiated distractions from the "business" of school

____ **29** Procrastination by some students who do not know how to set priorities or budget their time

____ **30** Putdowns which are used all too often by students when referring to their peers

____ **31** Rigidity among students who are unable to see the "gray" areas of life and the time and place for negotiation

____ **32** Rigor in the curriculum that is often undervalued by students in the courses they choose to take

____ **33** Skipping school or cutting classes, leading to student suspensions and dropouts

____ **34** Lack of sportsmanship in many types of competition, whether it be academic or athletic in context

____ **35** Taking turns, which requires students to be more patient and tolerant of others

____ **36** Lack of awareness or concern about prejudices and stereotypes among diverse school populations

____ **37** Ethnic, racial, religious, class, or sexual harassment

____ **38** Not taking responsibility for one's own learning or behavior

Basic Techniques for Dealing with Discipline Problems

The teacher can . . .

1 ignore the misbehavior.

2 delay taking action for the misbehavior.

3 use nonverbal actions.

4 use verbal actions.

5 give a gentle reprimand.

6 hold a mini-conference with the student.

7 hold a lengthy conference with the student.

8 work out a behavior contract with the student (signed by the student).

9 move a student's seat in the classroom.

10 arrange for a time-out placement for the student.

11 contact a parent or guardian to discuss the misbehavior.

12 arrange for a conference with the parents or guardians.

13 refer a student to the administration.

14 suspend the student.

15 expel a student for extreme misbehavior.

For more help, refer to: Thompson, J. G. (1998). *Discipline survival kit for the secondary teacher*. West Nyack, NY: Center for Applied Research in Education.

Which Discipline Option?

Basic Techniques for Dealing with Discipline Problems

Option	Name a problem for which you would use this option.	Circumstances under which you would use the option.
Ignore the misbehavior		
Delay taking action		
Nonverbal actions		
Verbal actions		
Gentle reprimand		
Mini-conference with student		
Lengthy conference with student		
Form behavior contract with student		
Move student seat		
Time-out placement		
Contact parent or guardian		
Conference with parent or guardian		
Refer to administration		
Suspend		

Wise Disciplinary Do's and Don'ts to Promote Effective Classroom Management

1 **DO** get students' attention before giving instructions or directions.

2 **DO** wait for students to focus rather than talk over chatter or conversations. Wait quietly until everyone is on task.

3 **DON'T** talk too much. Use the first few minutes of class for lectures and presentations and then get the students working.

4 **DO** break the class period into two or three different activities. Be sure each activity segues smoothly into the next.

5 **DON'T** stand still or sit at your desk. Circulate among students as they work in each quadrant of the classroom, and use proximity to improve overall classroom control.

6 **DO** establish eye contact periodically with each student if possible and give quiet reminders about behavior as needed.

7 **DON'T** yell. Use a quiet voice, not a loud one, in the classroom.

8 **DO** use a variety of cues to remind students of expected behavior, and teach students your cues in advance.

9 **DO** be aware of the effects of your own dress, voice, and movements on student behavior.

10 **DO** use students' names as low-profile correctors of inattention.

11 **DO** communicate positive expectations of good behavior to your class and reinforce it at every opportunity.

12 **DON'T** plead or threaten them about following the rules and play the judge and jury game.

13 **DO** establish logical consequences in advance for each classroom rule and consistently follow through with consequences to enforce those rules.

14 **DON'T** use "you" messages. Use "I" messages assertively to tell students what you want them to do.

15 **DO** discipline individual students quietly and privately. Never engage in a disciplinary conversation across the room.

16 **DO** respond to positive behavior you like with specific, personal affirmation.

17 **DON'T** be vague. When communicating a concern, be specific and descriptive.

18 **DO** pay attention to behaviors of students that look like they could become problematic, and quietly move in closer to their position in the classroom.

19 **DO** re-direct the student's attention when she or he is off task.

20 **DO** listen carefully to what students are thinking about and what they are feeling, especially in times of stress.

21 **DO** help low-ability students learn tricks and techniques to do such things as organize their notebooks, study for a test, and take good notes—so they are not unfairly punished for their current limitations.

22 **DO** start fresh every day and don't carry over yesterday's problems and mistakes.

Ways to Head Off
Potential Discipline Problems
(Before They Become Major Disruptions)

1 Provide consistent and meaningful positive reinforcement for students who behave appropriately that includes a combination of sincere praise, creative awards, group rewards, and informative phone calls or notes to home.

2 Develop a discipline plan or "ladder" of discipline offenses that correlates minor infractions with minor consequences and major infractions with major consequences. These might include some sort of prearranged warning system, conducting private talks with students, contacting parents for assistance, and scheduling conferences established by the teacher.

3 Experiment with alternative methods of classroom control, such as Time-Out Tables that last approximately 15 minutes, one-on-one talks with a student taken aside, or providing options for students to decide on their own consequences on predetermined behaviors established by the teacher.

4 "Walk the talk" by circulating around the room while teaching a lesson, pausing or stopping by problem students on a need basis.

5 Draw up a formal contract that specifies desired student behavior and that lays out timelines and penalties. Have the contract cosigned by student, teacher, and parent alike.

6 In cooperative or small group work sessions or settings, pull out misbehaving students and have them work in a group with the teacher as the leader for that class period or until they are ready to join their peers.

7 In extreme cases, invite a parent monitor to class and have him or her spend the entire day sitting and working with the student in a "monitoring" and not a "friendly" capacity.

8 Maintain a discipline log with each student's name listed in it. When a problem occurs, have the student sign the log next to or under his or her name. The student then completes a discipline sheet answering the following questions: What did I do? Why did this cause a problem? What can I do to prevent this problem from happening again? The discipline sheets are kept in a folder with the log and both serve as a method of accountability for anecdotal records and parent-guardian conferences.

Guidelines for Handling Inappropriate Behaviors

1 Place an emphasis on prevention through classroom rules and regulations that are clear, consistent, fair, and understood by all students.

2 Try to quickly "size up" the situation in order to determine if the behavior is indeed interfering with instruction or whether it is merely annoying to you as the teacher.

3 Be certain to attack the behavior problem or classroom interruption and not the student.

4 Whenever possible, count to ten before attacking the problem in order to minimize your reaction and to keep yourself cool, calm, and collected.

5 Deal specifically with the infraction at hand and do not refer to previous incidents or misconducts.

6 Always focus on orchestrating a win-win situation rather than a win-lose situation for all parties involved.

7 Remember and remind yourself that you, and you alone, are responsible for your words and your actions, so keep the discipline constructive and productive at all times.

8 Be fair in assigning consequences that fit the misbehavior, and apply those consequences as soon as possible after the misbehavior.

9 Provide the student who is being disciplined the opportunity and privilege of rejoining the ongoing classroom activities as soon as possible to avoid undue delay and limitations on task time.

10 If the student is out of control and unable to rejoin the group, isolate the student in some way, but emphasize when the privilege of class participation will be allowed again.

11 Emphasize to the student that you will offer support, feedback, guidelines, and limits to the student at any time, but that the ultimate responsibility for exercising proper behavior always rests with the student.

12 If certain misbehaviors are chronic among students, arrange for ongoing instruction and assistance that will involve the class in their solution.

The Definitive Middle School Guide, Revised Edition
Copyright © 2014 World Book, Inc./Incentive Publications, Chicago, IL

Discipline Mistakes to Avoid at All Costs

1 Never back a student into a corner, literally or figuratively, because the student will generally come out fighting.

2 Never discipline a student when you do not have your temper under control.

3 Never discipline the whole class when just a few are responsible for the misbehavior.

4 Never use sarcasm or put-downs when disciplining a student.

5 Never threaten a student with a penalty unless you are prepared to go through with it.

6 Never keep students overtime if it interferes with another teacher's classroom or timeline.

7 Always assign only one clear punishment per offense.

8 Always make the punishment fit the offense.

9 Never set unreasonable or arbitrary rules and procedures for students to follow.

10 Never engage in any form of verbal or physical abuse.

11 Never accuse or confront a student in front of the whole class, but take him or her aside to handle the misbehavior in private.

12 Never force a student to offer an apology in front of the class but rather handle it on a private one-to-one basis.

13 Never fail to respond to student questions about the nature of her or his behavior.

14 Never use grades as a punishment for student misbehavior.

15 Never threaten, punish, or humiliate a student in anger.

16 Never overlook or reward poor behavior in the classroom.

17 Never accept excuses to sensible rules and their consequences from students.

18 Never get into arguments with students that aren't likely to go anywhere.

19 Never hold a grudge against a student once an unacceptable behavior has been corrected.

20 Never fail to report any form of violence, verbal threats of aggression, or rumors of planned offenses on or off the school grounds.

21 Never fail to get involved when a student commits a disruptive act or threatens to do so in the halls or classrooms of the school.

22 Never forget that there are multiple causes of student misbehavior in the school, which include: students who have a need to seek attention, students who have unmet physical and psychological needs, students who have a need to avoid failure, students who have a need to seek power, students who do not know or understand teacher expectations, students who are unaware of their own behavior or how and when to display appropriate behavior, students who receive some sort of pleasure from misbehavior, students who have a strained relationship with the teacher, and students who have a need to seek revenge.

23 Never make a student stand in a corner, stay after school with nothing to do, or copy meaningless words or sentences.

Questions to Ask Yourself Before Taking Disciplinary Action

1 Is this action appropriate and reasonable for the misbehavior on the part of the student?

2 Is this action a short-term or long-term solution to the misbehavior?

3 Is this action compatible with both school and district policy?

4 Is this action consistent with my established rules for the classroom or interdisciplinary team?

5 Is this action likely to improve the future behavior of the student?

6 Is this action based on sound disciplinary theory and practice?

7 Is this action likely to be considered fair for those involved?

8 Is this action likely to make sense to the parents and to be supported by the parents of the student?

9 Is this action likely to be supported by the school's administration?

10 Is this action likely to discourage similar misbehavior in the future?

11 Is this action likely to make sense to other students in the class or school?

Side Effects of Punishment to Consider

1 It does not teach any replacement behavior in the form of a more effective behavior.

2 It often leads to anger, resentment, defensiveness, and retaliation or revenge-seeking.

3 It does not seek to solve the underlying conflict.

4 It often suppresses the behavior temporarily, but does not eliminate it.

5 It increases threat, which inhibits a student's ability to problem solve.

6 It frustrates all the basic psychological needs of belonging, power, freedom, and fun.

7 It is focused on past behavior rather than present and future behavior.

8 It sends the message that adults solve their problems by force, coercion, or power.

Tips for Conducting
a Classroom Meeting

Classroom meetings can be powerful tools for teaching student responsibility and solving behavior problems when they occur. Follow these basic steps for conducting class meetings in your own educational setting:

1 Introduce the concept of classroom meetings to your students. Determine who will assume the leadership role for both calling the meetings and establishing the time and place for these sessions. Consider whether the meetings should be held weekly, monthly, or "as needed."

2 Establish an acceptable format for these classroom meetings and clarify the roles of both teacher and students in this meeting process. Generally, the teacher acts as coach, takes the minutes, and participates as a group member offering help when needed. An appointed or elected student leader conducts the meetings by helping to identify problems, guide discussions, facilitate decisions, and get closure on solutions.

3 Clarify the roles of other students in the class as participants or nonparticipants in these meetings, and establish some ground rules for addressing the issues under discussion and for keeping the discussion on the designated topics.

4 Develop a seating plan to accommodate both participants and nonparticipants. Keep in mind that it is important to have participating students sit in a circle where they can see the faces of other participants and the teacher. Nonparticipants may serve as observers of the meeting and members of the audience.

5 Encourage all students to do some type of written follow-up activity after each meeting. Consider short reflective essays, mini-position papers, or simple journal entries that allow students to record their personal thoughts on topics discussed, problems addressed, or issues resolved.

Approaches to Conflict Mediation

APPROACH 1: Employ the following eight steps to resolve conflict situations:

1 Identify and define the problem or conflict.

2 Determine the circumstances, situations, and behaviors that led up to the problem or conflict.

3 Examine the feelings experienced by those involved.

4 Ask yourself, "Have I dealt with a problem or conflict such as this before? What did I do? Did it work? What would I do differently next time?"

5 List and reflect on many different alternatives for handling the problem.

6 Select one alternative and develop a plan of action.

7 Implement and monitor the plan.

8 Evaluate the plan to determine if it is working and, if not, what other alternatives need to be considered.

APPROACH 2: Design an information-gathering form similar to the sample on page 248 and use this with a group of trained mediators who follow these ground rules for mediating a conflict.

1 Get the conflicting parties to agree to solve the problem with the help of the mediator. This requires a voluntary "yes" from the involved parties.

2 Instruct disputants that they cannot engage in name-calling, but must be considerate and respectful of one another.

3 Inform disputants that they will each have an opportunity to state personal views of the conflict including what they want, how they feel, and what would be an acceptable solution.

4 Encourage disputants to be both honest and accurate in their descriptions of the conflict, including what they want, how they feel, and what would be an acceptable solution.

5 Stress to the disputants that they must agree to abide by the agreement or resolution.

6 Emphasize to disputants the importance of confidentiality and that all discussion at this meeting is confidential and will not be reported to authorities unless it involves child abuse, weapons, drugs, or alcohol-related incidents. It is important that the mediator listens closely to all disputants, finds out the facts causing the conflict, exhibits patience, and respects all parties.

The Definitive Middle School Guide, Revised Edition
Copyright © 2014 World Book, Inc./Incentive Publications, Chicago, IL

APPROACH 3: Organize a problem-solving team of teachers at each grade level to handle the difficult conflict situations that arise during the school year. These problem-solving teams should consider the following guidelines:

1 Teams should be composed of volunteers or participants who believe in the effectiveness of systematic, collaborative troubleshooting. Teams should include regular classroom teachers, an administrator, a support staff person (such as a school counselor, a psychologist, a social worker), parents, and possibly students.

2 School administrators must provide resources and support to facilitate team functioning, including such possibilities as release time, financial compensation, relief from other duties, and paperwork assistance.

3 Training in trust building, collaboration, interventions, and consultation should be provided for all team members.

4 Teams should be enabled to make use of their collective expertise and be encouraged to bring individual perspectives to the decision-making and problem-solving sessions.

5 Behavior contracts for use with students should be developed and used as part of this process. (See sample Behavior Contract on page 249 and sample Discipline Contract on page 250.)

6 Teams should consider a wide variety of interventions for improving student behavior, because different students respond to different interventions based on their needs and the causes of their behavior.

Some possible interventions include:

a. Opportunities to be a leader and contribute
b. A behavior-management contract
c. A mentor or buddy
d. An opportunity to "let off steam" via a physical outlet
e. A good role model
f. More one-to-one attention from volunteer, aide, peer, or tutor
g. Shorter or modified classroom assignments
h. More choices regarding classroom assignments and activities
i. More rigorous consequences
j. Parental support or involvement
k. More tangible rewards
l. Some quiet times or places
m. Conflict-resolution skills training

Information-Gathering Form for Mediation Meeting

Student signature_____ Date_____

Teacher signature_____ Date_____

1. **What is the basic conflict and who is involved?**

   _____
   _____
   _____
   _____
   _____

2. **What did you want that caused the conflict?**

   _____
   _____
   _____
   _____
   _____
   _____

3. **What did the other person(s) want that caused the conflict?**

   _____
   _____
   _____
   _____
   _____
   _____

4. **What are three possible solutions to the conflict that would satisfy you?**

   _____
   _____
   _____
   _____
   _____
   _____

5. **What are two things you might do if this conflict surfaces again?**

   _____
   _____
   _____
   _____
   _____
   _____
   _____

6. **What would you like to say to the other person(s) involved in this conflict?**

   _____
   _____
   _____

The Definitive Middle School Guide, Revised Edition
Copyright © 2014 World Book, Inc./Incentive Publications, Chicago, IL

Behavior Contract

Student Name: _____ Date: _____

I, _____ , agree to do the following things

during the time span from _____ to _____ .

1. _____

2. _____

3. _____

I can expect the following help from others in the school:

1. _____

2. _____

3. _____

When others and I have done the above, the following will happen:

1. _____

2. _____

3. _____

I understand that if I cannot or will not do the above, the following will happen:

_____

_____

_____

Signed by: _____ Date_____

Witnessed by: _____ Date_____

Discipline Contract

Who?_____ **When?**_____
(name of person(s) involved in the incident)   *(date and time)*

Where?_____ **In what situation?**_____
(location of the incident)   *(context in which the incident occurred)*

What happened? Who did what? *(specific actions of persons involved)*

_____
_____
_____
_____
_____

What did the teacher do? (actions teacher took)

How did the student(s) respond? (what the student(s) did in response to the teacher's actions)

What next? (the follow-up plan, or what student(s) and teacher will do next)

Student(s) signature(s): _____ Date_____

_____ Date_____

Teacher signature: _____ Date_____

Activities to Help Students Think About Behavior

ACTIVITY 1: "Dear Agony Aunt" Discussion Groups

Introduce this activity to students by having them bring copies of advice columns from their local newspaper. Discuss their purpose, format, and how they are used as a tool for problem solving. Next, instruct each student to write his or her own version of an advice column, focusing on a behavior problem or situation that the student finds inappropriate for the classroom or school setting. Divide the class into small cooperative learning groups and have them respond to the questions generated by members of their group by writing a response to each behavior problem area.

ACTIVITY 2: Acting Out Problem Situations

Create a set of scenarios that describe common behavior problems encountered by students of this age group. Assign students to cooperative learning groups and have each group create a skit, role-play, or case study to act out the solution or alternative solutions to their assigned problem.

ACTIVITY 3: A Picture Is Worth a Thousand Words

Collect assorted magazine pictures that feature groups of people in various settings—families, sporting events, work groups, social settings, etc. Give each student a picture and ask them to describe the various behaviors and feelings they detect in the picture by writing a paragraph about it. Mix up the finished paragraphs and pictures and ask students to match them correctly.

ACTIVITY 4: Inside and Outside Circle

Prepare a list of discipline or behavior-problem issues that are concerns in today's classroom and post them on the board or a large chart. Separate students in the classroom into two circles—one circle inside the other circle—with partners facing each other. Each pair of partners will discuss the first item on the list of problem areas with one another. After several minutes of discussion, play some recorded music for a few seconds and have students move their circles in opposite directions until the music stops. Facing a different person, students now discuss the second item on the list. The process repeats itself until the items on the list have been exhausted. Some possible discussion topics might be:

1. Why do some students cheat on class assignments and what should be done about it?
2. How can the teacher better motivate students to perform and do better work in school?
3. How do you feel about in- and out-of-school suspensions?
4 What classroom rules are hardest for you to follow and why?

ACTIVITY 5: The Gossip Danger

Choose six students to send out of the room for a short period of time. Select a student from the remaining class members and tell him or her a short story or anecdote. Call in one of the students from the removed group and ask the in-class student to repeat the story. Call in another student and have the first student called in repeat the story as he or she heard it.

Repeat this process several times so that the previously returning student tells each returning student the same story. Ask the rest of the class to take notes on where and when the original story takes on new details. End the activity with a discussion of "gossip" and how it can hurt others and become distorted over time.

ACTIVITY 6: A Century from Now

Divide the class into small cooperative learning groups and ask each group to create a time capsule for future generations of students that will tell them as much as possible about the norms, feelings, attitudes, lifestyles, and behavior patterns or preferences of today's teenager. In each time capsule, include such items as the following:

- a music CD
- a movie DVD
- newspaper articles of current events
- a series of journal entries about the day in the life of each group member
- photos or drawings of special places in the community where students hang out
- a restaurant menu from a favorite fast-food outlet
- a list of teenage heroes
- a book review or book cover
- an artifact from the school
- a series of magazine pictures showing what the lifestyle is like
- a movie advertisement

ACTIVITY 7: Me-Boxes

Give each student a small box. On the outside, they write, draw, or glue something about themselves on each face of the box. (Ideas: photo of self, family, or friends; poem; magazine cutouts of favorite things, favorite words, or colors.) On the inside, students write words, phrases, or notes or place objects that tell something about who they are "inside." This might include descriptors of their personality, feelings, behavior traits, or personal strengths and weaknesses.

ACTIVITY 8: You Are What You Wear

- Set aside one day in a given week where students are asked to wear to class a special outfit or pieces of apparel that best represents who they think they are or want to be.
- Discuss how clothes can tell a great deal about a person and the way he or she behaves.
- Ask students to design a new school uniform that they would wear if given the chance.
- Discuss how school uniforms often influence how a student behaves in school.

The Definitive Middle School Guide, Revised Edition
Copyright © 2014 World Book, Inc./Incentive Publications, Chicago, IL

Things to Know and Do About Bullying

WHAT IS BULLYING?

1 Bullying includes any deliberate, harmful, repetitive behaviors by one student toward another.

2 Bullying is unprovoked, and the intimidation, repeated over time, becomes harassment.

3 The victim feels defenseless and powerless.

4 Someone can be bullied physically, emotionally, or verbally, or with a combination of these.

5 Bullying may be seen as direct behaviors such as teasing, taunting, threatening, hitting or kicking, stealing or damaging things, calling names, taking away money, scattering a person's belongings around, derisive laughing, stalking, and forcing a student do something he or she does not want to do.

6 Bullying can be subtle and indirect. It can be gossiping, telling mean stories or rumors, leaving a person out of things, or "turning" others against that person. Girls often do this.

7 Bullying can be inflicted via the Internet. (This is called cyberbullying, and it is increasing in frequency.) Students can bully through e-mails, instant messages, and social networking sites.

8 Most children are bullied in some way during their years in school.

9 Bullying is prevalent in schools and out of school. Much of it is indirect, and often not even identified as bullying (social ostracizing, subtle harassment, cyberbullying).

10 Even if bullying occurs outside of school, its results find their way into the school.

POSSIBLE SIGNS THAT A STUDENT IS BEING BULLIED

1 has torn, damaged, or missing pieces of clothing or other belongings

2 shows up with unexplained cuts, bruises, and scratches

3 shows lack of interest in school and deteriorating school performance

4 seems isolated or withdrawn; has few friends

5 stays unusually close to the teacher or other adults during school

6 appears sad, moody, teary, irritable, or depressed

7 is afraid of going to school, walking to and from school, or riding the school bus

8 avoids school or certain other group situations

9 takes a different, or longer, or illogical route when walking to or from school

10 stops participating or contributing to class activities

11 does not seem to be "herself" or "himself"

12 chronically complains of physical ailments such as stomachaches or headaches

13 has frequent or recurring bad dreams or trouble sleeping

14 experiences a loss of appetite

15 is anxious and shows signs of sinking self-esteem

16 stops doing things he or she usually likes

17 becomes unexplainably hot-tempered, restless, annoyed, belligerent, or immature

18 begins to bully weaker students

19 displays suicidal behaviors or talks about suicide

20 talks about being useless or unlikable

WHAT TEACHERS AND OTHER SCHOOL STAFF MEMBERS CAN DO ABOUT BULLYING

1 Push for school-wide bullying policies, intervention procedures, and programs to help victims and bullies. Make sure all staff members know how to respond appropriately to bullying incidents.

2 Push for strong professional development antibullying training for all staff members. Make sure the training includes methods for helping victims of bullying to recover and to protect themselves.

3 Institute and follow through on a ZERO TOLERANCE policy toward bullying of ALL kinds.

4 Create the environment that clearly communicates bullying policies and procedures to students, makes consequences clear, and does not tolerate bullying behavior at all.

5 Provide parents and families with information about bullying and training to help a child who is bullied or a child who is a bully. Encourage them to watch for signs and to communicate with the school.

6 Examine the physical, social, and academic arrangements at school and adjust them to make it harder for bullying to take place on school grounds.

7 Conduct surveys and take other measures to get a clear picture of the bullying situation at your school.

8 Institute a strong program that teaches social skills that help bullied students feel more powerful and restore self-esteem, addresses the damage done to bullied students, and helps students create a culture where bullying is decreased.

9 Provide increased supervision in settings and situations where bullying occurs.

10 Encourage students to tell someone if he or she is bullied. Reassure the student that you will figure out together what to do about it. Affirm the student for talking about it.

11 If a student is bullied, take immediate action. Follow well-supported procedures for the protection of the victim and for the good of the bully.

12 Institute some kind of readily available support and counseling for students who are bullied and for students who are bullies.

13 Monitor student computers and equip them with filtering software. Create an online contract for students to sign regarding their computer use.

14 Provide students with a list of ways to avoid and respond to cyberbullying. Remind them to guard their personal contact information closely.

15 Give parents tips about how to stop and respond to online harassment.

16 Provide a safe place and way for students to report and talk about bullying.

17 Provide a safe place for bullies to discuss underlying behavioral, personal, and social issues.

18 Involve parents, community personnel, and law enforcement personnel in the discussion of the school program.

19 Make special efforts to include students who are withdrawn, and avoid shaming situations for all students.

Suggestions for Avoiding Discipline Problems with Particular Populations

Put a student into a situation in which he or she feels threatened by, insecure about, confused by, unprepared for, unchallenged by, or just unable to cope with the learning tasks expected of him or her—and you are bound to have some behavior problems. There are myriad factors that might bring a student to your classroom in this state of fear, embarrassment, or boredom. This collection of lists presents some characteristics, indicators, questions, and advice to help you consider the underlying issues, influences, and situations that can turn academic issues into discipline issues.

1 Characteristics of Underachievers

1. Harbor feelings of inferiority and failure
2. Feel rejected by family members
3. Take little responsibility for actions
4. Show hostility to authority figures
5. Resist adult influences
6. Feel victimized
7. Have negative feelings toward school
8. Appear rebellious
9. Lack academic skills and motivation
10. Demonstrate poor study habits
11. Withdraw from classroom challenges
12. Are less popular with peers
13. Demonstrate less mature behavior than achievers
14. Exhibit poor adjustment actions
15. Have little interest in outside hobbies, sports, or activities
16. Tend to be afraid of tests
17. Lack academic or vocational goals

2 Questions for Teachers of Ethnic and Language Minority Students to Ask Themselves

1. Do I have a clear and realistic sense of my own cultural and ethnic identity?
2. Do I firmly believe that students of all ethnic backgrounds can succeed?
3. Can I honestly bond with all types of students—with no "we-they" perceptions?
4. Am I committed to achieving equity with all my students and not just a few?
5. Do I use culturally relevant materials that promote contributions and perspectives of various ethnic groups?
6. Do I maintain a balance in promoting the school culture with the maintenance of my students' sense of ethno-cultural pride and identity?
7. Do I provide legitimate opportunities for students to work together in a wide variety of flexible social configurations?
8. Do I promote home-school partnerships as essential elements in academic programs and in the overall development of the individual student?
9. Do I give all students opportunities for leadership roles?
10. Do I identify and dispel prejudices, stereotypes, and inaccurate perceptions of individuals or groups as they are encountered in classroom materials?

3 A Gifted-Talented Student Often . . .

1 has a wide range of interests.

2 is eager to try new things.

3 seems very alert; gives rapid answers.

4 is self-motivated.

5 tends to dominate peers or situations.

6 has self-confidence.

7 is sensitive to situations and feelings.

8 can solve problems ingeniously.

9 is eager to complete tasks.

10 has a great desire to excel.

11 is very expressive verbally.

12 tells imaginative stories.

13 has a mature sense of humor.

14 is inquisitive; examines things closely.

15 can show relationships between apparently unrelated things or ideas.

16 tends to lose awareness of time.

17 likes to work alone.

4 Research Findings About Instructional Practices Toward Girls and Boys in the Classroom

Did you know that teachers. . .

1 tend to punish boys more frequently and more harshly than they do girls, even in similar situations?

2 expect boys to be more active and assertive and girls to be more passive and unassertive in the classroom?

3 give boys more direct instruction, attention, and approval-oriented gestures?

4 ask boys to handle more physical and leadership activities in the classroom?

5 ask boys more factual, closed, or low-level questions than girls?

6 ask girls to assume more supportive and housekeeping chores such as watering plants and writing thank-you notes than boys?

7 expect more from boys in math and more from girls in reading/language arts?

8 criticize boys more for behavior problems and girls more for skill limitations or deficiencies?

9 praise girls more for neatness and form and boys more for academic thoughts?

5 Some Ways to Help ELL Students in the Classroom

1 Have students sit in front of the classroom to avoid distractions and be closer to the interaction with the teacher.

2 Speak clearly, slowly, and naturally. Pause often to assist the student's comprehension.

3 Speak and write in shorter sentences, using simpler vocabulary.

4 Repeat, review and re-teach instructions several times.

5 Demonstrate concepts with a visual or tactile representation.

6 Show video presentations with volume down and tell the information in simpler terms.

7 Elicit short responses from students.

8 Assign a seat mate to each ELL student to serve as an informal tutor or study buddy during assignments.

9 Allow longer periods of silence after questions. Wait for student response.

10 Give opportunities for students to share their native language and customs with the class.

11 Keep a predetermined and set routine for delivering instruction and directions.

12 Use graphic organizers and technology as often as possible for clarification and motivation.

13 Adapt assignments by limiting number of examples and amount of work.

Characteristics of At-Risk Students
and
Characteristics of Schools That Meet Their Needs

Student Characteristics

An at-risk student

1 . . . demonstrates academic learning and achievement problems.

2 . . . tends to be inattentive.

3 . . . is easily distracted.

4 . . . displays short attention span.

5 . . . has low self-esteem.

6 . . . lacks social skills.

7 . . . reflects narrow range of interests.

8 . . . fears failure.

9 . . . lacks structure and organization.

10 . . . avoids responsibility and independence.

School Characteristics

A school that meets the needs of at-risk students

1 . . . focuses on students.

2 . . . challenges preconceived notions about certain kinds or groups of students.

3 . . . collaborates with parents and guardians.

4 . . . avoids strategies that intensify or perpetuate impediments.

5 . . . decentralizes instructional decisions.

6 . . . promotes success.

7 . . . reduces negative effects of large school size.

8 . . . values differences in students.

9 . . . minimizes mistakes and failures.

10 . . . adopts a "whatever it takes" stance.

RATE THE TEACHER!

(STUDENT INVENTORY)

Teacher's name_____   **Date**_____

RATING SCALE

4 = GREATEST   3 = VERY GOOD   2 = GOOD   1 = COULD BE MUCH BETTER

1.	My teacher has established clear guidelines for behavior in the classroom and consistently holds us to those guidelines.	4	3	2	1
2.	My teacher knows how to make allies with our parents.	4	3	2	1
3.	My teacher enjoys the subject matter and communicates this to the students most of the time.	4	3	2	1
4.	My teacher is well prepared every day.	4	3	2	1
5.	Most of the students find the teacher's lessons and activities interesting and informative most of the time.	4	3	2	1
6.	My teacher varies the instructional strategies and classroom activities on a regular basis.	4	3	2	1
7.	My teacher almost never belittles, lectures, nags, or embarrasses us in class.	4	3	2	1
8.	My teacher uses many different methods for evaluating what we know and can do.	4	3	2	1
9.	My teacher returns papers and tests quickly, teaches us why certain answers are right and wrong, and expects us to correct our mistakes.	4	3	2	1
10.	My teacher serves as a positive role model for the students in the class. She or he acts the way we are expected to act.	4	3	2	1
11.	When students need help with work, it is easy to approach the teacher for assistance.	4	3	2	1
12.	When a student misbehaves, my teacher tries to teach a more effective behavior instead of just punishing the students.	4	3	2	1
13.	My teacher is willing to help students with their work even if it means spending time before or after school.	4	3	2	1
14.	My teacher lets us make some choices about this class and our own learning.	4	3	2	1
15.	My teacher encourages and challenges each of us to be the best student possible and gives us support when we need it.	4	3	2	1

Directions to the student:
The purpose of this activity is to help you clarify (for yourself and others) what makes the ideal classroom experience, in your opinion. Complete the letter by finishing the thoughts or sentences.

Date _____

Dear _____ ,
             (Name of teacher receiving letter)

If I were designing the perfect classroom setting for me in your subject area, this is what I would like to see:

I would choose these two classroom rules for me to follow:
1.

2.

I would like these types of classroom assignments for my portfolio:

These are the kinds of homework tasks I prefer to do outside of class:

These kinds of tests or other assessments would be used to measure what I know and can do:

This grading scale would be used on my report card to parents:

The room arrangement and seating arrangement I prefer is diagrammed on the back of this letter.

Sincerely, _____
             (Your signature)

Levels of Parental Involvement in the Classroom

Think about the types of parent involvement represented and construct a profile of the different levels. Make it a goal of the team to place each family at some level on this hierarchy developed by Anne T. Henderson, Carl L. Marburger, and Theodora Ooms (1986).

LEVEL 7: Parents as Advisors and Co-Decision Makers
Parents provide input on school policy, procedures, and programs through active membership in ad hoc committees or permanent governance bodies.

LEVEL 6: Parents as Teachers
Parents form collaborative relationships with community resources, such as the public library, museums, businesses, parks, recreational facilities, and relevant cultural events important to the nurturing of the child.

LEVEL 5: Parents as Learners
Parents access workshops and parent information centers on topics relevant to the success of their child at school or in the community.

LEVEL 4: Parents as Supporters
Parents provide volunteer assistance to teachers, the parent organization, and other parents. These volunteer activities may take place during the school day, after school hours, on weekends, or even in the home.

LEVEL 3: Parents as Audience
Parents often attend and appreciate school performances, productions, and extracurricular activity offerings. They acknowledge invitations and make an effort to support the functions.

LEVEL 2: Parents as Collaborators and Problem Solvers
Parents consistently reinforce the school's efforts with their child and help to solve problems or make decisions as needed. Teacher and parent are positive "co-conspirators" in the school process and conference well together.

LEVEL 1: Parents as Partners
Parents perform basic obligations for their child's education, social development, and attendance. Students come to school regularly, on time, well-fed (or enrolled in free or reduced-cost meal programs), and with having had a reasonable night's sleep.

The Definitive Middle School Guide, Revised Edition
Copyright © 2014 World Book, Inc./Incentive Publications, Chicago, IL

Ways to Build a Good Parent-Communication Program

(Based on Williams' Taxonomy of Creative Thinking)

1 **FLUENCY ACTIVITY:** List as many communication products and performances as you can think of that your school develops or delivers in any given year to its families of students as a means of communicating information.

2 **FLEXIBILITY ACTIVITY:** Group or classify each of these products and performances from the Fluency list above in one of the following categories: Very Effective, Somewhat Effective, Not Effective, or Unknown.

3 **ORIGINALITY ACTIVITY:** Create an idea for a very unusual and unique product or performance that a school might implement to improve parent-student-teacher partnerships.

4 **ELABORATION ACTIVITY:** Elaborate on the good or poor qualities of each of the following products and performances offered yearly at your school: Monthly Newsletter, Open House, Parent-Teacher Conferences, Student Handbook, Parent Programs, Home Visits, Parenting Workshops, PTA or PTO Meetings, Parent Lounges or Resource Rooms, Parent Social Events, etc.

5 **RISK-TAKING ACTIVITY:** Write a mock letter as a teacher, student, or parent outlining your fear or concerns that could occur in either a school conference, an open house, or a home visit.

6 **COMPLEXITY ACTIVITY:** Discuss the desired role of parents as collaborators, advisers, and decision makers in the school.

7 **CURIOSITY ACTIVITY:** Design a survey to administer to parents and other adults in the community who serve as volunteers in the school. Use the results to develop a recruitment campaign, a thank-you celebration, or a training session for volunteers.

8 **IMAGINATION ACTIVITY:** Pretend you are in charge of scheduling a conference for absent parents. As an alternative for family members who simply cannot arrange their schedules to attend a conference at the school, plan to send home a videotape of a student-teacher conference. The conference is taped just as if the parent were there. Prior to the conference, the student and affected teachers outline what the conference will cover. While the tape rolls, the student reviews samples of own work, answers relevant questions asked by the teachers, discusses individual progress and problems, and shares special interests and accomplishments. Follow the videoconference with a personal telephone call for parent reactions.

Questions for Parent-Teacher Focus Group on Parent Involvement

Name of person conducting focus group

_____

Role_____

Target audience _____

Number of participants _____ Date _____

Time _____ Place_____

Directions:
The leader of the focus group should be someone familiar with focus groups as a tool for collecting information about a given topic. Focus groups should be limited to no more than ten participants and no longer than 60 minutes in duration. The focus group leader should record the session so that responses can be reviewed and edited at a later date. The discussion should be limited to these questions as much as possible and should encourage equitable input from all participants.

1 Is there a stated commitment and a written plan for parent involvement in this school? If so, what does it provide? If not, what should it provide?

2 How does the school make special efforts to involve parents and guardians from different racial and national origin in all parent activities? How successful is this effort? How could it be improved?

3 Do some parent involvement activities take place in the community, or do they all focus on the school as an official meeting place? Explain.

4 Is there a parent advisory council or governance group of some type in this school? Are members representative of the school population by race, gender, and national origin?

5 How active is the PTO or PTA in your school? What types of activities do they sponsor?

6 How does the school welcome parents on a daily basis as observers, visitors, volunteers, or resources? How could this be improved?

7 How do the administration and the teachers communicate with the parents on a regular basis? How effective are these communication efforts? How could they be improved?

8 How do parents participate in decisions affecting their child's education at the school? Give examples of this process.

9 Are meetings and conferences scheduled at times convenient to the parents and teachers? Are transportation, child care, or interpreters provided on a need basis?

10 On a 1 to 10 scale, with 1 being Very Poor and 10 being Outstanding, how would you rate the overall parent involvement efforts at this school? Give reasons and examples to support your rating.

Steps for an Effective Parent Conference

1 Keep in mind that many parents come to the conference with their own emotional baggage. They may have personal health, marital, or financial problems. They may have had negative and unsuccessful experiences with the schooling process as a student. A staff that is highly educated may intimidate them because of their own lack of literacy and academic skills. They may speak a language other than English. They may be overwhelmed by job or family responsibilities that limit their participation in school-sponsored functions. They may be concerned about their child being able to make it academically.

2 Document academic or behavior problems through use of observation checklists, anecdotal records, test scores, work samples, and teacher reports. Try to include positive as well as negative evidence in your portfolio.

3 Arrange the conference time and place so that both are convenient for parents and team members. Encourage parents or guardians and students to attend.

4 Approach the conference with a positive "can do" attitude. Discuss the student's strengths and successes before discussing problem areas. You should also share what you know about the student's learning style as well as information about her or his progress to date.

5 Encourage the parents or guardians to talk and share their perceptions while you listen carefully to what is being said. Take notes and ask clarifying questions. Some questions to consider are:

a) What are your child's strengths at home?

b) How does your child spend his time at home?

c) What responsibilities does your child have outside of school?

d) Where and when does your child do his homework?

e) What are your goals and hopes for your student both short term and long term?

6 Allow ample time for parents or guardians to air their frustrations and concerns without getting defensive or interrupting a train of thought. Try to use reassuring body language and verbal comments.

7 Make certain that all team members provide input at all stages of the conference, including preparation, implementation, and follow-up.

8 Develop an action plan that focuses on specific strategies and responsibilities for improving problem areas. Record decisions about who is to do what, when, and how.

9 Keep all team members and parents or guardians focused on the problem areas identified for this conference. Try to discourage digression from the task at hand.

10 Dismiss parents or guardians in a positive way so that they feel their time has been well spent and so that they know exactly what to do to help the student.

11 Above all else, make certain to follow the established plan of action in a timely fashion and arrange for a follow-up conference or discussion. Monitor the plan of action strategies in a consistent manner.

Things to Consider When Planning Student-Led Conferences

1 Compose a letter to parents that informs them how you are enhancing the role of students in the conference process. Emphasize the fact that in student-led conferences, students take ownership of their work, accomplishment, and plans for remediation, improvement, or enrichment. Also stress that the teacher plays an important role by providing students with the knowledge and strategies that will allow them to be self-sufficient on the day of their conference.

2 Talk with students about the multiple purposes of the student-led conference:

    a. It empowers students to take charge of their own progress and the reporting of that progress to parents.

    b. It provides leadership and communication skill practice for students.

    c. It demonstrates collaboration among student, teachers, and parents so that all hear the same message at the same time.

    d. It encourages students to be involved in the planning and selection process for what is to be discussed and displayed.

    e. It often provides extra incentive for parents to attend the conference.

3 Work with the students to prepare them for this activity by teaching the basic steps for conducting the conference, using an outline such as the following:

    a. Welcome parent to conference.

    b. Share portfolio of artifacts that represent student progress.

    c. Describe strengths, successes, and accomplishments.

    d. Talk about areas that need improvement.

    e. Ask parents for input, reactions, or questions.

    f. Write down any follow-up steps that need to be taken by student, parent, or teacher.

    g. Give parent a form or some other instrument for post-conference reflection and ask them to complete it as directed.

    h. Thank parent for coming.

4 Work with students as a group or individually to select items for inclusion in the conference portfolio. Consider worksheets, homework assignments, tests or quizzes, creative writing samples, journal entries, product or performance rubrics, artwork, etc.

The Definitive Middle School Guide, Revised Edition
Copyright © 2014 World Book, Inc./Incentive Publications, Chicago, IL

5 Give students an opportunity to role-play a mock conference where one student is the parent and the other student conducts the conference, and then reverse roles. Do this only after a demonstration has been done with the teacher playing the part of the student and a student volunteer playing the part of the parent.

6 A few days before the conference, sit down with each student and go over their portfolio of artifacts and the outline they are to follow during the conference itself.

7 Prepare a classroom Parent Post-Conference Reflection Sheet that asks parents to write a note to the student, commenting on such things as:

    a. I think you did a great job leading the conference because . . .
    b. I noticed that you are doing well in . . .
    c. I especially liked the work you did on . . .
    d. Something I would like you to work on or improve for next time is . . .
    e. I would like to help you with . . .
    f. I can see that you enjoy . . .
    g. The thing that surprised me most was . . .
    h. You could improve the conference by . . .

Ask the parent to return this reflection sheet within one week of the conference.

8 Prepare a Student Post-Conference Reflection Sheet that requires students to give feedback on the conference process they conducted, using such starter statements as:

    a. I think things went well today (or did not go well today) because . . .
    b. The best part of the conference for me was . . .
    c. Things might have gone better if I . . .
    d. Something I would do differently next time is . . .
    e. I think my parents enjoyed the conference most because . . .
    f. One thing I wish I had talked about at the conference was . . .

9 If one or more parents still feel a need to meet with the teacher privately, be sure to set up a time and place to do so.

10 Student-led conferences can be conducted one-on-one with the teacher as a close observer, or they can be conducted at a series of conference stations established around the room as the teacher facilitates the process.

Suggestions for Planning Open House Programs

1 Keep in mind that the open house for parents should

    a) focus on helping parents or guardians to become familiar and comfortable with the school, classroom, and teacher(s), as well as

    b) give teachers a specific time and place to communicate their expectations and routines to the parents.

2 Consider involving a few of your parents in the planning of the open house to get information about their needs and expectations.

3 Send out communications about the date, time, place, schedule, and purpose of the open house early in the school year. If possible, these mailings could be a combination of school-sponsored invitations as well as handwritten invitations by the students.

4 If your school has a significant number of parents who do not speak English, invite the district's foreign language teachers to attend and serve as interpreters for selected groups of parents.

5 Provide child care service for parents with young children.

6 Encourage all teachers to prepare and distribute information packets for each parent in attendance. These might include a list of curriculum plans and goals, a list of materials students need for class, and a calendar of upcoming events.

7 Teams of teachers should also prepare and distribute a specific Team Handbook to each set of parents or guardians that contains details about the operation of their team for the school year.

8 Make certain that the chairs and tables for the parent guests are adult size, comfortable, and in good condition. Make certain the classroom is clean and decorated with samples of student work and assignments.

9 Make the open house fun and enjoyable. You might try small cooperative learning group activities for parents, or you might have them write short notes to their children to be delivered the day after the open house, or you might provide them with a box of crayons and drawing paper and ask them to illustrate what they hope their child will experience in school this year.

10 Other options to consider as part of the open house plan are to show a visual presentation of the students working in classes or preparing a PowerPoint presentation to tell parents about the curriculum and expectations for the course.

The Definitive Middle School Guide, Revised Edition
Copyright © 2014 World Book, Inc./Incentive Publications, Chicago, IL

Findings from the Published Literature Related to Classroom Management and Discipline

FINDING #1:

Marion Johnson Payne concludes:

> What does an inviting, supportive, and safe environment feel like? Statements of encouragement and positive feedback outnumber disciplinary or correctional comments. Interactions among staff members and between students reflect democracy, fairness, and mutual respect. Teachers, staff, and students learn and put into practice the skills of direct feedback, mediation, healthy and appropriate confrontation, positive risk taking, and personal and collaborative goal setting. Students and adults have a shared language to discuss issues of diversity and equity. The essence of a happy, healthy school lies in the talk one hears.

Source: Erb, T. O. (Ed.). (2005). *This we believe in action: Implementing successful middle level schools.* Westerville, OH: National Middle School Association.

FINDING #2:

R. Marzano, J. Marzano, and D. Pickering write:

> Teacher-student relationships are critical to the success of two of the other aspects of effective classroom management—the rules and procedures, and disciplinary interventions. To build good relationships with students, it is important to communicate appropriate levels of dominance and to let students know that you are in control of the class and are willing and able to lead. It's also important to communicate appropriate levels of cooperation and to convey the message that you are interested in the concerns of students as individuals and the class as a whole. You may need to make a special effort to build positive relationships with high-need students, but using the proper techniques in working with these students can enhance the chance of successful classroom management.

Source: Marzano, R. J., Marzano, J. S., & Pickering, D. (2003). *Classroom management that works: Research-based strategies for every teacher.* Alexandria, VA: Association for Supervision and Curriculum Development.

FINDING #3:

Julia G. Thompson points out:

In spite of the encouraging changes that recent reforms have brought to education, one aspect of our jobs has not yet changed and probably never will—we still have discipline problems.

Here are just some of the discipline problems that many secondary teachers in today's schools have to handle in the course of their professional duties. The problems in this list are ones that are not always directly caused by students who misbehave, but are the result of other factors teachers have to manage in order to maintain a positive learning climate. They are as follows:

- Ineffective local discipline policies
- Overworked and unsympathetic administrators
- Parents who do not support school personnel
- Trendy but impractical solutions to discipline problems
- Overcrowded classes
- Buildings that need repairs and better maintenance
- Too little productive time with students
- Stacks of tedious paperwork
- Lax teachers whose problems with classroom management spill over into other classes
- A generation and culture gap between students and teachers
- Students who are unsupervised by their parents
- Uncertainty over the right action to take when problems occur
- Textbooks and other materials that are not relevant
- The loss of a feeling of safety at school
- Students with overwhelming family problems
- Lack of equipment
- Outdated technology
- Fatigue
- Being unable to contact parents easily by phone
- Exhausting class schedules
- Frequent class interruptions
- Teacher stress and burnout

Source: Thompson, J. G. (1998). *Discipline survival kit for the secondary teacher.* West Nyack, NY: Center for Applied Research in Education.

Review and Reflect

on Classroom Management and Discipline

Level 1: Remembering

Your Reflections

Task

Write down a list of several different tools or techniques that you do with your students (or know that you should do) that lead to effective management of your classroom and positive behavior management of your students.

My list:

Level 2: Understanding

Your Reflections

Task

Name a successful classroom activity or project you did with students this year that required students to work together in collaborative groups. Identify the things that made it effective from your viewpoint as the teacher and from the viewpoint of a student.

The activity:

Effective things (from teacher's viewpoint):

Effective things (from student's viewpoint):

Level 3: Applying

Your Reflections

Task

Construct and label a simple diagram or floor plan that shows the physical arrangement of your classroom. Attach the floor plan to this page. Think of some spaces that you might configure differently which might improve the layout. Make notes about these possible changes.

Notes about changes to make:

continued on page 270

Review and Reflect

on Classroom Management and Discipline

Level 4: Analyzing

Your Reflections

Task

Study the discipline plan, rules, or guidelines that your interdisciplinary team has developed for managing your classrooms. Identify which elements of the plan are working best and which elements need to be changed to reduce overall student behavior problems.

Working:

Not working:

Level 5: Evaluating

Your Reflections

Task

Prepare a report card that students can use to assess your effectiveness as a teacher and manager. List teacher behaviors and criteria. Try out the report card. How did you do? Summarize your results here.

Teacher behaviors or tasks for students to "grade":

How did I do?

Level 6: Creating

Your Reflections

Task

Plan to conduct a class meeting. Set guidelines and timelines for your plan. Make a list of problems and issues to address. Test your plan with a group, and get their feedback on the success of the meeting.

Describe the outcome of this experiment:

Module V

Advisory, Advocacy, *and* Affective Education

Contents of Module V

Overview of
Advisory, Advocacy, and Affective Education

An advisory, advocacy, or affective program is designed to:

- focus on the social, emotional, physical, intellectual, psychological, and ethical development of students.

- provide a structured daily or semi-weekly time as part of the school day during which special activities are designed and implemented to help adolescents find ways to fulfill their unique needs and characteristics.

- offer students consistent, caring, and continuous adult guidance through the organization of a supportive and stable peer group that meets regularly under a teacher advisor or advocate.

- nurture the fourth "R" of RELATIONSHIPS as a recognized and important element of the middle school curriculum and schooling process.

- play a major role in assisting our young people through the turbulence and hurdles of early adolescence.

- help students bridge the gap between elementary school and the independent world of high school. It offers middle school students the best of both worlds, because it provides every student with an advisor-advocate who has a special concern for the student as an individual and encourages independence and personal growth needed for high school success.

- help students build self-awareness and personal esteem.

- serve as a prescriptive antidote for the unmotivated learner, the ELL student, or the at-risk student who might otherwise be coerced into negative behaviors. At the same time, an advisory program may also be structured to meet the special needs of academically or otherwise talented students by accommodating a wide range of learning styles and interests.

- make students feel good about themselves and the contributions they can make to their school, community, and society as happy, fully functioning citizens of our global society.

> *Note: Programs that focus on this kind of development and student needs may have different labels. The terms **advisory**, **advocacy**, and **affective** are often used interchangeably in titles of programs. For the purposes of this book, the term **advisory program** will be used to describe programs and activities that encompass ALL THREE concepts.*

Terms Important for Understanding Advisory, Advocacy, and Affective Education

Advisor or advisor-advisee program: the unique organizational structure that contains one small group of students facilitated by an educator whose role is to nurture, advocate for, and guide students in the assigned group through the schooling process

Advocacy: that particular role that middle level educators play as active supporters and intercessors for early adolescents (While each student should have an adult who is primarily responsible for the academic and personal growth of that individual, advocacy should be inherent in the school's culture and in shared responsibility.)

Affective domain: the area of education that focuses on the attitudinal-emotional development of students, which includes a host of such "whole person" areas as self-esteem, emotional and social adjustment, and personal beliefs

Coaching: when teachers coach learners, they display a "cheerleader" attitude necessary to affirm positive personal growth and good deeds—characteristics these adolescent learners want to demonstrate and are capable of doing

Cognitive domain: the area of education that focuses on memory, reasoning, thinking, imagining, and the conscious intellectual activities associated with academics

Metacognition: the theory stating that learners benefit by thoughtfully and reflectively considering the things they are learning and the ways in which they are learning them (It is sometimes referred to as "thinking about thinking.")

Moral development: the theories postulating that individuals pass through various and predetermined stages of moral reasoning as determined by experts such as Lawrence Kohlberg

Self-esteem: the estimation individuals place on their own perceived attributes, capacities, intentions, and behaviors

Socialization: the process by which individuals are inducted into norms, values, rules, etc., of a group

Values and values clarification: the conscious attempt and process by which an individual is helped to make free value choices after studying a spectrum of options, to prize the choices made, and to behave in a manner that reflects his or her commitment to the value(s) chosen

> *Note: Programs that focus on this kind of development and student needs may have different labels. The terms **advisory**, **advocacy**, and **affective** are often used interchangeably in titles of programs. For the purposes of this book, the term **advisory program** will be used to describe programs and activities that encompass ALL THREE concepts.*

Guiding Questions for
Advisory, Advocacy, and Affective Education

1 How do we define "advisory, advocacy, and affective" education? How are they alike and how are they different? What is their relationship to one another? What are their parameters?

2 What is the relationship of affective growth to cognitive growth in an educational setting?

3 Why is affective education critical in today's complex, interdependent, global, and technological world?

4 Is it possible for affective attitudes and behaviors to be taught? If so, how is this best accomplished in the middle school setting?

5 What contradictions exist in today's early adolescent that are brought about by their unique needs and characteristics?

6 Why is it said that "all adolescents are at risk"? Do you agree with this statement? Why or why not?

7 How would you define and describe a teacher advisory or advocacy program?

8 What do the school's mission statement and the advisory program's mission statement say regarding advisory or advocacy programs? Do they support one another?

9 What are the basic responsibilities of an advisor?

10 Who in the school will manage and maintain the advisory program?

11 How will advisory groups be formed?

12 When do advisors meet with advisees in a group and when do they meet individually with advisees?

13 How will issues of confidentiality be handled?

14 Who will mediate differences of opinion among advisors regarding the resolution of problems with students?

15 What are some things advisors can do to become better prepared to meet individual needs in a group setting?

16 What happens when a student wants to switch from one advisory group to another?

17 Should advisory groups contain students all at the same grade level, or should more than one grade be represented?

18 Should the advisor continue with the same advisees all through middle school, or should students have new advisors each year?

19 How can parents be effectively involved in advisory activities?

20 What happens when parents want to meet with a teacher other than the child's advisor?

21 What are some pitfalls likely to be encountered by new advisors and how can experienced advisors help them avoid these pitfalls?

22 How, when, and by whom will the advisory program be evaluated?

Important Decisions to Be Made When Planning an Advisory, Advocacy, and Affective Program

1 Develop the overall mission or purpose of the program and make certain it interfaces well with the overall mission statement of the middle school.

2 Define the roles of administrators, counselors, teachers, and other staff members to be directly involved in the program.

3 Determine who can and should be advisors in the program.

4 Organize a carefully chosen Advisory Steering Committee comprised of administrators, teachers, parents, and students to help make key decisions in the organizational structure and implementation of the program.

5 Study alternative ways to schedule the advisory program time within the school day or week, as well as ways to assign students to advisory groups.

6 Develop a comprehensive plan for selecting and training advisors for the program.

7 Help teachers separate their roles as advisors from their roles as instructors in a specific discipline when participating in this program.

8 Develop a public relations plan for preparing both parents and students for participation in the program.

9 Identify multiple sources for quality advisory activities and experiences to be used in the program.

10 Develop a plan for evaluating the effectiveness of the program over time, as well as a process for making necessary changes as needed.

11 Determine ongoing ways to keep the advisory program viable and functioning over time.

12 Decide on the most important student and teacher outcomes to consider when validating the ultimate success of the advisory program.

The Definitive Middle School Guide, Revised Edition
Copyright © 2014 World Book, Inc./Incentive Publications, Chicago, IL

ADVISEE QUESTIONNAIRE
FOR THE FIRST WEEK OF ADVISORY

NOTE TO ADVISEE:
I will not share any of this information unless you give me permission to do so.

BASIC INFORMATION ABOUT YOU

What is your name?

What do you prefer to be called?

When is your birthday?

Where were you born?

How can I contact you?
(cell phone or e-mail or both):

With whom do you live?
(List names and relationships of each person in your home.)

YOUR INTERESTS

What do you usually do after school?

How do you like to spend weekends or free time?

What special interests or hobbies do you have?

YOUR LEARNING PREFERENCES

How would you describe your learning style (the way you learn best)?

What do you think is the purpose of advisory time?

What kinds of things would you like to do during advisory time?

If there is anything that might make advisory time difficult for you, what is it, and how could I help you?

OTHER STUFF TO KNOW ABOUT YOU

Who is someone you greatly admire, and why?

What are your greatest pet peeves?

What do you hope to be doing ten years from now?

If you could make one wish right now, what would it be?

Name_____ Date_____

The Definitive Middle School Guide, Revised Edition
Copyright © 2014 World Book, Inc./Incentive Publications, Chicago, IL

My Readiness to Be an Advisor

Teacher Self-Reflection

Name _____

Date _____

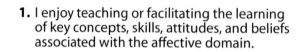

Readiness Indicators

Directions:
For each readiness indicator, circle one of the three responses. Choose the one that best describes your current state of readiness for acting as a student advisor. Be honest in your rankings, and be ready to share your reasons for each choice.

1. I enjoy teaching or facilitating the learning of key concepts, skills, attitudes, and beliefs associated with the affective domain.   usually sometimes rarely

2. I am comfortable with the idea of sharing my personal feelings and experiences with my advisees.   usually sometimes rarely

3. I show considerable interest in and enthusiasm for the advisory program.   usually sometimes rarely

4. I am willing to try new things and take reasonable risks with my advisory responsibilities.   usually sometimes rarely

5. I am prepared and organized when leading my advisory sessions.   usually sometimes rarely

6. I look forward to each advisory period.   usually sometimes rarely

7. I can spark students' interest in the challenges and purposes of the advisory concept.   usually sometimes rarely

8. I believe that all students can benefit from an advisory program.   usually sometimes rarely

9. I know how to help students apply problem-solving and decision-making skills to their daily lives.   usually sometimes rarely

10. I know how to help students identify and reach their academic potential.   usually sometimes rarely

11. I know how to help students build a strong and positive sense of self.   usually sometimes rarely

12. I am a positive role model as an advisor for my students.   usually sometimes rarely

The Definitive Middle School Guide, Revised Edition
Copyright © 2014 World Book, Inc./Incentive Publications, Chicago, IL

Teacher Advisory Issues Poll

Directions:

Please take a few minutes to fill out this poll and turn it in to a member of the Advisory Steering Committee. Note that the results of this poll will be made available at the next

_____ *(type of meeting)*

scheduled for _____ *(date, time)*

PART I.

Check three of the advisory-related areas that are of particular interest to you. The top priority issues from all advisors will be discussed in detail at the upcoming meeting.

_____ 1. Support from administration and social service specialists for my role as an advisor

_____ 2. Scheduling advisory time

_____ 3. Using the advisory period effectively

_____ 4. Implementing the advisory curriculum adequately

_____ 5. Defining expectations of advisory program, role of advisor, and role of advisees

_____ 6. Meeting with parents of advisees

_____ 7. Meeting with academic teachers of advisees

_____ 8. Supplementing the predetermined advisory curriculum with alternative materials and "teachable moment" opportunities

_____ 9. Maintaining records on advisees

_____ 10. Integrating advisory with the core academic areas of the curriculum

Part of this meeting's agenda will be devoted to a discussion of the results.

PART II.

Please indicate your preference for dealing with the poll results at the above meeting so that planning may be made accordingly.

_____ 1. I prefer a whole and large group discussion of results.

_____ 2. I prefer smaller cooperative learning groups for discussing the results.

_____ 3. I prefer hearing an expert's or consultant's input on the results.

_____ 4. I prefer a panel to discuss the implications of the results.

_____ 5. Other (please specify)

Name _____ Date_____

Levels of
Krathwohl's Affective Taxonomy

Much like other taxonomies, the Affective Taxonomy provides a useful way to describe and classify educational objectives. When used as a model for creating tasks in an advisory program, it makes possible the design of instruction that focuses on the nonintellective aspects of individual growth. Such practices as the improvement of self-concept, enhancing interpersonal relationships, and dealing with moral or value issues no longer need to be left to accident or chance.

LEVEL I — RECEIVING-ATTENDING

This level establishes an essential condition for learning to occur. The teacher prompts, gains, and guides the attention of the learner. Students are attending when they are being aware, being conscious of what is happening; being willing to receive, open to instruction; and controlling attention, focusing on the given task.

LEVEL II — RESPONDING

This level reflects a "willingness" on the part of the student. The student wants to understand, is willing to participate, and responds to instruction. The student participates, cooperates, contributes, and gains satisfaction in doing so. Students are responding by complying with given directions, participating willingly, and gaining in satisfaction or pleasure.

LEVEL III — VALUING

This level involves the determination of values, the worth of something established. The individual becomes associated with an attitude or belief. Students are valuing by determining the worth of something, expressing preferences, and making a commitment to beliefs.

LEVEL IV — ORGANIZATION

This level provides for the examination of evidence, the making of comparisons, and the prediction of outcomes. Attitudes and beliefs are weighted, ranked, and organized into a value system. Students are building a value system by comparing beliefs that are held; bringing values into an ordered relationship; and establishing a pattern of sentiment, beliefs, and values.

LEVEL V — CHARACTERIZATION

This level takes into account the behavior of the individual as guided by the attitudes, beliefs, and values that are held; values are internalized, acted upon, and reflected as one's philosophy of life. Students are acting on values by responding according to their beliefs, being consistent in their responses, and affirming their attitudes and beliefs.

Source: Krathwohl, D. R., Bloom, B. S., and Masia, B. B. (1964).
Taxonomy of educational objectives. Handbook II: Affective domain. New York: Longman.

The Definitive Middle School Guide, Revised Edition
Copyright © 2014 World Book, Inc./Incentive Publications, Chicago, IL

Steps to Using
Krathwohl's Taxonomy

To use Krathwohl's Taxonomy as a model for infusing affective values, beliefs, attitudes, and feelings into the advisory program, use the following steps:

STEP 1: Familiarize yourself with the five levels of the taxonomy, which are in hierarchical order.

STEP 2: Analyze several different advisory activities to determine which levels of Krathwohl's Taxonomy are being emphasized. During this review process, reflect on what distinguishes one level from the next.

STEP 3: Create some "teachable moment" advisory tasks from current events, news broadcasts, or community events. Try to include as many levels of Krathwohl's Taxonomy as you can for each lesson plan. Use the cue words in the chart on the next page to help with this activity.

STEP 4: Compare the cue words of Krathwohl's Taxonomy with those of Bloom and Williams. Reflect on why some behaviors occur in more than one level and in more than one taxonomy, remembering that it is the context for the behavior or cue word (verb) that makes the distinction.

> *Note: A bulletin board, mural, poster, or other visual model may be prepared to assist students with the understanding and application of Krathwohl's Taxonomy as a model for internalizing behaviors associated with attitudes, values, beliefs, and feelings.*

Affective Goals with Operational Definitions

AFFECTIVE GOAL	OPERATIONAL DEFINITION	CUE WORDS
RECEIVING Pays attention, is aware, takes information into account	The student displays attentiveness; listens, notices, and observes	listen, notice, see, observe, attend to, hear, follow, heed, regard, recognize, be alert to, consider, look for, examine, scan, review, inspect, scrutinize, smell, sense, touch, experience, absorb, be mindful of, be conscious of
RESPONDING Willingness to respond, motivated, gains satisfaction if responding	The student wants to discuss or explain.	show, tell, explain, express, answer, respond, follow, proceed, volunteer, practice, interact, contribute, attempt, perform, display, offer, complete, share, discuss, find, seek, consult, try, reject, inspire
VALUING Accepting, preferring, and making a commitment to a value	The student chooses a concept or behavior that he or she believes is worthy.	choose, select, rank, reject, adopt, decide, support, recommend, rate, defend, approve, pick, favor, challenge, specify, compare, estimate, state preference, judge, assess, appraise, subscribe to, turn down, state belief, oppose
ORGANIZATION Recognizes pervasive values, determines inter-relationships of values, organizes value system	The student reviews, questions, and arranges his or her values into an ordered system or plan.	review, determine, organize, compare, arrange, classify, sort out, systemize, rank order, figure out, consider, examine, advocate, design, group, propose, structure, prescribe, set in order, index, methodize, assign, prepare, dispose of, form
CHARACTERIZATION Internalization of a value; value system is consistent with behavior	The student voices beliefs and affirms personal values.	act out, resolve, practice, behave, treat, avoid, rely on, respond, honor, affirm, declare, resist, confide, adopt, recommend, reflect, accept, disclose, stand for, state, profess, announce, assert, acknowledge

The Definitive Middle School Guide, Revised Edition
Copyright © 2014 World Book, Inc./Incentive Publications, Chicago, IL

Checklist for Developmental Needs
to Be Addressed Through Advisory

Directions:
Note some activities you have used or could use to address each need during your advisory program. Check the item each time you include that in your planning.

✓ Developmental Needs	Activities to Address
_____ Need for movement and physical activity	
_____ Need for peer relationships and interactions	
_____ Need for active over passive learning experiences	
_____ Need to confront moral and ethical questions	
_____ Need for novelty and diversity	
_____ Need for adult approval and affirmation	
_____ Need for self-exploration and self-definition	
_____ Need for clear limits and structures that are fair and reasonable	
_____ Need for meaningful participation in school community	
_____ Need to know that body changes and growth spurts are normal	
_____ Need for introspection and self-reflection	
_____ Need to see relevance of what is learned in school	
_____ Need to think about the meaning of life with both idealism and ambiguity	
_____ Need for optimism and hope when it comes to the future	
_____ Need for competence and achievement	
_____ Need to explore options, make choices, and investigate alternatives	

Name_____ Date_____

The Definitive Middle School Guide, Revised Edition
Copyright © 2014 World Book, Inc./Incentive Publications, Chicago, IL

Questions to Guide Implementation of a Successful Advisory Program

1 Who is involved in the program?

. . . All students in the school are assigned to an advisory group that is facilitated by a teacher or an administrator. Advisory groups should have no more than 20 to 22 students in a group. The students may be assigned by grade level or across grade levels. The students may be assigned to a new advisor each year or the same advisor for three years. The principal and guidance counselor of the school are not advisors, because it is the job of these two people to coordinate and monitor the entire advisory process. The Advisory Steering Committee assists them in this role. Sometimes other staff members of the school may also serve as advisors-advocates if they are trained properly. These may include the secretary, the school nurse, the custodian, or a teacher's aide. No individual should be forced to serve as an advisor or advocate. Any educator who would not work or is very uncomfortable for an advisory situation should be given alternative responsibilities, which could range from supervisory to clerical tasks.

2 What is the purpose of the program?

. . . Advisory groups use the unique needs and characteristics of the early adolescent as the foundation for their organizational structure.

. . . These groups are designed to focus on the affective domain in which one small group of students identifies with and belongs to one advisor who nurtures, advocates, and guides through school the individuals assigned to this group. It is the goal of the advisory program to provide every student with an opportunity to know one adult in the school better than any other so that a special trust and bond is established in this relationship.

. . . Advisory groups also make it possible for students to belong and affiliate with a small group on a regular basis so that the advisor can express concern in a personal and more intimate setting, focusing on student feelings and attitudes as well as more academic needs.

3 When are advisory classes scheduled?

. . . Ideally, advisory groups should meet on a daily basis for 20 to 30 minutes a week. If this is not possible, advisory groups should meet at least a minimum of three times a week.

. . . Ideally, advisory groups should meet first thing in the morning to get the school day off to a good start and to establish the climate for the day's activities.

. . . Three traditional ways to schedule advisory time are:

1) The school day is extended for 30 minutes to provide additional minutes for advisory sessions and interactions.

2) Student begins each day with advisor. They spend ten minutes on housekeeping tasks. On two designated days each week, five to ten minutes are deducted from each class period so that an additional or longer advisory period is created and inserted between two other periods. It is during this time that the organized advisory curriculum is implemented.

The Definitive Middle School Guide, Revised Edition
Copyright © 2014 World Book, Inc./Incentive Publications, Chicago, IL

3) A school can also institute a "drop period" schedule to accommodate the program. For this option, a period is eliminated from the daily schedule on a rotating basis (either two, three, four, or ideally five days a week), and the advisory class is put in its place.

. . . Two alternative ways to schedule advisory time are:

1) Organizing teams in a type of block-time and modified self-contained program, where the teacher has the same students for two or three periods per day and teaches them two or more subjects, often referred to as an "extended time advisory program," which promotes trust and facilitates teacher guidance.

2) Planning full-day advisory experiences that include three to six full-day experiences throughout the year. These activities usually begin with a kick-off breakfast and can feature everything from community service projects and field experiences to artists-in-residence programs or city bus tours.

4 What is the content of the curriculum?

. . . The advisory curriculum content should focus on the affective, developmental, and social needs of the students within the context of the school setting. The specific topics range widely from physical development issues to social difficulties to study-organizational skills to moral-ethical issues.

. . . The curriculum should include both preplanned topics or themes along with "teachable moments" as they surface through local, regional, national, and global news events and human-interest stories.

. . . The curriculum should vary instructional strategies that are interdisciplinary and that complement the academic disciplines.

. . . The curriculum should infuse critical- and creative-thinking skills at all levels of the taxonomy, and should be applied both in the affective and the cognitive domains of knowledge.

. . . The curriculum should incorporate multiple learning styles and intelligences that cater to the diversity that exists among and between students.

. . . The curriculum should allow for "teachable moments" as they surface through local, regional, national, and global news events and human-interest stories.

. . . The curriculum should use as its foundation a research-based commercial program such as the ADVISORY program published by Incentive Publications, then supplement this resource with additional materials on a need basis. The commercial program offers the following advantages over a locally developed program, as it contains:

1) universal themes appropriate for the early adolescent;

2) scope and sequence of both content and skills to be taught;

3) a wide range of active learning tools and techniques that have been field-tested with target populations; and

4) infusion of quality educational models for addressing varied learning styles and thinking skills, such as Bloom's Taxonomy, Williams' Taxonomy, Krathwohl's Taxonomy, and Gardner's Multiple Intelligences.

Possible Goals
for an Effective Advisory Program

The following list may be used to help form a new advisory program or to reflect on the characteristics of an existing advisory program:

1 Teaching conflict-resolution skills among peers

2 Building a positive relationship among students and teachers

3 Assisting students in setting and achieving personal goals

4 Creating a climate and culture that is caring and encourages pride

5 Promoting attitudes of acceptance and collaboration among diverse groups

6 Enhancing abilities to make decisions and solve problems through the use of educational thinking-skill models such as Bloom's Taxonomy for Cognitive Development, Williams' Taxonomy for Creative Thinking, and Krathwohl's Taxonomy for the Affective Domain

7 Providing opportunities for self-exploration and the discovery of special interests, aptitudes, hobbies, and capabilities

8 Introducing and reinforcing healthy study habits and skills

9 Experimenting with technology and the Internet as important resources, but also recognizing their limitations and problem areas

10 Aiding in the building of personal friendships

11 Charting present and past academic and behavioral performances

12 Introducing and applying a variety of instructional delivery systems and thinking-skill models

13 Helping students become test-wise and gain practice in test-taking strategies

14 Investigating the world of work and career choices for the future

15 Planning and implementing service learning projects

16 Integrating art, music, and fitness into the schooling process

17 Understanding the elements of good communication skills, including reading, writing, speaking, and listening

18 Examining the media and the current events reported in the newspapers

19 Evaluating one's personal relationships, values, morals, and beliefs

20 Participating in self-assessment experiences, such as with learning style inventories and multiple intelligence reviews

The Definitive Middle School Guide, Revised Edition
Copyright © 2014 World Book, Inc./Incentive Publications, Chicago, IL

Key Elements
of a Successful Advisory Program

1 Each advisor plays the role of a child advocate representing that student at team meetings, screening meetings, parent conferences, and other student-staff sessions as needed.

2 Each advisor initiates intervention procedures and referrals both within the advisory setting and, if necessary, in collaboration with counseling services.

3 Each advisor maintains a line of communication with the advisee's academic teachers and with the advisee's parents or guardians.

4 Each advisor engages in individual conferences with advisees on a predetermined and consistent basis.

5 Each advisor maintains accurate records on advisees, including such tools as an advisee information folder, advisee academic plan card, advisee attendance and behavior record, advisee report card and progress report, and advisee test scores. The advisor follows all school, district, state, and federal confidentiality procedures when handling, using, and storing these records.

6 Each advisor supports the advisory concept and works to improve his or her own performance in the advisory role and setting.

7 Each advisor is well informed on the unique needs and characteristics of the early adolescent and of the advisees assigned in her or his advisory class.

8 Each advisor becomes a highly important adult in the school for his or her advisees.

9 Each advisory class has a reasonable teacher-student ratio.

10 Each advisory class has a specific time and place to meet that is regularly scheduled.

11 Each advisory class meets a minimum of three times a week for an average of 20 to 30 minutes a day, or meets on an alternative predetermined plan.

12 Each advisory class provides advisees with activities that are varied, active, and student-centered.

13 Each advisory class has a common core curriculum with flexibility in its implementation.

14 Each advisory class represents a place where both advisors and advisees look forward to advisory time and tasks.

15 Each advisory class places a high emphasis on individual learning styles.

16 Each advisory class maintains a balance of individual, small group, and large group activities.

17 Each advisory class infuses higher-order creative- and critical-thinking skills whenever able to do so.

18 Each advisory class emphasizes an advisee's academic, social, emotional, physical, psychological, or self-concept in its program.

Assets Crucial to a Child's Healthy Development for Life

The Minneapolis-based Search Institute, founded in 1958 to advance the well-being of children, has conducted research involving nearly 600,000 young people nationwide to formulate the *Healthy Communities–Healthy Youth* initiative. The goal is to provide the training and technical assistance needed to motivate and equip communities to nurture competent, caring, and responsible children. The average young person has fewer than half of the 40 developmental assets the institute has identified as necessary for healthy development.

This list of 40 assets may be used as a guide or checkpoint for planning or evaluating an advisory program's goals and objectives. The list also may be found helpful in determining how well a specific school and parent community currently meets these developmental needs young people have, keeping in mind that the more they are met, the less likely the young people are to use drugs and alcohol or to engage in sexual activity or violence. Activities and programs may be planned to promote these 40 assets and to help fill the gaps in character education, and thereby assume more responsibility for our nation's youth.

Keep these assets in mind as you plan advisory activities. Share the list with students. Build a discussion or activity around their response to the list or to individual items.

1. Family support
2. Positive family communication
3. Other adult relationships
4. Caring neighborhood
5. Caring school climate
6. Parent involvement in schooling
7. A community that values youth
8. A useful role in the community
9. An hour or more of community service per week
10. Feeling of safety at home, school, and in neighborhood
11. Clear rules and consequences at home
12. Clear rules and consequences at school
13. Neighbors take responsibility for monitoring behavior

14 Positive adult role models

15 Positive peer influence

16 High expectations from parents and teachers

17 Three or more hours a week in music, theater, or other arts

18 Three or more hours a week in sports, clubs, or organizations

19 One or more hours a week in religious activities

20 Time at home at least five nights a week

21 Motivation to do well in school

22 Actively engaged in learning

23 At least one hour of homework every school day

24 Cares about his or her school

25 Reads for pleasure at least three hours a week

26 Values helping others

27 Values equality and reducing hunger and poverty

28 Stands up for beliefs

29 Tells the truth even when it isn't easy

30 Accepts personal responsibility

31 Shows restraint from sexual activity, drugs, and alcohol

32 Can plan ahead and make choices

33 Has empathy, sensitivity, and friendship skills

34 Is comfortable with people of different backgrounds

35 Can resist negative peer pressure

36 Seeks to resolve conflict nonviolently

37 Sense of control over things

38 High self-esteem

39 Sense of purpose

40 Optimistic about the future

Major Roles of Individuals Responsible for an Advisory Program

1 ROLE OF ADMINISTRATOR

a) To generate a total school philosophy and mission statement that supports advisory as an essential element in the school's program

b) To promote and market the advisory program within the school and throughout the community

c) To establish an organized structure that facilitates the implementation of an advisement program, such as an Advisory Steering Committee

d) To assign competent personnel—students, parents, and community representatives—to the Advisory Steering Committee to coordinate the program

e) To provide time and space within the school for both planning and implementing advisory activities

f) To identify and provide quality in-service training for all individuals involved with the program

g) To participate actively in all in-service activities as a means of lending both support and expertise as needed

h) To monitor the progress of the program and visit advisement groups

i) To find ways to include the performance of staff, in their roles as advisors, as part of the annual performance evaluation process.

2 ROLE OF ADVISORY STEERING COMMITTEE

a) To facilitate the program, which involves scheduling, calendars, materials, in-service training, parent conferences, etc.

b) To establish goals and objectives for the program

c) To provide input and to serve as a liaison between the administration and faculty as well as between the faculty and the parent community

d) To monitor advisement procedures and activities

e) To provide support and enthusiasm for advisors

f) To design ongoing in-service necessary for continued growth

g) To assist in the assessment and evaluation of the advisory program

The Definitive Middle School Guide, Revised Edition
Copyright © 2014 World Book, Inc./Incentive Publications, Chicago, IL

3 ROLE OF GUIDANCE COUNSELOR

a) To assist in the development of advisory philosophy, themes, and activities

b) To coordinate the advisory program through leadership of the Advisory Steering Committee

c) To coordinate and conduct in-service training

d) To review and respond to referrals about advisees from advisors

e) To communicate with advisors about their advisees as needed

f) To meet periodically with advisors in conferences for the purposes of encouragement and for solving problems

g) To assist with monitoring and evaluating the program

4 ROLE OF ADVISOR

a) To provide a caring and nurturing relationship with advisees

b) To work with guidance counselor to ensure proper guidance services for all students

c) To attend all in-service training sessions

d) To plan and implement advisory activities

e) To provide a time and place for advisees to meet and share concerns

f) To respond to individual needs of advisees

g) To refer advisees for counseling or social services on a need basis

h) To communicate with parents and guardians of advisees

i) To provide increased academic and career advisement

j) To monitor academic progress and maintain accurate records on advisees

k) To encourage advisees' academic, personal, and social development

Possible Barriers
to Successful Advisory Programs

1 Insufficient planning time before implementing the program

2 Inadequate support of advisory concept by administrators, teachers, or parents

3 Incomplete curriculum of advisory topics, activities, and active learning strategies

4 Lack of budget for advisory training and materials

5 Poor scheduling of advisory time and space

6 Teachers uncomfortable with the role of advisor because of reluctance to share personal experiences and affective self

7 Teachers reluctant to take time from academic disciplines to teach affective content and skills

8 Teachers not embracing advisory activities with enthusiasm, energy, and creativity

9 Teachers taking on too much of the counseling role or unprepared to take advantage of referral options and services

10 Advisory program lacking adequate evaluation and assessment processes to determine its effectiveness with students

11 Students seeming to undervalue the advisory time

The Definitive Middle School Guide, Revised Edition
Copyright © 2014 World Book, Inc./Incentive Publications, Chicago, IL

Do's and Don'ts
of Advisory Programs

DO's

1 Do research the advisory concept through review of the literature, visitations to other school advisory programs, and dialogue with other teachers who serve as advisors, using the Internet as a resource.

2 Do allow plenty of time to plan for the implementation of the advisory concept.

3 Do a needs assessment to determine what programs and procedures are already in place at the school for meeting the affective needs and characteristics of students. The advisory program can either enhance these elements or fill in the gaps.

4 Do organize an active Advisory Steering Committee to oversee the development, implementation, and evaluation of the advisory program.

5 Do create a quality-marketing plan to promote the advisory concept with all stakeholder groups including administrators, teachers, support staff, students, and parents.

6 Do develop a realistic timeline with checkpoints for planning and implementing the advisory program from the very beginning of its inception.

7 Do arrange for open forum meetings and get-togethers with constituent groups to present tentative plans and to encourage input and feedback.

8 Do spend quality time and dollars arranging for comprehensive in-service and training programs designed to meet the needs of advisors and steering committee members.

9 Do seek out a comprehensive curriculum for the advisory program that combines the materials of an established publishing house with supplementary materials for those "teachable moments" that occur during any given school year.

10 Do plan an ongoing evaluation program to monitor the progress of the advisory program that includes a variety of assessment tools, including interview forms, observation checklists, and individual surveys or questionnaires.

11 Do interface the advisory program with other successful program options in the school so that they complement one another rather than compete with one another.

12 Do be flexible and consider changes and modifications to the program as it progresses.

DON'Ts

1 Don't expect the planning, implementation, and evaluation process for advisory to progress without problems to be solved, plans to be altered, and timelines to be adjusted.

2 Don't try to censor suggestions for improvement, feedback for change, or criticisms of existing policies. Keep the lines of communication open and encourage two-way exchanges at all times.

3 Don't get discouraged or frustrated when setbacks and disappointments occur. Think of these as creative tensions to be resolved.

4 Don't duplicate another school's program and expect it to work without considerable modification.

5 Don't skimp on the training for advisors and don't fail to offer ongoing assistance and in-service throughout the advisory program's implementation and evaluation phases.

6 Don't attempt to implement an advisory program without a predetermined curriculum, complete with themes, topics, activities, strategies, and supplementary or optional materials.

7 Don't overlook alternative methods for scheduling and using advisory time. Try out different ways of delivering the program until a satisfactory formula has been achieved.

8 Don't focus on the quantitative dimensions of the advisory program, but consider the quality of the advisory experiences and activities.

9 Don't expect all advisors to handle their advisory responsibilities in like manner, but allow for differences in personalities and learning or teaching styles.

10 Don't doom the program to failure by complaining about it, especially during the developmental and early implementation phases. Make the criticism constructive about potential for improvements in the program.

11 Don't expect each advisee to respond to the program in like manner, as students, like teachers, have different needs and perceptions of what advisory is supposed to accomplish.

12 Don't forget to have fun with the students and learn from your mistakes as well as your successes.

The Definitive Middle School Guide, Revised Edition
Copyright © 2014 World Book, Inc./Incentive Publications, Chicago, IL

Name _____ Date _____

Alternative Ways to Use Advisory Time

Directions: Examine each of the activities listed here as potential uses for a quality advisory period. Describe a particular task that you have done successfully in the classroom for each of the given categories. Be ready to share the task with others who might want to field-test it with their own group of advisees.

1 Small and whole group discussion

2 Impromptu and mini-speeches or talks

3 Games or simulations

4 Book, movie, and television reviews

5 Role-plays and case studies

6 Study and test review sessions

7 Community field trips and experiences

8 Speaker's bureau of adults from the community at large

9 Virtual field trips to special websites

10 Learning log or journal entries

11 Learning stations or portable desktop centers

12 Spelling bees, contests, and other academic competitions

13 Skits and plays

14 Silent sustained reading sessions with follow-up book dialogues

15 Demonstrations or exhibits

16 Experiments or investigations

17 Interviews, surveys, or questionnaires

18 Conflict-resolution exercises

19 Panels, debates, and round-table conversations

20 Current events

21 Movies, movie clips, or other visual presentations

22 Holiday celebrations

23 Special club or activity days

24 Career and workplace explorations

25 Individual counseling and conference sessions

Springboards for Discussions and Journal Entries in Advisory

Opinions, beliefs, observations, comments to share

1 A reaction to a particular point with which you strongly agree or disagree

2 A question about a concept that confuses you

3 A description about a situation that frustrates you

4 A paraphrase of a difficult or complex idea that interests you

5 A summary of a special time or feeling

6 A comment on what you think about a given person, place, or thing

7 A reaction to an idea that confirms or questions a particular belief you hold

8 A discussion of the pros and cons of an issue important to your well-being

9 A comparison and contrast of two opposing ideas that intrigue you

10 A history of a significant emotional event you experienced

Questions to answer

1 Which is the stronger gender—male or female? (Why?)

2 Is it easier in today's world to be a kid or an adult? (Why?)

3 Would you rather have good looks or good grades? (Why?)

4 If you could see into your future, would you want to? (Why or why not?)

5 Which is better for you—cooperation or competition? (Why?)

6 How would you define maturity? (Why?)

7 What makes an ideal hero? (Why?)

8 How would you recognize a perfect day?

9 Do people learn more from their mistakes or from their successes?

10 What would be the best thing that could happen to you? (Why?)

Quotes to spark discussions

1 Golda Meir:
You cannot shake hands with a clenched fist.

2 Winston Churchill:
The price of greatness is responsibility.

3 Albert Einstein:
The most beautiful thing we can experience is the mysterious.
It is the source of all true art and science.

4 Dwight D. Eisenhower:
Leadership is the art of getting someone else to do something
you want done because he wants it done.

5 Henry Ford:
Failure is only the opportunity to begin again more intelligently.

6 Mohandas Gandhi:
No culture can live if it attempts to be exclusive.

7 Henry Van Dyke:
Use what talents you possess; the woods would be very silent if no birds
sang there except those that sang best.

8 Martin Luther King, Jr.:
Injustice anywhere is a threat to justice everywhere.

9 Vince Lombardi:
It's not whether you get knocked down, it's whether you get up.

10 Margaret Thatcher:
Being powerful is like being a lady.
If you have to tell people you are, you aren't.

11 John Mosley:
All things are difficult before they are easy.

12 Alexander Pope:
A man should never be ashamed to say he has been wrong, which is
but saying in other words that he is wiser today than he was yesterday.

Discussion questions to consider

1 Do you generally agree or disagree with this quotation? Explain.

2 Give an example from history or personal experience to illustrate
the idea behind this quotation.

3 Why do you think the author of this quotation chose to say what
he or she said?

4 How might you restate the quote in your own words?

STUDENT INTEREST INVENTORY

Write a spontaneous personal reaction to complete each sentence below.

1. Something I do that I am most proud of is _____

   I'm proud of this because

   _____

2. My favorite leisure time activity is

   _____

3. I would like to make improvements in _____ because

   _____

   _____

4. My favorite book is

   _____

5. One thing I enjoy doing with my family is _____ because

   _____

6. I think my family's rules are _____ because

   _____

7. One thing I enjoy doing with my friends is

   _____

   _____

8. One thing I would change about my life is _____ because

   _____

9. I would like for my friends to think I am _____ because

   _____

   _____

10. When I am an adult, I would like to _____ because

   _____

   _____

continued on page 299

Name_____ Date_____

The Definitive Middle School Guide, Revised Edition
Copyright © 2014 World Book, Inc./Incentive Publications, Chicago, IL

11. One thing I would change about my community is _____ because
_____

12. When I think of school, I feel _____ because
_____

13. The thing I like best about school is _____ because
_____
_____

14. The thing I like least about school is _____ because
_____
_____

15. The trait I admire most in a teacher is _____ because
_____

16. I think homework is _____ because
_____

17. I think our school rules are _____ because
_____

18. My favorite school subject is _____ because
_____

19. One thing I would change about my school is _____ because
_____
_____

20. I hope ADVISORY will help me to _____
_____
_____

Name_____Date_____

Options for Advisory Program Scheduling

OPTION 1:

Student begins each day with advisory teacher for a designated 20- to 30-minute period of time.

Advantages:

1 Student starts the day on a positive note with small advisory group and teacher advocate.

2 Academic school day is not broken up by affective advisory program.

3 Schedule is consistent and easy to follow.

Disadvantages:

1 Advisory time can too easily be used up for housekeeping and administrative tasks with little time left for advisory activities.

2 Student has no time to report or reflect on how school day is going.

3 Advisory preparation time adds to burden of school-day preparation.

OPTION 2:

Student begins each day with advisor. They spend 10 minutes on housekeeping or administrative tasks. On two designated days each week, 5 to 10 minutes are deducted from each class period so that an additional or longer advisory period is created and inserted between two other periods. It is during this time that the organized curriculum is implemented.

Advantages:

1 Two advisory periods are available on selected days, one for advisory tasks and one for administrative tasks.

2 Student begins each day on a positive note with advisory group and teacher advocate.

3 Administrative or housekeeping tasks are not taken away from academic time.

4 Advisory is easy to schedule, as advisory time can be scheduled between any two periods.

Disadvantages:

1 Advisory tasks possible only two days a week, so advisory becomes more administrative than affective in nature.

2 Advisory adds to school-day preparation time.

3 Teacher must teach an additional period two days per week.

The Definitive Middle School Guide, Revised Edition
Copyright © 2014 World Book, Inc./Incentive Publications, Chicago, IL

OPTION 3:

A school can institute a "drop period" schedule to accommodate the advisory program. For this option, a period is eliminated from the daily schedule on a rotating basis (either two, three, four, or, ideally, five days a week), and the advisory class is put in its place.

Advantages:

1 The planner has a fair amount of scheduling freedom. When advisory time is scheduled daily, two days can be devoted to formal advisory curriculum activities. One day is set aside for administrative tasks, and the remaining two days may be used for alternative advisory activities. When fewer days are allotted for advisory classes, the scheduler will, of course, plan other combinations of advisory activities.

2 The burden of giving up academic time to make room for advisory time is shared among the teachers.

3 Scheduling is easy, as a period is eliminated from the daily schedule on a rotating basis.

4 Advisory time is scheduled in place of something else and not in addition to everything else.

Disadvantages:

1 Some effort is required to plan a rotating schedule.

2 May be difficult to meet state guidelines for prescribed academic day.

Name _____ Date _____

Alternatives for Advisory Staff Development

> *Directions: There are many alternatives to the traditional workshop or in-service training session designed for improving the attitudes and skills of teachers serving as advisors. In fact, learning styles of staff members in any school setting differ as widely as they do for the students they teach.*
>
> *Advisors should be given several options for improving their effectiveness in advisory classrooms by choosing one or more alternative methods of staff development. Consider each of the following methods for improving competencies in the advisory classroom. Record a benefit or a problem (or both) for each of the alternatives from your perspective as an advisor.*

1 Conduct an action research project with your group of advisees.

Benefit or Disadvantage: _____

2 Observe an advisory classroom and analyze it as a teaching case.

Benefit or Disadvantage: _____

3 Plan and critique an advisory lesson with an advisor colleague.

Benefit or Disadvantage: _____

4 Be a mentor and coach a colleague advisor.

Benefit or Disadvantage: _____

5 Conduct research or visit advisory websites on the Internet.

Benefit or Disadvantage: _____

6 Give an advisory presentation or a model lesson before an audience of peer advisors at a conference.

Benefit or Disadvantage: _____

7 Read journal articles or professional monographs on the advisory concept. Try writing an advisory-related article of your own.

Benefit or Disadvantage: _____

8 Maintain an advisory reflection log or learning journal of your own.

Benefit or Disadvantage: _____

9 Design a self-assessment tool around your advisory role and use it to analyze your own behavior and teaching in the advisory classroom.

Benefit or Disadvantage: _____

10 Videotape your performance in an advisory session and ask a group of peers to view the tape and give you feedback.

Benefit or Disadvantage: _____

The Definitive Middle School Guide, Revised Edition
Copyright © 2014 World Book, Inc./Incentive Publications, Chicago, IL

Evaluation Tools to Measure Effectiveness of Advisory Programs

Overview

TOOL 1: Searching for Feelings

Advisors use this "autograph" list to examine feelings related to their experiences being advisors and leading an advisory program.

TOOL 2: Making Advisory Tasks Accountable and Measurable

This tool describes steps for aligning advisory curriculum or activities with subject-area standards.

TOOL 3: The Whole-Faculty Study Group

This checklist guides a whole faculty in forming an on-site study group. The purpose of this particular study group would be to examine and evaluate your school's advisory program.

TOOL 4: Classroom Observation Form for an Advisory Session

A qualified observer can use this form to reflect on and rate an educator leading an advisory session. The observer uses a simple rating scale to score the advisor's implementation of twelve straightforward characteristics of an effective advisory session.

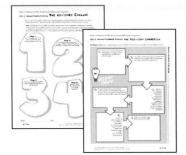

TOOL 5 and TOOL 6: Student Feedback Activities

Students use two active strategies to give feedback about how they perceive the advisory class that they are experiencing. They give reflections, evaluations, insights, and opinions through these two tactile-audio-visual-writing-creative activities.

TOOL 7: Questions for Parent-Teacher Focus Group on Advisory

A well-planned and well-implemented focus group session can provide valuable assessment and suggestions for improvement in any program. This series of questions helps a parent-teacher focus group give feedback on the advisory program.

TOOL 8: Teacher Self-Evaluation of Advisory Program Effectiveness

Each teacher participating in an advisory program can use this tool to reflect on sixteen aspects of an effective program and decide how the program is working in her or his classroom and the school in general.

Tool 1: SEARCHING FOR FEELINGS

Directions:

Circulate throughout the room and try to locate a colleague who experienced each of the designated feelings below in a work-related advisory session during the past week. Ask them to sign your list and briefly describe why they felt as they did. Record a comment or two as a memory aid for discussion purposes in a sharing session. If possible, try not to use any individual for more than one response.

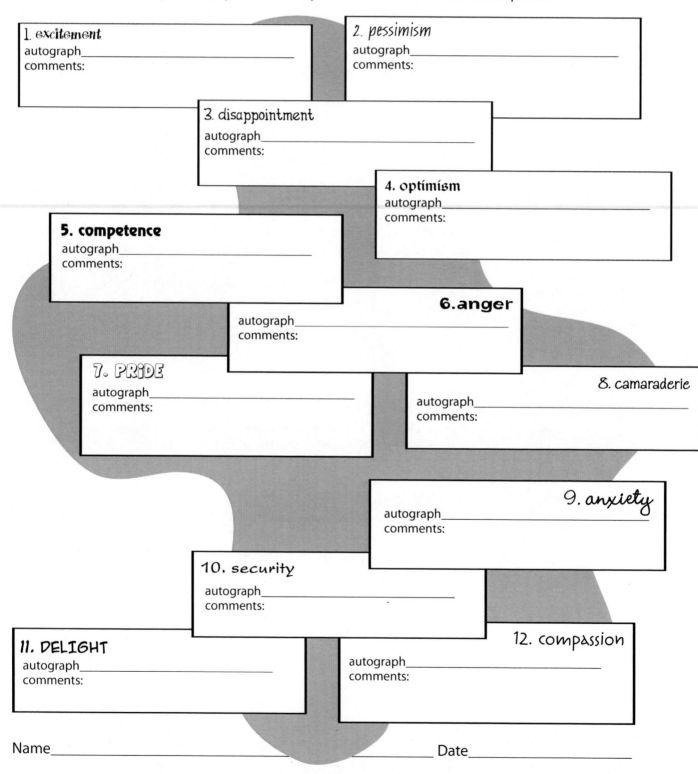

1. excitement
autograph_____
comments:

2. pessimism
autograph_____
comments:

3. disappointment
autograph_____
comments:

4. optimism
autograph_____
comments:

5. competence
autograph_____
comments:

6. anger
autograph_____
comments:

7. PRIDE
autograph_____
comments:

8. camaraderie
autograph_____
comments:

9. anxiety
autograph_____
comments:

10. security
autograph_____
comments:

11. DELIGHT
autograph_____
comments:

12. compassion
autograph_____
comments:

Name_____ Date_____

The Definitive Middle School Guide, Revised Edition
Copyright © 2014 World Book, Inc./Incentive Publications, Chicago, IL

TOOL 2: Making Advisory Tasks Accountable and Measurable

Designing advisory activities for students in such a way that they also meet standards-based curricular requirements is both a necessity and a challenge.

Advisory must never be viewed as a "frills" time-out period for students, but rather as a support program for the various core discipline areas. One way to accomplish this goal is to gather samples of student work that result from assigned advisory tasks. These student work samples can then be used to help judge the worth or value of both the advisory assignments and the quality of student responses to these activities.

Directions:

Organize a group of advisors by grade level, team level, or department level. Provide these advisors with a set of guidelines for aligning classroom work in advisory with standards from one or more of the other designated subject areas. Allow sufficient time for this process to take place. Repeat the steps outlined below on a variety of advisory tasks as needed to validate a variety of curricular outcomes.

STEP	INSTRUCTION	COMMENTS or EXPLANATION
1.	Instruct advisors to have students complete a designated advisory task according to the directions given.	Briefly describe the task:
2.	Together, advisors identify each of the curricular standards that apply to this particular task, designating subject area(s) to which it applies.	List standards and subject areas on the back of the paper. Write an example here:
3.	Advisors work together to develop a scoring guide derived from both the standards and the assigned task.	List the traits or categories in your scoring guide:
4.	Advisors collectively score the student work using this scoring guide.	Write a sentence to describe the usefulness of your scoring guide in the scoring experience:
5.	Discuss and determine whether or not the work meets the standards, making any adjustments necessary to ensure that it does.	Summarize what you learned:
6.	Discuss the process that you did in steps 1–5.	Write a statement about the process:

TOOL 3: **The Whole-Faculty Study Group**

Study groups within individual schools have become excellent tools for determining the value of a program, the success of a concept, or the affective and academic growth of a student. It is strongly suggested that the advisory program become the basis for a series of study group projects as part of the evaluation process for judging the worth of advisory in the secondary school program.

Carlene U. Murphy and Dale W. Lick, study group researchers, recommend these steps to organize a study group. Use the group to examine strengths and weaknesses of the existing advisory curriculum or overall advisory program with a given school setting.

✓ Study Group Checklist

_____**1.** Keep the size of the group to no more than six people.

_____**2.** Let the content dictate the membership (composition) of the group.

_____**3.** Establish and keep a regular schedule on a weekly basis. (Regular and shorter meetings are preferable to irregular and longer meetings.)

_____**4.** Establish group norms at the first meeting of the study group so that every member understands and supports the rules and follows the acceptable standards for behavior.

_____**5.** Agree on an action plan for the study group and adjust the timeline and tasks at regular intervals on a need basis.

_____**6.** After each study group meeting, complete a log that summarizes what happens at the meeting. This will provide a history for the group. Encourage members to keep individual logs of their personal reflections.

_____**7.** Establish a pattern of study group leadership that encourages each member to serve as the leader on a rotating basis.

_____**8.** Give all study group members equal status and equal responsibilities.

_____**9.** Keep the group focused on curriculum and instruction. The functions of study groups are to support curricular and instructional innovations, to integrate instructional practices, to target instructional needs, and to monitor the impact of instructional changes.

_____**10.** Plan ahead for transitions, as most study groups stay together for a school year.

_____**11.** Make a comprehensive list of learning resources, both material and human.

_____**12.** Consider a variety of data sources as part of the action plan, including such options as student work; student grades; attendance or discipline reports; parent participation in school events; student or staff surveys; promotion, detention, and suspension records; student participation in school events, activities, projects, and courses; teacher observations; or state assessments.

_____**13.** Include training in the study group's agenda.

_____**14.** Evaluate the effectiveness of the study group.

The Definitive Middle School Guide, Revised Edition
Copyright © 2014 World Book, Inc./Incentive Publications, Chicago, IL

TOOL 4: Classroom Observation Form for an Advisory Session

Name of person conducting the observation

_____

Job or role

_____

Date and time of observation period

_____

Directions:
This form should be used by a knowledgeable administrator, staff member, or consultant to actively observe an advisor-advocacy session with students. Indicate the degree of implementation for each item by choosing the one descriptor below that best corresponds to your observations.

Rating Scale	5 = very much	4 = pretty much	3 = somewhat
	2 = not really	1 = not at all	

Rating   Factor to Observe

1. [ ] The number of students in today's session is appropriate.

2. [ ] There were minimal or no outside interruptions during today's session.

3. [ ] The teacher was well prepared for today's session.

4. [ ] The students appeared to be prepared for today's session.

5. [ ] The planned activity or task seemed appropriate for the group in terms of curricular content and advisory time available.

6. [ ] The teacher's preparation and delivery of the activity or task was interesting and well received by the students.

7. [ ] The students were active participants in the activity or task.

8. [ ] The students appeared to enjoy and relate to the activity or task.

9. [ ] The teacher effectively brought the activity or task to a logical and meaningful conclusion.

10. [ ] The activity or task related directly or indirectly to an affective need of the students.

11. [ ] The activity or task related directly or indirectly to one or more cognitive standards of importance to the students.

12. [ ] Both the teacher and the students seemed pleased with the results of the task or activity.

Tools to Measure Effectiveness of Advisory Programs

TOOL 5: Student Feedback Activity: THE ADVISORY COLLAGE

For an advisory program to be successful, the advisor needs feedback from students as to how things are going. So your response to the activities and process of advisory class is crucial!

Task: The teacher has provided you with materials such as old magazines, newspapers, markers, poster board, fabric scraps, newsprint, scissors, glue. You will work with your small group to create a collage that represents some things that you have learned in the advisory sessions. You will cut out words and phrases, pictures, or other graphics and add words, phrases, and illustrations as needed.

Step 1:
Use this space to write some ideas that you will graphically portray.

Step 2:
Look for good words and images. Write a few of the best phrases or words that you found.

Step 3:
Put your collage together. Did everybody take part in the process?

Step 4:
Write a brief description of your final product.

Names of students in this group:

Name_____ Date_____

The Definitive Middle School Guide, Revised Edition
Copyright © 2014 World Book, Inc./Incentive Publications, Chicago, IL

Tools to Measure Effectiveness of Advisory Programs

TOOL 6: Student Feedback Activity: THE TELEVISION COMMERCIAL

Directions: Work with a small group of peers and follow these steps to complete the task outlined below:

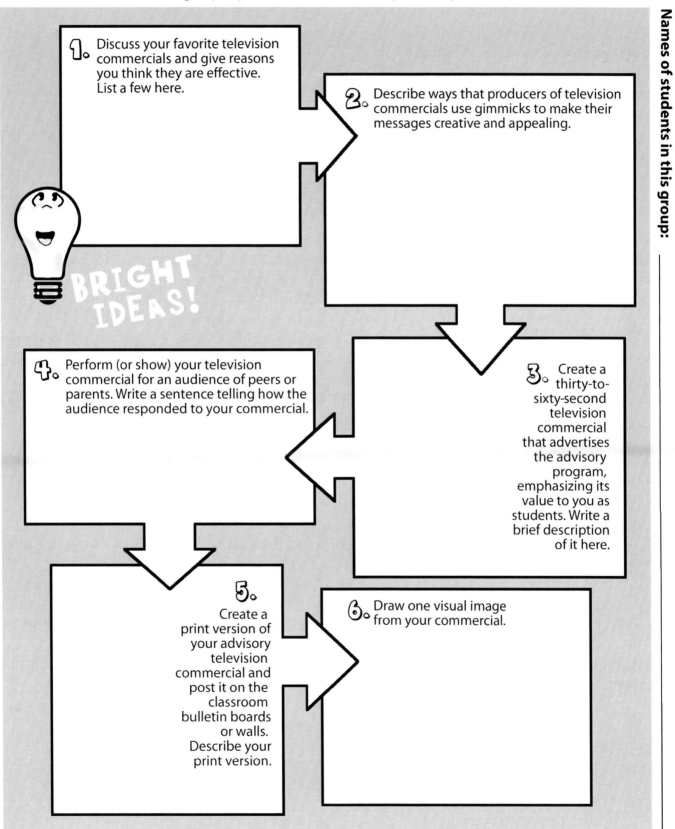

1. Discuss your favorite television commercials and give reasons you think they are effective. List a few here.

BRIGHT IDEAS!

2. Describe ways that producers of television commercials use gimmicks to make their messages creative and appealing.

3. Create a thirty-to-sixty-second television commercial that advertises the advisory program, emphasizing its value to you as students. Write a brief description of it here.

4. Perform (or show) your television commercial for an audience of peers or parents. Write a sentence telling how the audience responded to your commercial.

5. Create a print version of your advisory television commercial and post it on the classroom bulletin boards or walls. Describe your print version.

6. Draw one visual image from your commercial.

Names of students in this group:

TOOL 7: Questions for Parent-Teacher Focus Group on Advisory

Directions:
Plan to record this focus group session so that responses can be reviewed and edited at a later date. Limit the discussion to these questions as much as possible to stay on track. Encourage equitable input from all participants.

Name of person conducting focus group

_____

Role_____

Target audience _____ Number of participants_____

Date_____ Time_____ Place_____

1.
What do you see as the primary purpose of an advisory program for students in this school?

2.
What do you see as the major benefits of an advisory program for students in this school?

3.
What do you see as the biggest barriers to the advisory program in this school?

4.
What types of activities seem to work best for students in the advisory program? What types are most problematic?

5.
How much do you think teachers enjoy and look forward to advisory sessions they teach?

6.
How does the advisory program help to make the students better people or citizens?

7.
How does the advisory program in the school help to make the students better students?

8.
How can you tell whether or not the advisory program in the school is an effective one?

9.
What suggestions do you have for improving the advisory program in the school?

The Definitive Middle School Guide, Revised Edition
Copyright © 2014 World Book, Inc./Incentive Publications, Chicago, IL

TOOL 8: Teacher Self-Evaluation of Advisory Program Effectiveness

Name_____ Date _____

Question	Yes	No	Comments
1. My school or district has a comprehensive advisory program complete with philosophy statement, goals, objectives, and activity suggestions._____			
2. I have a copy of the full program plan for my grade level._____			
3. The program in my school has a name and logo that are easily recognized. _____			
4. Each student in my school has regular contact with his or her program teacher._____			
5. There is a person or group who coordinates, monitors, and evaluates the program._____			
6. The program activities are appropriate for students at my grade level._____			
7. The weekly schedule of events for the program is appropriate._____			
8. I have more than enough program activity options for most given topics._____			
9. I have flexibility in my program to take advantage of teachable moments._____			
10. There are few outside interruptions during the program time._____			
11. The number of students in my advisory program is appropriate._____			
12. The majority of students enjoy this program time._____			
13. The majority of parents seem to be supportive of the program._____			
14. The majority of faculty members enjoy the program time._____			
15. I enjoy this program time._____			
16. I feel that the program is beneficial to students both affectively and academically._____			

Findings from the Published Literature Related to Advisory, Advocacy, and Affective Education

FINDING #1:

Burkhart and Kane remind us:

> Advocacy lies at the heart of middle level education, and every middle level educator needs to be an advocate for young adolescents. National Middle School Association (2003, pp.64–65) in its paper, *This We Believe: Successful Schools for Young Adolescents*, asserts that successful schools for young adolescents are characterized by, among other things, "an adult advocate for every student," one "who is knowledgeable about young adolescent development in general, who self-evidently enjoys working with young adolescents, and who comes to know students well as individuals." Advocacy and advisory are closely related. If advocacy is an operational mindset, an attitude about how to engage with and support young adolescents during these important years of growth, then advisory refers to specific programs designed by middle level educators to address the needs and interests of students.

Source: Burkhart, R. M., & Kane, J. T. (2005). An adult advocate for every student, In Erb, T. O. (Ed.), This we believe in action: Implementing successful middle level schools. Westerville, OH: National Middle School Association.

FINDING #2:

Goldberg gives advice for the design of an advisory program:

> An advisory system in any middle school helps overcome the impersonality and alienation that secondary students often feel. Using staff as advisors guarantees that each student has an advocate who knows the student well. Those who know this process can say with certainty that an advisory system makes school a more personal place; gives all advisors a chance to share something powerful; provides students and parents a specific person in the school to whom they can turn with questions, concerns, or offers of help; and has a generally salutary effect on the overall culture of a school. As time goes by, an advisor becomes a combination mentor, advisor, and adult friend—but always a mature professional with a student's best interest in mind and an understanding of who that student is. An advisory system gives each student the support young people crave and helps defeat an alienation from school that too many students feel in an educational bureaucracy.

Source: Goldberg, M. F. (1998). How to design an advisory system for a secondary school. Alexandria, VA: Association for Supervision and Curriculum Development.

FINDING #3:

Michael James and Nancy Spradling (2002) add:

When defining advocacy we must shift from

. . . advising to advocacy

. . . teaching to coaching

. . . guidance to guiding

. . . activities to accomplishments

. . . technicalities to caring in action

. . . quantitative accountability to acting responsibly
and, most importantly,

. . . others-generated mandates to concern-driven causes.

When we *advocate* for our middle school students, we support who they are and what they do to the same degree we expect them to support who we are and what we do as well as their peers and significant others.

When we *coach* our learners, we display the "rah-rah" attitude necessary to affirm positive personal growth and good deeds—characteristics these learners want to demonstrate and are capable of doing if we let them.

When we *guide* we serve as an adult role-model—no lightly accepted responsibility.

When our students *accomplish* something, no matter how small or seemingly insignificant, we need to lead the celebration to establish a success-breeds-success cycle.

When our students *act out of caring* by doing an unselfish deed or successfully completing a service learning project, we need to be ready with the blue ribbons or kind words showing our genuine caring for both the person and the act.

When our students *act responsibly* they are saying in effect, I know what is expected and I can act on that opportunity because I am "response-able."

When our students *act out of concern* for others, they demonstrate a very perceptive stance of knowing what is really important to self and others (before doing something about it).

Source: James, M., & Spradling, N. (2002). *From advisory to advocacy: Meeting every student's needs.* Westerville, OH: National Middle School Association.

FINDING #4:

According to Kathleen Cushman:

Fairness builds trust and respect. Students know that by coming to school they are making a bargain with teachers, and they want it to be a fair one. Here's how students define it:

  . . . If you will show and care about the material, then we will believe the material can be important for us to learn.

  . . . If you will treat us as smart and capable of challenging work, then we will feel respected and rise to the challenge of demanding work.

  . . . If you will allow us increasing independence but agree with us on clear expectations, then we will learn to act responsibly on our own, though we will sometimes make mistakes in the process.

  . . . If you will model how to act when you or we make mistakes, then we will learn to take intellectual risks and learn to make amends when we behave badly.

  . . . If you will show respect for our differences and individual styles, then we will let you limit some of our freedoms in the interest of the group.

  . . . If you will keep private anything personal we tell you, then we will trust you with information that could help you teach us better.

Source: Cushman, K., & What Kids Can Do (Organization). (2003). *Fires in the bathroom: Advice for teachers from high school students.* New York: New Press.

FINDING #5:

So what should Advisory look like today? Debra Pitton suggests:

It is not a good option to simply use advisory time for a study hall or revert to an administrative homeroom model. Students at this age need opportunities to talk about issues that they are concerned about, they need to feel a sense of belonging, and they need to connect with an adult who cares. If teachers view their students as emerging adults and acknowledge the needs and concerns of young adolescents, then it makes sense that the teacher's role must also include facilitating opportunities for student discussion and skill building in the social and emotional areas. All of these things happen in a well-developed and carefully facilitated advisory program.

Source: Pitton, D. E. (2001). The school and the child and the child in school. *Middle School Journal, 33*(1), 14-20.

Review and Reflect
on Advisory, Advocacy, and Affective Programs

Level 1: Remembering	Your Reflections

Task

Define the concepts of "affective, advisory, and advocacy" as they relate to advisor-advisee types of instructional programs in today's middle schools.

affective

advisory

advocacy

Level 2: Understanding	Your Reflections

Task

Briefly, list reasons why you feel you would or would not make a good student advisor or advocate in your educational setting.

Describe what types of training you think would be of the most benefit to you at this time to improve your advisory skills.

Would I make a good advisor?

Training that would benefit me:

Level 3: Applying	Your Reflections

Task

List what you believe to be the major elements of a successful advisory program.

My list:

continued on page 316

Review and Reflect

on Advisory, Advocacy, and Affective Programs

Level 4: Analyzing | Your Reflections

Task	
Compare and contrast the notion of teacher as teacher versus teacher as a coach. Tell which approach works best for you.	**What works best for me is:** **Why?**

Level 5: Evaluating | Your Reflections

Task	
Review the merits of the different evaluation tools suggested in this module (chapter) to measure the effectiveness of advisory programs. Identify the most interesting to the least interesting and give reasons for your choices.	**Most interesting:** **Why?** **Least interesting:** **Why?**

Level 6: Creating | Your Reflections

Task	
Design an original advisory lesson plan that you think would work well in most middle school settings. Test it with a group of students and see how it works for both you and for them!	**Describe the plan:** **How did it work for you?** **How did it work for students?**

The Definitive Middle School Guide, Revised Edition
Copyright © 2014 World Book, Inc./Incentive Publications, Chicago, IL

Module VI

Student
Assessment

and

Evaluation

Contents of Module VI

Overview of
Student Assessment and Evaluation

Assessment is . . .

- the ongoing testing or grading of students according to a given set of criteria.

- considered to be authentic when methods of assessing achievement or performance are as close to real-life situations as the setting allows.

- valuable to both teachers and students as feedback on the effectiveness of classroom delivery systems and expected outcomes.

- the development and implementation of a wide variety of instructional tools and techniques as well as multiple assessment strategies.

- the process of measuring individual student growth in both cognitive and affective areas.

- the effective implementation of student products, performances, and portfolios for purposes of stimulating student interests, student self-esteem, and student learning.

- the measurement of innovative and alternative delivery systems in the classroom that includes everything from cooperative learning and exploratory courses to teacher-directed lesson plans and lectures.

- essential to the successful implementation of state and national standards.

Effective assessment tools and techniques characteristically . . .

. . . identify both student strengths and weaknesses.

. . . make provisions for ongoing and personal student involvement in the overall assessment process.

. . . take into account differences in student learning styles, interests, attitudes, and aptitudes.

. . . make provisions for collaborative efforts while taking into account individual differences within the group.

. . . employ multifaceted scoring procedures rather than a single rigid grading system to satisfy all stakeholders in the assessment process.

. . . provide timely and specific feedback for teacher evaluation and future planning.

. . . contribute to the student's feelings of self-worth and his or her academic achievement.

Terms Important for Understanding Student Assessment and Evaluation

Achievement test: a test that measures what has been taught and learned, as well as the extent to which an individual has achieved or mastered a set of defined objectives or learning outcomes

Alternative assessments: assessments that differ from the multiple-choice, timed, "one-shot" approaches that characterize most standardized tests and some classroom assessments

Aptitude test: a test that measures or predicts what a person will be able to do in the future and the likely effects of future learning experiences

Assessment: a broad term referring to the process of gathering and synthesizing data and information to find out the current level of student achievement

Authentic assessment: methods of assessing student achievement levels that simulate real-life situations and that include portfolio, product, and performance measures

Benchmark: a standard for judging a performance (Schools develop benchmarks to tell what students should know by a particular stage of their schooling.)

Checklist: a list of behaviors, attributes, or tasks with which teachers tally students' evidence of mastery

Criteria: guidelines, rules, or principles by which student responses, products, or performances are evaluated

Criterion-referenced: using standards, objectives, or benchmarks as the reference points for determining student achievement

Diagnostic test: a test that assesses specific skills to determine an individual's strengths and weaknesses used by teachers to guide them in planning instruction that is based on student needs

Evaluation: the process of making a judgment regarding quality, value, or worth, based upon criteria

Feedback: the process of telling students what or how they did as compared with what they were assigned or supposed to do

Formative evaluation or assessment: assessment that is both frequent and ongoing and which provides important checkpoints or benchmarks in measuring what students know and can do at any given time during a learning process (Formative assessments provide ongoing information to help teachers adjust instruction and improve student performance.)

High-stakes test: a test whose results will have a significant impact on the life of the student, teacher, administration, or school

Learner outcomes: clearly defined content knowledge, skills, and behaviors related to the topic being studied that students are expected to demonstrate through completion of authentic tasks

The Definitive Middle School Guide, Revised Edition
Copyright © 2014 World Book, Inc./Incentive Publications, Chicago, IL

Measurement: the assignment of a numerical quantity to a given assessment or evaluation procedure

Metacognition: a theory which states that learners benefit by thoughtfully and reflectively considering the things they are learning and the ways in which they are learning them

Naturalistic observations: sometimes called "kid watching," this is a process whereby teachers observe individual and group behaviors related to academic tasks, work habits, thinking processes, and other activities that influence performance

Norm-referenced test: a test constructed to compare students to one another and to the performance of others in the standard by which the student is measured

Norms: statistics used by test designers to represent specific populations and how the average person in that population would do on a specific test

Percentage: the score on a test that a student receives based on a number of points or on a given part out of 100

Percentile: one of the points on a 99-point scale that shows a person's relative standing within a particular group

Performance assessment: an assessment based on the professional judgment of the assessor through observation of the student performing a predetermined task

Portfolio assessment: an assessment based on a meaningful collection of student work that exhibits the student's overall efforts, progress, and achievements in one or more areas

Pre-assessment: any type of assessment prior to teaching a lesson that a teacher uses as a basis for making instructional decisions

Product assessment: an assessment that requires tangible indicators of the application of knowledge and skills through written, visual, or aural products

Reliability: the consistency of performance on the test from one taking of the test to another by the same individual

Rubric: a set of guidelines containing criteria based on stated performance standards and a descriptive rating scale for purposes of distinguishing between performances or products of different quality

Standardized test: a norm-referenced and systematic sample of student performance obtained under prescribed conditions developed for state or national use

Standards: specific indicators of what students should know and be able to do as a result of their classroom or schooling experience

Summative evaluation: assessment that follows multiple learning experiences and which measures what the student has completed or mastered over an extended period of time

Validity: the extent to which a test measures what it was intended to measure

Guiding Questions for Student Assessment and Evaluation

1 What are some essential terms or concepts to know and understand when dealing effectively with today's assessment issues, options, and concerns?

2 What things must be considered when examining the middle school's grading and reporting program for assessing student progress?

3 How do we define and justify authentic assessment practices in today's middle schools?

4 What are the major differences between a traditional assessment program and an authentic assessment program? The advantages and disadvantages of each approach to measuring what students know and can do in the classroom?

5 How can teachers assigned to the same team work together to develop a plan to more effectively assess individual students within the group?

6 What are some commonalities of portfolio, performance, and product assessment? Explain the strengths and weaknesses of each and give one example of a situation in which each would be a valid means of assessment.

7 Why are student products good assessment tools? How can they be used to encourage creativity?

8 What are some things to keep in mind when designing, scoring, and using performance tests and evaluating their results?

9 What are the most valuable components of a student portfolio as viewed by the teacher? As viewed by the student?

10 What are some advantages of including student self-evaluation as an ongoing part of a structured assessment program?

11 What can teachers do to make sure that assessment results are reported and interpreted in a manner that is actually meaningful and useful to parents and students?

12 What steps can teachers take to become more proficient in selecting, administering, recording, and making use of assessment tools and results?

13 How does one prepare for and conduct a successful student-led or teacher-led parent conference?

14 What are some informal or alternative methods teachers can develop and use for assessing student understanding of material covered during instruction?

15 What are some guidelines for developing different types of questions for a traditional test? For an essay test?

16 What are some effective ways to help students both prepare for a test and complete a test with success?

17 How can a teacher use observations, checklists, and rubrics successfully in the assessment process?

18 What does the current research tell us about the most effective ways to measure what students know and can do in today's middle school classrooms?

The Definitive Middle School Guide, Revised Edition
Copyright © 2014 World Book, Inc./Incentive Publications, Chicago, IL

Characteristics of Traditional and Authentic Assessment Measures

Traditional Assessment

1. Purpose is accountability.

2. Objectives tend to be specific, clear, and generally require low-level thinking.

3. Features structured assessment tasks that are the same for all students.

4. Administration is efficient, quick, and easy.

5. Tests have high reliability with low cost.

6. Computer does the scoring with a single score on each test or subtest.

7. Desired responses are fixed and limited.

8. Impact on students is varied depending on student attitude, learning style, and stress level.

9. Assessor bias is not a problem.

10. Does not require teacher planning time for preparation.

11. Results are easy to explain to parents and public.

12. Can be readily designed to reflect district objectives or mandates.

Authentic Assessment

1. Purpose is to show improvement, growth, and what a student knows and can do.

2. Objectives are integrated, cover multiple subject areas, and generally require high-level thinking skills.

3. Features open-ended tasks, which are different for different students.

4. Administration and scoring tends to be time consuming.

5. Reliability is difficult to achieve and requires training for scorers.

6. Complex scoring depends on checklists and rubrics.

7. Students are in charge of own response, which is either product or performance based.

8. Student is less threatened by assessment because it is an integral part of instruction.

9. Assessor bias is more difficult to control.

10. Requires considerable planning time for teachers to develop and grade assessment tool or outcome.

11. Results shown to parents through a portfolio or conference setting.

12. More difficult to tie directly to a given district objective or mandate.

Design Elements of a Quality Alternative Assessment Task

An alternative assessment task

1 simulates a meaningful, relevant, and real-life situation as much as possible.

2 is open-ended and engages students in higher-order creative- and critical-thinking skills.

3 has an answer to the student's question of "Why do I need to know or do this?"

4 has a variety of different options or choices for students to consider and for evaluating student learning. One size doesn't fit all.

5 is interdisciplinary and integrates varied subjects and skills.

6 establishes a specific set of multiple criteria and scoring options for judging the results of the product or performance outcome.

7 addresses a set of specific learning objectives and competencies that are measurable.

8 involves the student in both its design and in its evaluative process.

Source: Coil, C., & Merritt, D. (2001). *Solving the assessment puzzle piece by piece.* Marion, IL: Pieces of Learning. (Note: an updated and revised ed. of this book was published in 2011.)

> *Note: Review this list of elements of a quality, alternative assessment measure and use it as a checklist for those alternative assessment measures you either use or design.*

Ways to Guarantee Good Assessment in a Differentiated Classroom

According to Rick Wormeli (2006), good assessment . . .

1 advances learning, not just documents it. It is accepted as integral to instruction, not outside instruction.

2 determines what's being assessed. We assess what's important, not just what is possible.

3 provides enough information to the teacher to inform instructional practice.

4 is ongoing and emphasizes formative over summative information. It is never saved for the end of a unit.

5 is open and never secretive. It begins with the end in mind.

6 focuses on developmentally appropriate, enduring, and essential content and skills or KUD (what students Know, Understand, and are able to Do).

7 is authentic to the learning experience—the assessments are similar to what students experience during the lessons.

8 is a highly valid indicator of what students know and are able to do, not something diluted by inappropriate testing formats. It answers "Yes!" to the question: "Can we conclude what we want to know with this assessment?"

9 is reliable. It answers "Yes!" to the question: "Will the assessment yield the same accuracy when repeated over time?"

10 occurs because it's at this point in the learning to assess mastery, and not because it is test day.

11 often engages more than one discipline because life is rarely compartmentalized.

12 often calls for the use of different tools and products. It's better to learn three ways to do one thing than it is to learn one way to do three things.

13 often uses tasks that reveal common misunderstandings so teachers can see whether students have truly learned the material.

14 often includes those being assessed in determining its form and criteria and in analyzing their personal progress to encourage student ownership in the process.

15 is often conducted with multiple experiences over time to increase accuracy.

Source: Wormeli, R. (2006). *Fair isn't always equal: Assessing & grading in the differentiated classroom.* Portland, ME: Stenhouse Publishers.

Formative and Summative Assessment Formats to Use in the Classroom

1. Teacher observations and daily recordings on note cards

2. Student learning logs or journal entries

3. Peer observations

4. Anecdotal comments or records

5. Peer assessments and reviews

6. Student self-assessment or reflective comments

7. Student or teacher interviews

8. Role-playing or case studies

9. Small or large group projects, presentations, or participation studies

10. Teacher-assigned or teacher-directed formal tasks

11. Written pre-tests and post-tests

12. Oral quizzes

13. Open-ended or guided responses

14. Interactive lectures

15. Teacher-led or student-led discussions

16. Panel presentations

17. Independent study sessions

18. Checklists and rubrics

19. Learning contracts

20. Real-life events as mock performances (trials, debates, historical reenactments)

21. Choral or poetry readings

22. Readers' theater

23. Skits, plays, and dramas

24. Game and simulation outcomes

25. Inquiry challenges where students are problem posers and problem solvers

26. Student performance tasks (speeches, oral presentations, reports, demonstrations, talk shows, travel logs, audiovisual reports)

27. Portfolios and work samples

28. Visual products (brochures, data sheets, essays, forecasts, models, puzzles, scrapbooks, software reviews, annotated bibliographies)

29. PowerPoint, podcasts, or other computer-generated presentations

Note: This list represents examples of both formative and summative assessment formats. Remember that formative assessment measures are generally ongoing classroom assignments, activities, and practice exercises, which serve as checkpoints for how a student is doing. The information from formative assessment helps you adjust instruction. Summative assessments are generally more formal in nature and measure the accumulated performance or knowledge at end of a unit, product, or performance, course, or class.

The Definitive Middle School Guide, Revised Edition
Copyright © 2014 World Book, Inc./Incentive Publications, Chicago, IL

Things to Keep in Mind About Portfolios

1 Portfolios are collections of a student's work assembled over time to document individual growth and academic progress.

2 Portfolio assessment measures require the student to assume primary responsibility for making decisions about what goes in the portfolio, how the portfolio is organized, and what type of self-reflection experiences are to be included.

3 Portfolios provide students with opportunities for goal setting, for tools of discussions with peers and adults, for demonstrations of student skills and acquisition of concepts studies, for evidence of student learning, for making connections between varied subject areas, and for invitations to reflect on work that has been done.

4 Portfolio contents can be housed in a number of different containers, including file boxes, shoe boxes, shopping bags, cardboard magazine holders, photo albums, scrapbooks, and expandable file or pocket folders.

5 Portfolios should contain front and back covers and information about time span represented by artifacts. They should also contain a Table of Contents, an overview of the organizational structure employed by the portfolio, a collection of at least ten different artifact formats, reflections on all included artifacts, and a self-evaluation to analyze overall student strengths and weaknesses.

6 Portfolios can be graded in many ways. Individual pieces can be graded over a predetermined time period. A completed portfolio can be graded on such criteria as visual appeal, organization, creativity, reflections, form or mechanics, evidence of growth, knowledge of concepts or skills demonstrated, and completeness.

7 Some performance-type activities to be considered for portfolios might be: debates, exhibitions, displays, skits or plays, speeches, audio or visual presentations, choral readings, dances, presentations, oral lab reports, newscasts, court trials, panel discussions, travelogues, surveys, role-plays, case studies, or personal interviews.

8 Some product-type activities to be considered for portfolios might be: poems, booklets, charts, graphs, diagrams, flowcharts, reviews, newspapers, editorials, collages, posters, banners, glossaries, journal entries, letters, lists, murals, puzzles, games, book reports, transcripts, scrapbook, stories, experiments, magazines, games, or models.

9 Some test-type activities to be considered for portfolios might be: teacher-made tests, student-generated quizzes, take-home tests, criterion-referenced tests, standardized tests, open book exams, oral tests, textbook tests, cooperative learning group tests, or district or state-mandated tests.

10 Portfolios are important assessment tools to use because:

a) they are tools for discussion.

b) they provide opportunities for students to demonstrate what they know and what they can do.

c) they provide a vehicle for students to reflect on their work.

d) they document the growth of a student's learning over time.

e) they cater to alternative student learning styles and multiple intelligences.

f) they allow students to make decisions on what to include or exclude.

g) they make it easier for students to make connections and transfers between prior knowledge and new learning.

11 Some questions that need to be addressed in planning and implementing a portfolio assessment process include:

a) What are the major purposes of a portfolio for both student and teacher?

b) How should the individual pieces in the portfolio be selected, and should there be a limit to the number of student work samples allowed?

c) What specific pieces should be included in the portfolio and how do they represent the student's acquisition of content and skills?

d) What are the options for evaluating the portfolio's content?

e) How should the portfolio work samples be organized?

f) In what ways can the portfolios be shared through parent-teacher conferences?

12 Here are some things to think and talk about with both students and peer teachers:

a) Think of five careers or job opportunities for which people might use a portfolio to demonstrate or show their expertise in a given area.

b) If you were going to create a personal portfolio about you outside of school, what things would you choose to put in it?

c) How might a student use a portfolio to help get a job after graduating from high school or college?

The Definitive Middle School Guide, Revised Edition
Copyright © 2014 World Book, Inc./Incentive Publications, Chicago, IL

Steps for Planning a Portfolio System

1 Determine the overall purpose and intended audience of the portfolio.

 . . . How will the portfolio document student growth and learning?

 . . . What is the timeline for this portfolio?

 . . . Who will view the portfolio?

2 Specify the curricular areas to be included in the portfolio.

 . . . Will this be a single course portfolio or a team portfolio?

3 Decide on the selection criteria for items placed in the portfolio.

 . . . Who selects the pieces—student, teacher, parent, or some of each?

 . . . How many pieces should be represented?

 . . . What types of pieces should be represented?

 . . . How often should pieces be included?

4 Plan a management system for the portfolio process.

 . . . What type of container will house the portfolio?

 . . . How will students organize and maintain their portfolio?

 . . . How will students update their portfolio?

5 Establish a set of priority uses for the portfolio.

 . . . How can I make certain that students see the value of the portfolio?

 . . . How can I oversee the selection of the most appropriate pieces to accurately reflect student growth over time?

 . . . How can I make optimal use of the portfolio with parents?

 . . . How can I use the portfolio for celebration of work done well?

 . . . How can I interface the portfolio process with grading of report cards?

 . . . How can I use the portfolio to provide me feedback as a teacher? As a parent?

6 Focus on a manageable assessment process for measuring the success of portfolios.

 . . . How will I know the portfolio assessment process is working?

 . . . How do I grade the portfolios?

 . . . How do I get students to apply self-evaluation and metacognitive techniques?

 . . . What is done with the portfolios at the end of the grading period, semester, or school year?

Questions to Ask
During a Portfolio Conference

1 How is your portfolio organized and how did you decide on this organizational pattern?

2 How did you go about selecting your portfolio pieces?

3 What pieces are you most proud of in this portfolio and why do you feel as you do?

4 What piece in the portfolio do you wish was not there and how could you improve it?

5 Of all the assignments represented by the pieces in the portfolio, which one was hardest for you to do and which one was easiest? What makes this so?

6 How do these pieces reflect your overall growth this grading period, semester, or year?

7 What makes you feel proud when you review the work in this portfolio?

8 How would you improve this portfolio process for next time?

9 What does this portfolio say about you, the student, and you, the person?

10 What do you hope happens to the contents of this portfolio?

11 What advice would you give to another student about to begin the portfolio process?

12 How does the work in this portfolio affect your grade in this class or course? How should it affect the grade in this class or course?

The Definitive Middle School Guide, Revised Edition
Copyright © 2014 World Book, Inc./Incentive Publications, Chicago, IL

Things to Know About Performance Assessment

1 A performance-assessment task involves using real-life applications to real-life problems or at least in simulated settings. Performance tasks are realistic, complex, and comprehensive in nature, requiring extended time to complete, and involve greater use of judgment in scoring.

2 Some important characteristics of performance tasks include:

   a) student choice,

   b) elaboration of core knowledge content,

   c) application of process and higher-order thinking skills,

   d) an explicit scoring system,

   e) a broad audience, and

   f) a structured plan to fit a specific instructional objective or performance standard.

3 Performance tasks are often preferred over more traditional assessment tasks because:

   a) educators are dissatisfied with selected response and paper-pencil tests;

   b) educators feel that process or procedural knowledge is as important as content knowledge, and this can best be measured through performance tasks; and

   c) educators feel that conventional tasks are harmful because they encourage high-stakes testing and a focus on low-level instructional tasks.

4 Educators should follow these steps when designing a performance test:

Step 1: Identify content area to be assessed, including factual-conceptual understandings.

Step 2: Select the process or inquiry or thinking skills you wish to measure.

Step 3: Write a detailed description of the performance task.

Step 4: List the criteria to be used to evaluate the task.

Step 5: List the resources required to complete the task.

Step 6: Write directions for the students that include appropriate language for clarity.

Step 7: Decide on how to interpret results—comparison with other students or self.

Step 8: Develop scoring procedures that focus on performance, not content.

Step 9: Determine who will rate or evaluate performance—teacher, peers, or self.

Step 10: Administer a trial test wherever possible to do so.

5 Students benefit significantly from performance-assessment measures because:

a) they can show originality and creativity that go beyond what is taught.

b) they can use all or most levels of Bloom's Taxonomy (cognitive thinking) and Williams' Taxonomy (creative thinking) in a single outcome.

c) they can reflect growth in social and academic skills and attitudes that are not easily reflected in paper-and-pencil kinds of tests.

d) they can motivate or engage students who are reluctant learners or at-risk performers in school.

e) they can make learning more relevant and memorable for students.

f) they can demonstrate what the student knows and can do in a very concrete way.

g) they can more easily allow for integration of reading, writing, and speaking skills.

h) they can give students more flexible time to do more thoughtful work.

i) they can permit students to interact collaboratively with other students.

j) they can cater to students with varied learning styles.

Steps for Designing a Performance Task

A performance-assessment task focuses on real-life applications or real-life problems where possible to do so. Performance tasks are realistic, complex, comprehensive, time consuming, and most often scored using rubrics. Performance tasks are characterized by high levels of student choice, elaboration or core knowledge and content, application of higher-order thinking skills, explicit scoring systems, broad audiences, and structured plans that fit a specific set of instructional objectives or performance standards.

Educators should follow these steps when designing a performance task:

1 Identify content area(s) to be assessed, including factual-conceptual understandings.

2 Select the process, type of inquiry, or thinking skill you wish to measure.

3 Write a detailed description of the performance task.

4 List the criteria to be used to evaluate the performance.

5 List the resources required to complete the task.

6 Write directions for the students that include appropriate language for clarity.

7 Decide on how to interpret results—comparison with other students or with self.

8 Develop scoring procedures that focus on performance, not content.

9 Determine who will rate or evaluate the performance—teacher, peers, or self.

10 Administer a trial test wherever possible to do so.

11 Modify or revise elements of the performance task according to trial test results.

Descriptions of Performance Task Options to Consider

1 COMPARISON-AND-CONTRAST TASK:
The student is asked to compare two or more people, places, or things by presenting both similarities and differences.

2 DEMONSTRATION TASK:
The student is asked to show or perform a specific skill or act.

3 INFERENCE TASK:
The student is asked to look for and identify subtitles and between-the-lines meanings when reviewing ideas and information.

4 PREDICTION TASK:
The student is asked to make realistic guesses about what could have happened or will happen in the future.

5 APPLICATION TASK:
The student is asked to use his or her knowledge or skill in a new context or situation different from the one in which it was learned.

6 EXPERIMENTAL TASK:
The student is asked to set up an experiment to test a hypothesis.

7 GENERALIZATION TASK:
The student is asked to draw conclusions from a given set of data.

8 INVESTIGATION TASK:
The student is asked to follow a reasonable set of guidelines for conducting an inquisition or in forming generalizations about an assigned topic or problem.

9 ANALYSIS TASK:
The student is asked to break down a whole into its component parts, looking for relationships between parts or the recognition of the organizational principles involved.

10 PERSPECTIVES TASK:
The student is asked to consider two or more different perspectives, then to choose the perspective he or she supports.

11 INVENTION TASK:
The student is asked to create, compose, design, develop, or produce something new and unique.

12 APPRAISAL TASK:
The student is asked to determine the worth or value of a person, place, thing, event, or idea.

13 DECISION-MAKING TASK:
The student is asked to identify the factors or variables that caused a certain decision to be made.

14 PROBLEM-SOLVING TASK:
The student is asked to create a solution to a specific problem.

15 EVALUATION TASK:
The student is asked to identify the pros and cons or advantages and disadvantages of a given situation.

The Definitive Middle School Guide, Revised Edition
Copyright © 2014 World Book, Inc./Incentive Publications, Chicago, IL

Reasons Student Products Make Good Assessment Tools

Students' original products are valuable tools for assessment because:

1 they come in a variety of sizes, shapes, colors, and formats. They may involve learning logs, video or audio recordings, computer demonstrations, dramatic performances, informative bulletin board displays, debates or panels, formal speeches or presentations, student experiments and inventions, investigation reports, physical constructions, or role-playing and case study scenarios.

2 they are more likely to be initiated or generated by students rather than teachers, which then reflect individual student learning styles and interests.

3 they can show dimensions of student creativity and originality not always evident in more traditional kinds of assessment, such as quizzes and paper-pencil tests.

4 they can demonstrate student grasp or understanding of academic content or knowledge in new and different ways.

5 they can improve student attitudes toward learning because of their hands-on approach and emphasis on action.

6 they can make the classroom come alive as students interact collaboratively with one another sharing ideas, resources, and know-how during activity periods.

7 they lend themselves to subject matter integration more easily than other forms of evaluation.

8 they require more flexible time frames for completion, which in turn allows for better differentiation of instruction between and among students.

9 they represent more concrete expressions of what has been learned in the eyes of the students who do not always see evidence of knowledge demonstrated in test-taking situations.

10 they encourage mutual goal setting and planning between both student and teacher.

Things to Know About
Rubrics and Checklists

1 A checklist is used to identify the critical attributes of specific end products and most often has a simple "yes" or "no" box to check that follows each identified attribute. Most checklists focus on these main assessment categories:

. . . Organization and preparation

. . . Content

. . . Mechanics

2 A rubric is a generic scoring tool used to evaluate a student's performance in a given outcome area. Rubrics consist of a fixed measurement scale and a list of criteria that describe the characteristics of products or performances for each score point. Criteria are the guidelines, rules, or principles by which student responses, products, or performances are evaluated.

3 Three tips for scoring rubrics are:

. . . When reading a response or examining a product, refer to the rubric frequently to keep the criteria in mind.

. . . Remember that a specific level such as a "2" includes work that is an exact "2" or a "plus 2" or a "minus 2," and a plus or minus could be helpful in this process.

. . . Focus only on the criteria specified in the rubric, and not on other elements.

4 Some characteristics of effective rubrics are:

. . . They reflect the most significant elements related to the assigned task.

. . . They help to be more accurate and consistent when pinpointing competence levels.

. . . They help teachers grade student work more accurately and fairly.

. . . They encourage student self-evaluation as part of the process.

. . . They provide more information than a checklist of skills or attributes.

5 Some preliminary guidelines to consider before constructing quality rubrics are:

. . . Define quality performance in a given subject or content area.

. . . Determine what distinguishes quality work from mediocre or unacceptable work.

. . . Collect samples of rubrics from various disciplines to examine and critique.

. . . Collect samples of student work that reflect varied degrees of competence.

. . . Generate a master list of potential criteria (descriptors) for several degrees of proficiency in student work.

The Definitive Middle School Guide, Revised Edition
Copyright © 2014 World Book, Inc./Incentive Publications, Chicago, IL

Steps to Follow in Creating and Using Rubrics with Students

1 Determine the overall objectives and proficiencies expected of students at completion of task.

2 Decide on specific criteria to be demonstrated by students.

3 Create a rubric with four to six degrees of proficiency of each criterion and express in language common to students.

4 Weight each criterion to determine percentage or number of points each criterion is worth.

5 Distribute and explain purpose and contents of rubric to students.

6 Require students to set goals for themselves and determine what level of proficiency they are most comfortable with at this point in time.

7 After assigned task is completed, ask students to self-evaluate using the rubric sheet.

8 After task is completed, teacher evaluates the student using the rubric sheet and discusses any discrepancies between the two sets of results.

9 Instruct students to revise work that does not meet minimum standards.

10 Encourage students to collaboratively develop rubrics with criteria for their future projects as they gain experience in their use and purpose.

11 Experiment with three types of scales when constructing rubrics with the students. Consider these options:

. . . Numerical Scale *Example*:	1	2	3	4
. . . Verbal Scale *Example*:	Not Yet	Needs Improvement	Making Progress	Proficient
. . . Numerical or Verbal Scale *Example*:	1 Whoops!	2 Not Good	3 OK	4 Cool!

Advantages for Using Rubrics in the Classroom

1 They are easy to use and explain.

2 They focus, streamline, and standardize assessment planning.

3 They make scoring of complex work products more manageable.

4 They establish consistent criteria for student self-assessments.

5 They identify steps students must take to improve a performance.

6 They offer specific information to share with parents.

7 They can readily be coordinated to school or state standard expectations.

8 They provide criteria for writing report cards.

9 They make teacher expectations very clear.

10 They provide students with more informative feedback about their strengths and areas in need of improvement when compared with more traditional forms of assessment.

11 They support and do not inhibit learning from a student and parent perspective.

12 They support the combined development of skills, concepts, and good thinking.

13 They can determine how well students are meeting school and district performance standards.

14 They can inform and improve one's teaching.

15 They are both visual and graphic, which appeals to multiple learning styles.

16 They provide quality alternatives to other assessment measures and make excellent artifacts for portfolios.

The Definitive Middle School Guide, Revised Edition
Copyright © 2014 World Book, Inc./Incentive Publications, Chicago, IL

CONSTRUCT A RUBRIC

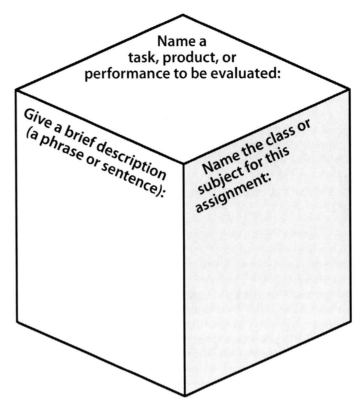

Name a task, product, or performance to be evaluated:

Give a brief description (a phrase or sentence):

Name the class or subject for this assignment:

Directions:
Use this form to plan and construct a rubric for an assessment task.

THE KEY ELEMENTS (OR COMPONENTS) OF THE TASK, PRODUCT, OR PERFORMANCE	CRITERIA BY WHICH THE SUCCESS OF THE ELEMENT WILL BE JUDGED

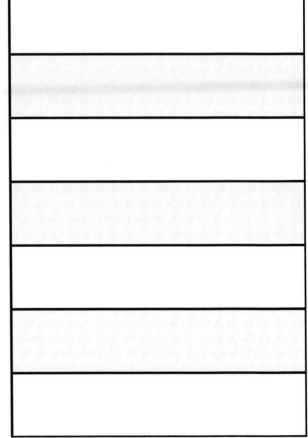

See the next page for the scoring component of the rubric.

Scoring Guide for Judging Success of Task

Directions:
Make copies of this page so that you have one copy for each of the elements you identified on the previous page. Referring to the criteria you outlined for evaluation, describe what the performance, product, or task will look like for each of these levels:

5 What constitutes a STRONG performance?

_____

_____

_____

4 What constitutes a SATISFACTORY performance?

_____

_____

_____

3 What constitutes a performance that NEEDS SOME IMPROVEMENT?

_____

_____

_____

2 What constitutes a performance that NEEDS CONSIDERABLE IMPROVEMENT?

_____

_____

_____

1 What constitutes a performance that is NOT ACCEPTABLE?

_____

_____

_____

Benefits of Self-Evaluation for Students

Self-evaluation

1 places the assessment burden (or privilege) on the individual.

2 answers students' two most basic questions: "How am I doing?" and "Where do I go from here?"

3 provides the basis for agreement between student and teacher on academic priorities.

4 improves effectiveness, as opposed to efficiency, in the schooling process.

5 encourages objective analysis of one's own attitudes and aptitudes.

6 expands students' metacognitive experiences because it asks students to think about what they were thinking and to evaluate their own mental processes.

7 relates progress to performance by answering such questions as "Are we doing the right things?" and "Are we doing the right things right?"

8 assists in preparation for added growth and responsibility.

9 promotes a feeling of personal accomplishment and self-esteem.

10 encourages individual goal setting.

11 acknowledges differences in learning styles.

12 gives student a sense of ownership of the learning process.

Teacher-STUDENT Conference Form

Student _____ Date _____

Teacher _____ Class _____

Purpose of conference _____

Record the important points that were discussed and decided at the conference. Make a copy for the teacher and a copy for the student.

WHAT DID WE DISCUSS?

What were the student's reactions?

What were the teacher's reactions?

What will the student do to follow up?

What will the teacher do to follow up?

When is the next conference? _____ What will happen there?

The Definitive Middle School Guide, Revised Edition
Copyright © 2014 World Book, Inc./Incentive Publications, Chicago, IL

STUDENT SELF-ASSESSMENT CHECKLIST

Student name _____ Date_____

Assigned task (Describe briefly)

_____

_____

_____

Directions:
Use this form to record the individual tasks you do on a daily basis to complete a particular assignment. Check off each task as you complete it. Make a comment about how well or how completely you did the task.

✓

When completed	Date completed	Tasks to Do	Comment

Skill Observation Form

Use this form as a guide for observing individual or small groups of students in a specific learning situation or behavior setting.

Make notes that give evaluative comments about the performance of the skill or process.

Learning situation or setting _____

Date _____ Subject or class _____

Student observed	Skill or process observed	Time period	Comment
1.			
2.			
3.			
4.			
5.			
6.			
7.			
8.			
9.			
10.			

PEER REVIEW

Directions:
Join with a peer partner who will review your work on a piece of writing or other product or performance. Ask your partner to use this form for responding to your work.

Title of work
_____

Type of work
_____

_____

_____

1. The part of this piece I like best is . . .

2. A part of this piece that is not clear and that is confusing to me is . .

3. A question I have about this piece is . . .

4. A suggestion I have for improving this piece is . . .

5. To me, the strength of this piece is . . .

Work created by_____   **Reviewed by** _____

RATE A GROUP PRESENTATION

Your name_____ Date_____

Other group members: _____

The presentation: (give a short description of what the group did)

_____

_____

1 Not Acceptable
2 Somewhat Acceptable
3 Acceptable
4 Mostly Acceptable
5 Completely Acceptable

Reflect on a product or performance that was presented by your group. On each of the ten items, give a score of **1, 2, 3, 4,** or **5** and a comment. Score yourself and your group separately.

Self-evaluation   Characteristics of Presentation   Group-evaluation

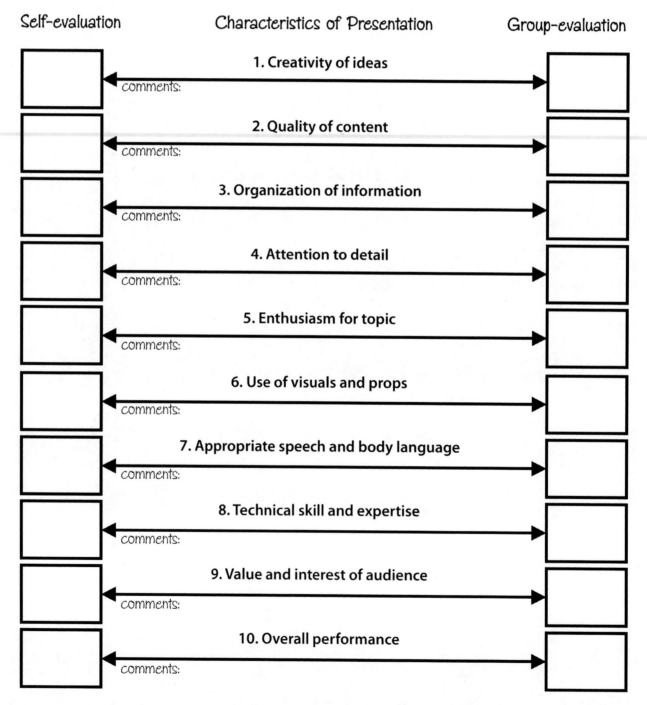

1. Creativity of ideas
comments:

2. Quality of content
comments:

3. Organization of information
comments:

4. Attention to detail
comments:

5. Enthusiasm for topic
comments:

6. Use of visuals and props
comments:

7. Appropriate speech and body language
comments:

8. Technical skill and expertise
comments:

9. Value and interest of audience
comments:

10. Overall performance
comments:

Reflective Questions
to Use with Students

1 What would you like to tell me about this piece of work?

2 How did you begin this task?

3 How did you plan this project?

4 What did you want to happen as a result of this idea?

5 What evidence do you have to support the notion that this work is the best you can do?

6 What would you do differently next time?

7 How would you describe this project to another student?

8 What questions or concerns about your work do you want to discuss today?

9 Was the work on this task satisfying to you and why or why not?

10 What is something you can do now that you could not do as well before?

11 What can I learn about you from this piece of work?

12 What is something you want people to notice about this project?

13 Do you feel that this product reflects your abilities?

14 What else might you want to say about . . . ?

15 How pleased are you about . . . ?

16 I am not clear what you mean by . . . Could you give me an example?

17 Why do you think . . . ?

18 How would you go about improving . . . ?

19 What advice would you give somebody who wanted to replicate your work?

20 What did you most enjoy (or least enjoy) about this assignment?

Statements to Ponder About Grading, Reporting, and Assessing Student Progress in Your School

Note: Teachers and administrators should spend adequate time reacting to each of these statements to determine where they stand on the issues of grading, reporting, and assessing student progress in today's typical middle school setting. Which ones can you agree on and what problems do you have with those that bring about disagreement?

1 Conventional practices in school grading, reporting, and assessing are compatible with the middle school concept.

2 Most teachers have common agreement on what a particular grade means in the school.

3 The grading system as it stands now encourages students to cheat on tests.

4 The grading system we have now serves students well.

5 The competitiveness among adults in today's society justifies the conventional competitive system we operate in assessing student progress in the school.

6 The grading approach in the school does much to support students' learning.

7 The grading system in the school is fair and developmentally appropriate for most students.

8 The importance placed on grades in most schools causes students to believe that getting good grades is a major aim of education.

9 Grades, for all their limitations, do provide the motivation needed for all students to apply themselves.

10 Grades provide teachers, parents, and students with the best means for measuring a student's success in school.

11 A teacher's subjective, but professional, judgment of a student's academic standing is probably more valid than the score on a standardized test.

12 Students should be graded on their citizenship and conduct as well as on their academics.

13 Numerical grades are more accurate than letter grades and therefore should be the basis for deciding letter grades.

14 Our report card format accurately portrays what we are doing and teaching in the classroom.

15 Every student, teacher, and parent attaches the same importance to a letter grade.

Adapted from: Lounsbury, J. H., & Schurr, S. (2003). *Assessing student progress: Moving from grades to portfolios.* Westerville, OH: National Middle School Association.

Ways to Make Tests and Grades More Student-Friendly

TESTS

1 Encourage students to submit possible test questions for the test as long as they can also provide an acceptable answer. Then include some of these student-generated questions on a legitimate teacher-made test.

2 Provide two or three optional, but quality, questions for students to answer on a test and allow them to substitute one of these for another on the test that is too difficult for them to complete.

3 Design a Jeopardy-style test that gives the answers and requires students to come up with an appropriate question or questions for each of these answers.

4 On occasion, allow students to use a 3" x 5" file card of personal notes for a test as long as the notes are in the student's own handwriting and as long as it is turned in with the test.

5 Prepare a Form A and a Form B for a given test and let students choose which form to use in the testing situation. One form might be an essay-type test, while the other is an objective-type test.

6 Allow students to get partial credit for a question marked wrong on the test if they can justify their thinking to the satisfaction of the teacher.

7 Encourage students to prepare a critique of a test that the teacher has required them to take. Discuss comments by the students as a group to encourage both better test design and test taking.

8 Design a special test-passing certificate for those who succeed in passing an important test.

9 Challenge students to answer this question as individuals or within a small group: "What makes a test worth taking?"

10 Organize a "test-taking" rally for your class before taking an important test or exam.

11 Invite students to write a humorous children's book on the subject of "How to Flunk a Test." Use this as a tool for reviewing key test-taking tips and tidbits.

GRADES

1 Consider the practice of allowing the student to redo an assignment and receive a grade that is the average of the two. Both copies of the assignment should be turned in or be part of the portfolio process.

2 Write selected assignment grades in pencil and tell the students that these penciled grades can be changed if improvement is seen by the teacher on related, future assignments.

3 In advance, decide what concepts and skills are most important to do. Weight these from most important to least important when it comes to assigning grades.

4 Each grading period, allow the students to throw out one low test grade, homework grade, and/or classroom assignment grade or redo one of these assigned tasks.

5 Challenge students to respond to this question as individuals or in a small group: "When is a grade not a fair grade to measure what you know and can do?" Give specific examples to support your position.

6 During report card time, design and distribute a Report Card for the Teacher that can be used to elicit input in the form of letter grades from students as they reflect back on the performance of the teacher during the grading period.

7 From time to time, encourage students to discuss such topics as:

   a) How should grades be determined on a given assignment or on a given report card?

   b) Are there some things about a student's progress that are not easy to grade and measure? If so, what are they?

   c) What would happen if all grades were eliminated from a school for three years?

   d) What things have you learned in class this year, and what evidence besides grades do you have that such learning took place?

8 Establish a procedure for students to safely question grades and test practices without fear of retribution.

9 Minimize the assigning of grades to practice tasks in class or as part of homework. Students should have considerable time to practice new skills before they are graded on mastery of them.

The Definitive Middle School Guide, Revised Edition
Copyright © 2014 World Book, Inc./Incentive Publications, Chicago, IL

Questions Students Need to Have Answered Before a Test

1 Is this going to be a quiz, test, or exam?

2 What type of quiz, test, or exam will it be? (Take-home, oral, collaborative, individual, or open-book?)

3 What kind of questions will it have? (Multiple-choice, essay, fill-in-the-blank, true-false, or short answer?)

4 How much time will I be given to complete the quiz, test, or exam?

5 How long will it be? How many questions will it have?

6 What information will be covered? (Notes, textbook, lecture, outside readings, or discussions?)

7 Do the answers have to be written in complete sentences, and will spelling count?

8 Can I hand in the test as soon as I finish?

9 How can I best review for the quiz, test, or exam?

10 How will the test be graded or scored?

11 How important is this test to my overall grade?

The Definitive Middle School Guide, Revised Edition
Copyright © 2014 World Book, Inc./Incentive Publications, Chicago, IL

Ways Students Can Use
Test Time Wisely

1 Skim through the entire test before you begin writing the answers.

2 Budget your time by setting time limits for each section of the test.

3 Complete all questions for which you know the answers first. Then go back and work on those questions you are not as certain about.

4 Read through each set of directions twice.

5 Underline or circle key words and phrases in each set of directions on the test.

6 Use intelligent guessing strategies for those questions you do not know. Try not to leave any questions unanswered, unless there are penalties for making a "best guess."

7 Never go back and change an answer unless you are absolutely sure you made a mistake.

8 Allow a few minutes at the end of the test to go back and review all questions and answers.

9 Be sure your name is on each page of the test.

10 Do not worry about what other students are doing on the test or how they are pacing their time.

11 If you had to transpose answers from one place to another on the test or answer sheet, double-check to make sure you were not careless in doing so.

The Definitive Middle School Guide, Revised Edition
Copyright © 2014 World Book, Inc./Incentive Publications, Chicago, IL

Ways to Prepare Middle Level Students for Taking Essay Tests

1 Define the concept of "essay test" for students and discuss how it differs from other types of test questions and formats.

2 Give examples of various question types including multiple-choice, matching, short-answer, true-or-false, and essay questions. Examine the strategies used by students when answering each type of question.

3 Point out the benefits and challenges of taking essay tests over other types of more traditional tests.

4 Review the process for taking an essay test with students, emphasizing what constitutes good writing for essay questions.

5 Provide students with multiple examples of essay questions from past years, along with student responses that were both satisfactory and unsatisfactory as models for what to do and what not to do.

6 Encourage students to develop their own essay-type questions on a given topic and then write possible responses to their own student-generated efforts. Critique student responses and have them rewrite their question accordingly.

7 Show students how essay questions are related to the required student performance standards for the language arts or English curriculum in the school and for the standards of the particular subject you teach.

8 As a group, make a list of "do's and don'ts" for writing quality responses to essay questions. Impress upon students how correct grammar principles, spelling, and readable handwriting can influence the grade given to essay question responses.

9 Consider giving extra points or extra credit to students who voluntarily elect to rewrite unacceptable or inadequate responses to essay questions on a given test or exam.

10 Begin the process of administering essay tests to students on either open-book tests or take-home tests when students have more time and some study aids to help with the writing of responses.

11 Provide students with copies of the Essay Direction Words charts on pages 354–355 of this book to use as helpful tools during essay test situations.

Essay Direction Words

If you are asked to:	You should do this:	Examples:
1. Analyze	Break down or separate a problem or situation into separate factors or relationships. Draw a conclusion, make a judgment, or make clear the relationship you see based on your breakdown.	Analyze the main story line in Chapter 2 and tell how it sets the stage for Chapter 3.
2. Categorize	Place items under headings already labeled by your teacher.	Categorize the items on the left under the proper headings on the right.
3. Classify	Place items in related groups; then name or title each group.	Listed below are 20 items. Classify them into 4 main groups.
4. Compare & 5. Contrast	Tell how things are alike; use concrete examples. Tell how things are different; use supporting concrete examples.	Compare and contrast the American government system with that of the German government.
6. Criticize	Make a judgment of a work of art or literature and support your judgment.	What do you think about the end of Shakespeare's tragedy, Romeo and Juliet? Explain your answer.
7. Deduce	Derive a conclusion by reasoning.	Deduce the logic problem to arrive at one of the conclusions listed below.
8. Defend	Give enough details to prove the statement.	Defend the statement "innocent until proven guilty."
9. Define	Give the meaning.	Define the word *plankton*.
10. Describe	Give an account in words; trace the outline or present a picture.	Describe Grand Coulee Dam.
11. Diagram	Use pictures, graphs, charts, mind maps, and flowcharts to show relationships of details to main ideas.	Diagram the departments of the federal government.
12. Discuss	Consider the various points of view by presenting all sides of the issue.	Discuss the use of chemotherapy in the treatment of cancer.
13. Distinguish	Tell how this is different from others similar to it.	Distinguish the three types of mold we have studied in class.
14. Enumerate	List all possible items.	Enumerate the presidents of the United States since Abraham Lincoln.
15. Evaluate	Make a judgment based on the evidence and support it; present the good and bad points.	Evaluate the use of pesticides to keep farmers from losing crops.

The Definitive Middle School Guide, Revised Edition
Copyright © 2014 World Book, Inc./Incentive Publications, Chicago, IL

If you are asked to	You should do this:	Examples:
16. Explain	Make clear and plain; give the reason or cause.	Explain how a natural disaster can help humans.
17. Illustrate	Give examples, pictures, charts, diagrams, or concrete examples to clarify your answer.	Illustrate the use of a drawbridge.
18. Interpret	Express your thinking by giving the meaning as you see it.	Interpret the line "Water, water everywhere and not a drop to drink."
19. Justify	Give some evidence by supporting your statement with facts.	Justify the decision to drop an atomic bomb on Nagasaki, Japan.
20. Outline	Use a specific and shortened form to organize main ideas supporting details and examples.	Outline the leading causes of World War II.
21. Paraphrase	Put in your own words.	Paraphrase the first paragraph of the Gettysburg Address.
22. Predict	Present solutions that could happen if certain variables were present.	Predict the ending of the short story written below . . .
23. Prove	Provide factual evidence to back up the truth of a statement.	Prove that the whaling industry has caused the near-extinction of certain varieties of whales.
24. Relate	Show the relationship among concepts.	Relate humans' survival instincts to those of animals.
25. Review	Examine the information critically. Analyze and comment on the important statements.	Review the effects of television advertisements on the public.
26. State	Establish by specifying. Write what you believe and back it with evidence.	State your beliefs in the democratic system of government.
27. Summarize	Condense the main points in the fewest words possible.	Summarize early man's methods of self-defense.
28. Synthesize	Combine parts or pieces of an idea, situation, or event.	Synthesize the events leading to the Civil War.
29. Trace	Describe in steps the progression of something.	Trace the importance of the prairie schooner to the opening of the West.
30. Verify	Confirm or establish the truth or accuracy of point of view with supporting examples, evidence, and facts.	Verify the reasons for the writing of the Declaration of Independence.

Informal Methods of Assessing Student Understanding of Material Covered During Instruction

1 THE IN BASKET

Ask each student to write at least one good question on an index card about a key topic or set of concepts previously taught in class. Place each of these cards in a box or envelope and randomly select one card at a time to read aloud to the class. Students volunteer to respond to the questions presented and earn "points" for each correct answer. Students may gain additional points for embellishing or adding to someone else's response as well. Several of these student-generated questions could be used on a test to be given at a later date.

2 GROUP PROFILE

Distribute one index card to each student and have each record a number from 1 to 10 that best describes how well he or she understands ideas recently taught during a lecture, discussion, textbook reading assignment, video, homework task, etc. Provide students with at least three benchmarks on the rating scale to use in making their decisions. For example, one continuum might look like this:

1   2   3   4   5   6   7   8   9   10

1 = I don't understand much of anything I read or heard.   5 = I understand about half of the ideas presented.   10 = I understand the material well enough to take a test on it or to teach it to someone else.

Collect the file cards (no names on them, please) and record all responses on the board, a transparency, or a large sheet of chart paper. Use this to determine the percentage of the class that has knowledge of the material that was assigned or taught.

3 SMALL-GROUP CONSENSUS REPORT

Divide students into small groups of three or four. Instruct them to reach consensus on the five most important facts they have learned and should remember from the day's lecture, discussion, or assigned reading. Have each group write responses on a large piece of newsprint and post around the room for all to see. Ask each group's recorder to share his or her small group's responses and justify its choice of five facts.

Look for similar responses from each group and reach a large-group consensus on the most important information recorded on the charts. Have students copy these in their notebooks to study for a test at a later date.

4 PICTURE CARDS

Provide each student or small group of students with a duplicate set of picture-symbol cards that you have prepared in advance. Make picture-symbol cards by drawing, pasting, printing, or photocopying a series of individual pictures or symbols on index cards or sections of card stock. Possible pictures or symbols for this activity might include a heart, eagle, dollar sign, hourglass, flag, globe, light bulb, bell, star, firecracker, etc.

Have students select one or more picture-symbol cards from the set and use them as springboards or catalysts for use in expressing feelings or emotions in any given area. This works well in getting students to use analogies when making informal judgments about people, places, or things. For example, one might instruct the students to select a picture-symbol card from the set that represents their feelings about a recent court decision, about an editorial from the newspaper, about a historical event from the textbook, or about an incident from a novel.

The Definitive Middle School Guide, Revised Edition
Copyright © 2014 World Book, Inc./Incentive Publications, Chicago, IL

5 STUDENT PANEL

Divide students into small groups and have them generate a list of tasks in school that they find difficult to do and a list of tasks they find easy to do. Have them graph the results of their brainstorming. Share graphs with the entire class. Next, choose a task with which many students have difficulty. Form a panel of students from the class who felt the task was easy for them and use this group to share concrete ideas about how they mastered this task. Allow time for the class to ask questions of this "panel of experts."

6 CONVINCE THE PANEL OF EXPERTS

Each student is instructed to prepare for class one well-written summary paragraph stating his or her position or collection of facts on a key concept, issue, idea, problem, or situation related to a given unit of study. Each person reads or shares the paragraph with a panel of "student experts" (three selected class members).

The panel "rates" the information on prepared flashcards (1–10, with 10 being highest). The teacher tabulates each total and announces the "best performances" at the end of the time period.

This activity should be followed with a large-group discussion using such questions as:

a) How many students gained at least one new idea or perspective today?

b) Did this process spark any additional ideas in your minds?

c) What criteria were used by the "panel of experts" to judge the summary paragraphs?

d) How could we help each other on our presentations so that all would receive 10s?

7 CAKEWALK

Prior to this activity, write ten important questions about a topic being studied in the classroom. Write these questions on a blackboard, transparency, or large sheet of chart paper so they are visible to everyone in the room.

Students then form two concentric circles in which each person of the outer circle faces another person of the inner circle to form pairs.

Instruct the students in each group to move counter to one another while background music is being played. When the music stops, the students also stop moving, still facing one another. They then have two minutes to discuss the answer to the first question on the board, overhead, or chart paper.

When the music starts again, the students move again until the music stops and they are facing a new partner. This time they are to discuss the answer to the second question given. The process is repeated until all ten questions have been addressed. This makes an excellent review activity at the end of a unit of study.

8 EQUATION QUIZ

The teacher prepares a series of equations that represent a variety of important concepts being studied as part of an instructional unit. Students are given the equations and asked to use their notes, textbooks, or worksheets to figure them out. If time permits, students should also be given the opportunity to create their own equations representing information that they think is important. Examples of equations for several content areas are given below.

Math Examples

2,000 = P. in a T.	(2,000 = Pounds in a Ton)
90 = D. in an R. T.	(90 = Degrees in a Right Triangle)
23 Y. – 3 Y. = 2 D.	(23 Years minus 3 Years = 2 Decades)
32 = D. F. at which W. F.	(32 = Degrees Fahrenheit at which Water Freezes)

Social Studies Examples

T. = L. S. State	(Texas = Lone Star State)
7 = W. of the A. W.	(7 = Wonders of the Ancient World)
M. + M. + N.H. + V. + C. + R.I. = N.E.	(Maine + Massachusetts+ New Hampshire + Vermont + Connecticut + Rhode Island = New England)
S. + H. of R. = U.S. C.	(Senate + House of Representatives = United States Congress)

9 RESPONSE CARDS

Provide each student with two feedback cards of different colors. On one card, the word TRUE is printed in large letters; on the other card is the word FALSE, also in large letters. Inform the class that the cards will be used to show individual responses to questions that the teacher asks about material they have studied.

Proceed to make a series of statements that can be answered TRUE or FALSE. Students should hold up the card that shows their best response to the question or statement.

Variations of this activity include using other card options, such as sets of cards with answers A, B, C, and D for response to multiple choice questions, or sets of blank cards on which students can write short answers.

10 ALPHABET REPORTS
Students are given a sheet of paper with the 26 letters of the alphabet printed vertically down one side. They are directed to select 26 related concepts, terms, events, or persons that show what they have learned about a given topic. Each item should begin with a different letter of the alphabet, and students should be encouraged to think of more than one word for each letter as they record their ideas. Next, students should try creating meaningful phrases with each cluster of words recorded next to the appropriate letter of the alphabet, so that the reading of the report flows like a free-verse poem.

11 CONCEPT PUZZLES
Students are instructed to select the most important terms, concepts, or ideas associated with a textbook chapter or teaching unit. They are to develop brief definitions or identifying phrases for each as well. Next, students are told to construct a crossword puzzle that incorporates each of the items and to fill in the appropriate numbers, crossword-puzzle style. These can be exchanged among peers to "test" one another on their understanding of information taught.

12 BINGO BONANZA
Students are directed to generate a set of 25 questions and answers that are important to their understanding of a completed textbook chapter, lecture, assigned reading, or instructional unit. The questions should be organized or sorted into five major categories, and students should create some identity for each category name using the letters B, I, N, G, and O. Next, BINGO cards should be designed according to one of these formats:

a) Generic cards (like traditional BINGO cards) using a 5" by 5" matrix with numbers in the 24 designated cells and the FREE spot designated in the center. In this case, the teacher reads a question with an associated number, and if the student has the number and can correctly write in the answer, he or she fills in the appropriate cell.

b) Specific cards with the cells previously filled in using 24 of the key concepts, ideas, terms, etc. If the student believes that one of the answers on the card fits the question being read, he or she writes the question number next to it. As in BINGO, the first student to complete the answers in a row horizontally, vertically, or diagonally calls out BINGO and wins the game!

Assessment Tips, Tools, and Test Formats

1 Use oral and open-book tests. Have students demonstrate reference and research-location skills while taking an open-book test and then share their knowledge through an oral quiz. Oral exercises are more accurate and less threatening than paper-and-pencil tests.

2 Encourage students to write and submit test questions for an upcoming exam. This serves as an excellent review technique.

3 Show students how to solve problems through a wide variety of techniques, including:

— Looking for patterns
— Constructing a table
— Making an organized list
— Guessing and then checking
— Drawing a picture or diagram
— Using objects or acting out the scenario
— Working backwards from end to beginning
— Changing one's point of view or perspective
— Writing an equation in words, symbols, or numbers
— Simplifying the problem by breaking it into components

4 Offer teacher-made percent tickets worth from 1% to 5%. A percent ticket is a document worth percentage points for tests, essays, or reports. Students earn tickets for good behavior or good work and then can turn them in to raise a grade on an assignment.

5 Create a legitimate "test-type" paper-and-pencil question sheet to serve as a review for an upcoming classroom quiz or test. After each question, write down the page number in the textbook where its answer can be found if the student does not know it.

6 Write a series of open-ended test items that require the student to apply critical-thinking skills. For example, select a topic and instruct the students to do one of the following analytical tasks:
Compare and contrast;
Give pros and cons;
State advantages and disadvantages;
Think of causes and effects.

7 Require students to maintain scrapbooks of all their work assignments for a given unit of study. Students glue their worksheets, homework, quizzes, reports, etc., in the scrapbook as they are assigned or graded and then use these items for review at the end of the unit.

8 When reviewing for a test, provide the students with a series of topics related to a unit of study. Students, one at a time, draw a topic out of a hat and give a one-minute speech on all they know about it. Distribute the topic slips of paper at the beginning of class so that students have some time to think about and plan their impromptu speeches.

9 Divide students into pairs and give each pair of students three chairs for their group, placed side by side. All sets of chairs are placed in a circle around the room. The first set of chairs (Group 1 chairs) is the only cluster that has someone sitting in all three chairs. The teacher prepares a set of test review questions and asks the first question to Group 1. The first student to blurt out the answer moves to the empty chair in Group 2. The teacher then asks a question of Group 2, and the first person to blurt out the correct answer moves to the empty chair in Group 3. The process is continued, and the first person to get back to their original group chair wins the game.

The Definitive Middle School Guide, Revised Edition
Copyright © 2014 World Book, Inc./Incentive Publications, Chicago, IL

10 On every test, allow students to argue for any two questions they missed or answered incorrectly. In order to win the argument, the student must write a detailed explanation supporting the answer from her or his perspective. All or partial credit can be given to the question if the argument is logical and convincing to the teacher. This strategy is helpful because students perceive it as fair, as an opportunity to control or raise a grade, and as an invitation to go back and review the material.

11 Create a Test Substitute Form where a student can explain why he or she is not able to take a test and what he or she will do in place of the test. Once or twice a year, excuse a student from a quiz or test after receiving and reviewing the Test Substitute Form.

12 Give students a prorated test of about twenty questions that requires all students to answer the first ten questions, then gives the option of answering additional questions from the remaining ten. Inform students that they can stop after ten, answer one or more of the optional questions (in any sequence), or complete all twenty.

13 Design a simple quiz on a topic being studied that asks the student to

   a) write a fact about the topic;
   b) state an opinion about the topic;
   c) give an example related to the topic;
   d) draw a conclusion about the topic;
   e) make an inference about the topic;
   f) issue a judgment on the topic; or
   g) compose a summary statement on the topic.

14 Design a single test question on a topic of study that requires the student to record only his or her learnings: "What am I taking away from this study (or unit, or lesson)?"

15 Prepare a set of review questions and use them to simulate the tic-tac-toe game show format of Hollywood Squares. Arrange students so that three sit on the floor, three sit on chairs, and three stand behind the chairs. All nine "celebrities" are given cards with a big X printed on one side and a big O printed on the other side. Two volunteers serve as contestants (designated as either an X or an O) and pick members of the celebrity squares to answer the game's questions read by the teacher. Celebrities answer the questions, and contestants either AGREE or DISAGREE with their responses. Contestants try to form a tic-tac-toe through this process.

16 Prepare a set of 5" x 8" index cards so that one half of the card has a question and the other half of the card has the correct answer or answers. Cut the cards in half and randomly distribute them to members of a class. Ask students to mingle around the room and match up the correct question with its corresponding answer(s).

17 Prepare a set of statements about a topic under study (some of which are facts, some of which are opinions, some of which are true, and some of which are false). Write these on large cards and have students determine the answers through discussion and debate.

18 Provide each student in the class with an index card and have them write out a question (to which they know the answer) on the topic being reviewed for a test. Collect cards and then randomly redistribute them to students. Ask each student to read the question and attempt to answer it as best they can. Require the question's author to certify whether the question has been answered adequately or not.

Authentic Assessment Tools to Evaluate Classroom Assessment

Overview

TOOL 1: Questions on Authentic Assessment for Teacher Focus Group

This tool is designed to obtain teacher input within a given school on personal perspectives and experiences with both traditional high-stakes testing methods and with authentic assessment measures. It requires an outside observer who is trained in both traditional and authentic assessment practices at the middle grade level, as well as someone trained in conducting focus group sessions. Building administrators, team leaders, district level staff, and outside consultants may be used successfully for this purpose. Focus groups of teachers should be limited to no more than five or six in number and are often most effective when teachers represent varied subject areas. It then becomes more of a learning situation for participants as they hear their colleagues discuss student assessment measures across multiple disciplines. Each person conducting the focus group should plan to record the session, which should be limited to no more than an hour in length. It is also important that the focus group facilitator ensure that each teacher in the group shares personal experiences and that no single individual monopolizes the discussion. Input from the focus group questions should be compiled by the observer and shared openly with the teachers involved.

TOOL 2: Student Self-Checklist of Preferred Assessment Tools and Techniques

The student uses this form to review and reflect on the kinds of assessment options offered in the classroom and the types preferred. As students think about the assessment options, they consider why they prefer certain approaches or tools, and also consider other types they may be willing to try.

TOOL 3: Teacher Self-Checklist of Preferred Assessment Tools and Techniques

The focus of this tool is an individual self-checklist, which can be used by the teacher to review her or his assessment choices. After checking the options that are frequently used, the teacher can make comments about why those are chosen and think about using other options. The teacher can then set some goals for varying assessment options in the classroom.

TOOL 4: Classroom Interview Form

This interview form is to be used by an outside observer with the individual teacher after the teacher has completed the Teacher Self-Checklist of Preferred Assessment Tools and Techniques. Responses to the questions or tasks may either be recorded on a separate piece of paper or recorded. The purpose of the interview process is to encourage both professional dialogue about current assessment practices that are taking place in this classroom, as well as self-reflection by the teacher on academic reasons for the choices.

The Definitive Middle School Guide, Revised Edition
Copyright © 2014 World Book, Inc./Incentive Publications, Chicago, IL

Questions on Authentic Assessment for Teacher Focus Group

Name of person conducting focus group

_____

Role_____

Date_____ Time _____ Place _____

Directions:
Plan to record this focus group session so that responses can be reviewed and edited at a later date. Limit the discussion to these questions as much as possible, and encourage equitable input from all teacher participants.

1. How has high-stakes testing influenced both your teaching and your evaluating of students in the classroom?

2. How do you incorporate authentic assessment measures in your classroom?

3. Under what circumstances are teacher-generated tests or authentic assessment measures more effective than standardized or state-mandated tests when assessing what students know and can do? Less effective?

4. What are some advantages of product, performance, and portfolio assessment measures over traditional testing methods? Some disadvantages?

5. How do you feel about the use of rubrics as an integral part of student assessment?

6. What are the benefits of student self-assessment measures as an ongoing and integral part of a structured assessment program?

7. What are some informal methods of assessing student understanding of material covered during instruction?

8. How have technology tools, techniques, and programs affected the overall assessment program in your classroom and school?

9. What can teachers do to make sure that assessment results are reported and interpreted in ways that are meaningful and useful to both parents and students?

10. How can current assessment options be better used to help students develop a positive self-image and capitalize on individual learning styles, strengths, and weaknesses?

11. What steps can teachers take to become more proficient in selecting, administering, recording, and making use of multiple assessment tools and results?

STUDENT SELF-CHECKLIST OF PREFERRED ASSESSMENT TOOLS AND TECHNIQUES

Name _____

Date _____ Class _____

Directions:
1. Write a **P** (for preferred) next to those types of assessment tools and techniques that work best for you to show what you know and can do in a given subject or classroom setting. Write in other items as needed.
2. For each **P**, write a comment telling why you chose that item.
3. Then, write a **T** (for try) next to any tool or technique you would be willing to try.

TOOL OR TECHNIQUE	P OR T	COMMENTS:
Multiple-choice test questions		
True-false test questions		
Matching test questions		
Short-answer test questions		
Essay test questions		
Teacher observations		
Daily journal recordings or entries		
Anecdotal teacher comments		
Peer observations and assessments		
Student projects and products		
Student performance tasks		
Self-assessment checklists or reflections		
Teacher-student conferences		
Oral quizzes		
Written reports		
Computer-generated presentations		
Demonstrations or exhibits		
Discussions, panels, or debates		
Illustrations, diagrams, or other graphics		
Oral presentations		
Multimedia presentations		
Dramatizations		
Three-dimensional constructions		
Investigations or experiments		
Games and simulations		
Case studies or role-plays		
Portfolios		
Other:		

Teacher Self-Checklist of Preferred Assessment Tools and Techniques

Name _____

Date _____   Class _____

Directions:
1. Write a **P** (for preferred) next to those types of assessment tools and techniques that work best for you to find out what your students know and can do in your classsroom. Write in other items as needed.
2. For each **P**, write a comment telling why you chose that item.
3. Then, write a **T** (for try) next to any tool or technique you would be willing to try.

Tool or Technique	P or T	Comments:
Multiple-choice test questions		
True-false test questions		
Matching test questions		
Short-answer test questions		
Essay test questions		
Teacher observations		
Daily journal recordings or entries		
Anecdotal teacher comments		
Peer observations and assessments		
Student projects and products		
Student performance tasks		
Self-assessment checklists or reflections		
Teacher-student conferences		
Oral quizzes		
Written reports		
Computer-generated presentations		
Demonstrations or exhibits		
Discussions, panels, or debates		
Illustrations, diagrams, or other graphics		
Oral presentations		
Multimedia presentations		
Dramatizations		
Three-dimensional constructions		
Investigations or experiments		
Games and simulations		
Case studies or role-plays		
Portfolios		
Other:		

Classroom Interview Form

Teacher_____

Date & time of interview_____

Interviewer_____

Role or Position_____

Directions:
This interview form is to be used by an outside observer in discussion with the teacher after the Teacher Self-Checklist has been completed. Responses may be written on a separate piece of paper.

1. How do you generally determine your assessment format for each lesson you teach?

2. How do you generally match content standards with assessment options on any given lesson?

3. Do you prefer traditional assessment measures (paper-pencil quizzes, tests, or exams) to more authentic assessment measures (product, performance, or portfolio outcomes)? Why or why not?

4. How often do you require students to produce a product or project or participate in a performance as a major assessment tool or technique? How successful are the results?

5. How often do you use rubrics as part of your assessment process, and for what purposes do you use them?

6. How do you go about developing or creating your typical teacher-made tests?

7. How often do you use pre-tests and post-tests in your classroom to assess what students know and can do before and after instruction takes place?

8. How often do you involve students in self-assessment efforts?

9. How do you prepare your students for standardized or high-stakes testing required by the district or the state?

10. How do you help students develop study skills in the classroom?

11. How would you describe an ideal student assessment activity from your perspective?

The Definitive Middle School Guide, Revised Edition
Copyright © 2014 World Book, Inc./Incentive Publications, Chicago, IL

Findings from the Published Literature Related to Student Assessment and Evaluation

FINDING #1:

Sue C. Thompson and Dan French conclude:

Meaningful learning experiences occur through the complexity of integrated thematic instruction that focuses on the questions, issues, and concerns of early adolescents in relation to their world. Consequently, assessing these kinds of learning experiences should entail a wide range of authentic assessments, including projects where students are actually demonstrating what they know and can do through collaborating, exploring, making, investigating, acting, and being fully engaged in the learning experience. Such projects need not be subject specific but may use skills and knowledge from several content areas.

Source: Erb, T. O. (Ed.). (2005). *This we believe in action: Implementing successful middle level schools.* Westerville, OH: National Middle School Association.

FINDING #2:

Grant P. Wiggins emphasizes:

I would prefer that school systems develop an Assessment Bill of Rights to project the inherently vulnerable student from the harms that testing easily leads to. It would be supported by explicit audit or oversight policies to ensure that the rights were protected. Here is my rough draft of such a set of rights:

All students are entitled to the following:

1) Worthwhile (engaging, educative, and authentic) intellectual problems that are validated against worthy "real-world" intellectual problems, roles, and situations;

2) Clear, apt, published, and consistently applied teacher criteria in grading work and published models of excellent work that exemplifies standards;

3) Minimal secrecy in testing and grading;

4) Ample opportunities to produce work that they can be proud of (this means ample opportunity in the curriculum and instruction to monitor, self-assess, and self-correct their work);

5) Assessment, not just tests; multiple and varied opportunities to display and document their achievement, and options in tests that allow them to play to their strengths;

6) The freedom, climate, and oversight policies necessary to question grades and test practices without fear of retribution;

7) Forms of testing that allow timely opportunities for students to explain or justify answers marked as wrong but that they believe to be apt or right;

8) Genuine feedback: usable information on their strengths and weaknesses and an accurate assessment of their long-term progress toward a set of exit-level standards framed in terms of essential tasks; and

9) Scoring or grading policies that provide incentives and opportunities for improving performance and seeing progress against exit-level and real-world standards.

Source: Wiggins, G. P. (1993). *Assessing student performance: Exploring the purpose and limits of testing.* San Francisco: Jossey-Bass Publishers.

FINDING #3:

Philip Schlechty writes:

Ten critical qualities of student work should be:

a) PRODUCT FOCUS: Work that engages students almost always focuses on a product or performance of significance to students.

b) CLEAR AND COMPELLING STANDARDS: Students prefer knowing exactly what is expected of them, and how those expectations relate to something they care about. Standards are only relevant when those to whom they apply care about them.

c) PROTECTION FROM ADVERSE CONSEQUENCES FOR INITIAL FAILURES: Students are more engaged when they can try tasks without fear of embarrassment, punishment, or implications that they are inadequate.

d) AFFIRMATION OF THE SIGNIFICANCE OF PERFORMANCE: Students are more highly motivated when their parents, teachers, fellow students, and "significant" others make it known that they think the student's work is important. Portfolio assessments can play a significant role in making student work "more visible."

e) AFFILIATION: Students are more likely to be engaged by work that permits, encourages, and supports opportunities for them to work interdependently with others.

f) NOVELTY AND VARIETY: Students are more likely to engage in the work asked of them if they are continually exposed to new and different ways of doing things. New forms of work and new products to produce are as important as new techniques.

g) CHOICE: When students have some degree of control over what they are doing, they are more likely to feel committed to doing it. Schools, however, must distinguish between giving students choices in what they do and letting them choose what they will learn.

h) AUTHENTICITY: When students are given tasks that are meaningless, contrived, or inconsequential, they are less likely to take them seriously and to be engaged by them. If the task carries real consequences, it is likely that engagement will increase.

i) ORGANIZATION OF KNOWLEDGE: Students are more likely to be engaged when information and knowledge are arranged in clear, accessible ways, and in ways that let students use the knowledge and information to address tasks that are important to them. Content should be organized so access to the material is clear and relatively easy, and the students' work has enough attractive qualities to keep them engaged.

j) CONTENT AND SUBSTANCE: Educators should commit themselves to inventing work that engages all students and helps them attain rich and profound knowledge.

Source: Sparks, D., & Schlechty, P. (1998). The educator examined. *Journal of Staff Development, 19*(3), 38-42.

FINDING #4:

John Lounsbury and Sandra Schurr stress:

Students in the middle grades fear the testing and evaluation process more than most adults realize. However, this condition is not really surprising given the unique needs and characteristics of the age group. After all, young adolescents, whose physical growth is often erratic, whose self-confidence and self-discipline leave much to be desired, whose conceptual and abstract thinking abilities are in a perpetual state of flux, and whose compulsion to socialize or seek peer approval causes extreme conflict are ones whose evaluations are not easy to prepare.

Source: Lounsbury, J. H., & Schurr, S. (2003). *Assessing student progress: Moving from grades to portfolios.* Westerville, OH: National Middle School Association.

Review and Reflect
on Student Assessment and Evaluation

Level 1: Remembering   Your Reflections

Task	My list:

List several possible product, performance, and assessment items that would be good artifacts for a student portfolio in your particular classroom and subject area.

Level 2: Understanding   Your Reflections

Task

Explain the major difference between traditional and authentic assessment measures as well as the advantages and disadvantages of each.

Differences:

Traditional Assessment

Advantages | Disadvantages

Authentic Assessment

Advantages | Disadvantages

Level 3: Applying   Your Reflections

Task

Choose a typical product or performance task that you might assign students in your classroom or subject area, and construct a rubric you could use for assessing its effectiveness. List a few of the criteria you used in the rubric.

Product or performance:

Criteria:

continued on page 370

continued

Review and Reflect
on Student Assessment and Evaluation

Level 4: Analyzing
Your Reflections

Task

Develop a portfolio of artifacts that show the unique characteristics, achievements, and opportunities representative of both your classroom and of you as a middle school teacher this year. List some of the things you will put into that portfolio.

List of portfolio artifacts:

Level 5: Evaluating
Your Reflections

Task

Which is easier for you to develop, assess, and grade for students in your class—a product requirement or a performance requirement? Give reasons for your answer.

Which is easier?

Why?

Level 6: Creating
Your Reflections

Task

Design a test-taking and study guide for students in your class. Make notes about some of the advice or tips you will include.

Sample tips, advice, contents:

The Definitive Middle School Guide, Revised Edition
Copyright © 2014 World Book, Inc./Incentive Publications, Chicago, IL

APPENDIX

Selected Bibliography

SCHOOL STRUCTURES AND CLIMATE

Arnold, J. F., & Stevenson, C. (1998). *Teachers' teaming handbook: A middle level planning guide.* Fort Worth, TX: Harcourt Brace College Publishers.

Beane, J. (1999). Middle schools under siege: Points of attack. *Middle School Journal, 30*(4), 3-9.

Breeden, T., & Egan, E. (1997). *Positive classroom management.* Nashville, TN: Incentive Publications.

Classroom Connections (Vol. 4, No. 1). (2001). Westerville, OH: National Middle School Association.

Connors, N. A. (2000). *If you don't feed the teachers, they eat the students!: A guide to success for administrators and teachers.* Nashville, TN: Incentive Publications. (Note: the 2nd ed. of this book was published by World Book, Inc./Incentive Publications in 2013.)

DuFour, R., & Eaker, R. E. (1998). *Professional learning communities at work: Best practices for enhancing student achievement.* Bloomington, IN: National Education Service.

Erb, T. O. (Ed.). (2005). *This we believe in action: Implementing successful middle level schools.* Westerville, OH: National Middle School Association.

French, D., Rothman, S., & Massachusetts. (1990). *Structuring schools for student success: A focus on ability grouping.* Quincy, MA: Massachusetts Dept. of Education.

Hackmann, D., & Valentine, J. (1998). Designing an effective middle level school. *Middle School Journal, 29*(5), 3-13.

Implementing the middle school concept: Middle school 101. (2000). Westerville, OH: National Middle School Association.

Jackson, A., Davis, G. A., Abeel, M., Bordonaro, A., & Carnegie Council on Adolescent Development. (2000). *Turning points 2000: Educating adolescents in the 21st century.* New York: Teachers College Press.

Lipka, R. P., & National Middle School Association. (1998). *The Eight-Year Study revisited: Lessons from the past for the present.* Columbus, OH: National Middle School Association.

Lounsbury, J. H. (2002). Understanding and appreciating the wonder years. Retrieved from http://web.archive.org/web/20020701045805/http://www.nmsa.org/moya/new2002 /pk_related_understanding.html.

National Middle School Association. (1995). *This we believe: Developmentally responsive middle level schools : A position paper of National Middle School Association.* Columbus, OH: National Middle School Association.

Schurr, S., Thomason, J. T., Thompson, M., & Lounsbury, J. H. (1995). *Teaching at the middle level: A professional's handbook.* Lexington, MA: D. C. Heath.

INTERDISCIPLINARY TEAMING AND BLOCK SCHEDULING

Arnold, J. F., & Stevenson, C. (1998). *Teachers' teaming handbook: A middle level planning guide.* Fort Worth, TX: Harcourt Brace College Publishers.

Arnold, J. Teams and curriculum. (1997). In Dickinson, T. S., & Erb, T. O. (Eds.), *We gain more than we give: Teaming in middle schools.* Columbus, OH: National Middle School Association.

Carr, C. (1992). *Teampower: Lessons from America's top companies on putting teampower to work.* Englewood Cliffs, NJ: Prentice Hall.

Epstein, J. L., Mac, I. D. J., & United States. (1990). *Education in the middle grades: Overview of national practices and trends.* Columbus, OH: National Middle School Association.

George, P. S. (1992). *The Middle-school - and beyond.* Alexandria, VA: Association for Supervision and Curriculum Development.

George, P. S., & Alexander, W. M. (1993). *The exemplary middle school* (2nd ed.). Fort Worth, TX: Harcourt Brace Jovanovich College Publishers. (Note: the 3rd ed. of this book was published by Thomson/Wadsworth in 2003.)

Hackmann, D., & Valentine, J. (1998). Designing an effective middle level school. *Middle School Journal*, *29*(5), 3-13.

Hackmann, D. G. (1995). Ten guidelines for implementing block scheduling. *Educational Leadership*, *53*(3), 24-27.

Harrington-Mackin, D. (1994). *The team building tool kit: Tips, tactics, and rules for effective workplace teams.* New York: American Management Association. (Note: the 2nd ed. of this book was published in 2007.)

Irvin, J. L. (1992). *Transforming middle level education: Perspectives and possibilities.* Boston: Allyn and Bacon.

Katzenbach, J. R., & Smith, D. K. (1994). *The wisdom of teams: Creating the high-performance organization.* New York, NY: HarperBusiness.

Lounsbury, J. H. (Ed.). (1992). *Connecting the curriculum through interdisciplinary instruction.* Columbus, OH: National Middle School Association.

Merenbloom, E. Y., & National Middle School Association. (1991). *The team process: A handbook for teachers* (3rd ed.). Columbus, OH: National Middle School Association.

NEA Special Committee on Time Resources. (1994). It's about time. In Dalheim, M. (Ed.), *Time Strategies.* West Haven, CT: NEA Professional Library.

Romano, L. G., & Georgiady, N. P. (1994). *Building an effective middle school.* Madison, WI: WCB Brown & Benchmark Publishers.

Rettig, M. D., & Cannizzaro, J. (1996). *Block scheduling.* Upper Saddle River, NJ: Prentice-Hall.

Schurr, S., & Lounsbury, J. (2001). *Revitalizing teaming to improve student learning.* Westerville, OH: National Middle School Association.

Thompson, R. (2008). *Get fit! The personal trainer for academic teams.* Nashville, TN: Incentive Publications.

CURRICULAR MODELS AND INSTRUCTIONAL METHODS

Anderson, L. W., & Krathwohl, D. R. (2001). *A taxonomy for learning, teaching, and assessing: A revision of Bloom's taxonomy of educational objectives.* New York: Longman.

Beane, J. A., (1993). *A middle school curriculum: From rhetoric to reality* (2nd ed.). Columbus, OH: National Middle School Association.

Breeden, T., & Mosley, J. (1992). *The cooperative learning companion.* Nashville, TN: Incentive Publications.

Brodhagen, B., & Gorud, S. (2005). Multiple learning and teaching approaches that respond to their diversity. In Erb, T. O. (Ed.), *This we believe in action: Implementing successful middle schools.* Westerville, OH: National Middle School Association.

Caldwell, B. J. (1999). Education for the public good: Strategic intentions for the 21st century. In Marsh, D. D. (Ed.), *Preparing our schools for the 21st century*. Alexandria, VA: Association for Supervision and Curriculum Development.

Clark, D. N. (2000). Developmentally responsive curriculum and standards-based reform: Implications for middle level principals. *NASSP Bulletin, 84*(615), 1-13.

De Bono, E. (1999). *Six thinking hats*. Boston: Back Bay Books.

Drapeau, P. (2004). *Differentiated instruction: Making it work*. New York: Scholastic/Teaching Resources.

Eberle, B. (1996). *Scamper on: Games for imagination development*. Waco, TX: Prufrock Press.

English, F. W. (1992). *Deciding what to teach and test: Developing, aligning, and auditing the curriculum*. Newbury Park, CA: Corwin Press. (Note: the 3rd ed. of this book was published in 2010.)

Fogarty, R., & Bellanca, J. Cognition in practice. (1995). In Fogarty, R. (Ed.), *Best practices for the learning-centered classroom*. Palatine, IL: IRI/Skylight Publishing.

Forte, I., & Schurr, S. (2008). *Curriculum & project planner: Integrating learning styles, thinking skills & authentic assessment* (Rev. ed.). Nashville, TN: Incentive Publications. (Note: the 2nd ed. of this book was published by World Book, Inc./Incentive Publications in 2013.)

Gardner, H. (1983). *Frames of mind: The theory of multiple intelligences.* New York: Basic Books.

Glatthorn, A. A. (1999). *Performance standards and authentic learning*. Larchmont, NY: Eye on Education.

Heacox, D. (2002). *Differentiating instruction in the regular classroom: How to reach and teach all learners, grades 3-12*. Minneapolis, MN: Free Spirit Publishing. (Note: an updated edition of this book was published in 2012.)

Hill, S. E., & Hill, T. (1990). *The collaborative classroom: A guide to co-operative learning*. Portsmouth, NH: Heinemann.

Johnson, D. W., & Johnson, R. T. (1999). *Learning together and alone: Cooperative, competitive, and individualistic learning* (5th ed.). Boston: Allyn and Bacon.

Parnell, D. (1995). *Why do I have to learn this? Teaching the way children learn best*. Waco, TX: CORD Communications.

Santa, C. M. (1988). *Content reading including study systems: Reading, writing and studying across the curriculum.* Dubuque, IA: Kendall/Hunt Pub. Co.

Silver, D. (2005). *Drumming to the beat of different marchers: Finding the rhythm for differentiated learning* (Rev. ed.). Nashville, TN: Incentive Publications. (Note: the 2nd ed. of this book was published by World Book, Inc./Incentive Publications in 2014.)

Spear, R. C. Appropriate grouping practices for middle level students. (1992). In Irvin, J. L. (1992), *Transforming middle level education: Perspectives and possibilities*. Boston: Allyn and Bacon.

Thompson, R., & VanderJagt, D. (2003). *Fire up! for learning: Active learning projects and activities to motivate and challenge students*. Moorabbin, VIC: Hawker Brownlow Education.

Tomlinson, C. A. (1999). *The differentiated classroom: Responding to the needs of all learners*. Alexandria, VA: Association for Supervision and Curriculum Development.

Tomlinson, C. A. (2001). The role of the teacher in a differentiated classroom. In *How to differentiate instruction in mixed-ability classrooms*. Alexandria, VA: Association for Supervision and Curriculum Development.

Urquhart, V., & McIver, M. (2005). *Teaching writing in the content areas.* Alexandria, VA: Association for Supervision and Curriculum Development.

Waterman, S. S. (2005). *Handbook on differentiated instruction for middle and high schools.* Larchmont, NY: Eye On Education.

Wiederhold, C. W., & Kagan, S. (1998). *Cooperative learning & higher-level thinking: The Q-Matrix.* San Clemente, CA: Kagan Cooperative Learning.

Williams, F. E. (1970). *Classroom ideas for encouraging thinking and feeling.* Buffalo, NY: D.O.K. Publishers.

Winebrenner, S. (2006). *Teaching kids with learning difficulties in the regular classroom* (Rev. and updated ed.). Minneapolis, MN: Free Spirit Publishing.

Wormeli, R. (2007). *Differentiation: From planning to practice, grades 6-12.* Portland, ME: Stenhouse Publishers.

CLASSROOM MANAGEMENT AND DISCIPLINE

Cushman, K., & What Kids Can Do (Organization). (2003). *Fires in the bathroom: Advice for teachers from high school students.* New York: New Press.

Erb, T. O. (Ed.). (2005). *This we believe in action: Implementing successful middle level schools.* Westerville, OH: National Middle School Association.

Gossen, D. C. (1996). *Restitution: Restructuring school discipline.* Chapel Hill, NC: New View Publications.

Marzano, R. J., Marzano, J. S., & Pickering, D. (2003). *Classroom management that works: Research-based strategies for every teacher.* Alexandria, VA: Association for Supervision and Curriculum Development.

Thompson, J. G. (1998). *Discipline survival kit for the secondary teacher.* West Nyack, NY: Center for Applied Research in Education.

ADVISORY, ADVOCACY, AND AFFECTIVE EDUCATION

Burkhart, R. M., & Kane, J. T. (2005). An adult advocate for every student. In Erb, T. O. (Ed.), *This we believe in action: Implementing successful middle level schools.* Westerville, OH: National Middle School Association.

Cole, C. G. (1992). *Nurturing a teacher advisory program.* Columbus, OH: National Middle School Association.

Cushman, K., & What Kids Can Do (Organization). (2003). *Fires in the bathroom: Advice for teachers from high school students.* New York: New Press.

Forte, I., & Schurr, S. (1991). *Advisory: Middle grades advisee/advisor program.* Nashville, TN: Incentive Publications.

Goldberg, M. F. (1998). *How to design an advisory system for a secondary school.* Alexandria, VA: Association for Supervision and Curriculum Development.

James, M., & Spradling, N. (2002). *From advisory to advocacy: Meeting every student's needs.* Westerville, OH: National Middle School Association.

Krathwohl, D. R., Bloom, B. S., and Masia, B. B. (1964). *Taxonomy of educational objectives. Handbook II: Affective domain.* New York: Longman.

Pitton, D. E. (2001). The school and the child and the child in school. *Middle School Journal, 33*(1), 14-20.

STUDENT ASSESSMENT AND EVALUATION

Asp, E. (2000). Assessment in education: Where have we been? Where are we headed? In Brandt, R. S. (Ed.), *Education in a new era.* Alexandria, VA: Association for Supervision and Curriculum Development.

Brandt, R. S. (Ed.). (1992). *Readings from educational leadership: Performance assessment.* Alexandria, VA: Association for Supervision and Curriculum Development.

Burke, K. (1999). *How to assess authentic learning* (3rd ed.). Arlington Heights, IL: SkyLight Training and Publishing. (Note: the 5th ed. of this book was published by Corwin Press in 2009.)

Coil, C., & Merritt, D. (2001). *Solving the assessment puzzle piece by piece.* Marion, IL: Pieces of Learning. (Note: an updated and revised ed. of this book was published in 2011.)

Erb, T. O. (Ed.). (2005). *This we believe in action: Implementing successful middle level schools.* Westerville, OH: National Middle School Association.

Fogarty, R. (1998). *Balanced assessment.* Arlington Heights, IL: SkyLight Training and Publishing.

Forte, I., Schurr, S., & Incentive Publications, Inc. (1995). *Making portfolios, products, and performances meaningful and manageable for students and teachers.* Nashville, TN: Incentive Publications.

Griswold, P. A. (1990). Assessing relevance and reliability to improve the quality of teacher-made tests. *NASSP Bulletin, 74*(523), 18-24.

Herman, J. L., Aschbacher, P. R., & Winters, L. (1992). *A practical guide to alternative assessment.* Alexandria, VA: Association for Supervision and Curriculum Development.

Jacobs, H. H. (1997). *Mapping the big picture: Integrating curriculum & assessment, K-12.* Alexandria, VA: Association for Supervision and Curriculum Development.

Lounsbury, J. H., & Schurr, S. (2003). *Assessing student progress: Moving from grades to portfolios.* Westerville, OH: National Middle School Association.

McTighe, J., & Ferrara, S. (2000). *Assessing learning in the classroom.* Washington, DC: National Education Association.

Paris, S. G., & Ayres, L. R. (1994). *Becoming reflective students and teachers: With portfolios and authentic assessment.* Washington, DC: American Psychological Association.

Paulson, F. L., Paulson, P. R., & Meyer, C. A. (1991). What makes a portfolio a portfolio? *Educational Leadership, 48*(5), 60-63.

Sparks, D., & Schlechty, P. (1998). The educator examined. *Journal of Staff Development, 19*(3), 38-42.

Wiggins, G. (1991). A response to Cizek. *Phi Delta Kappan, 72*(9), 700-703.

Wiggins, G. P., & McTighe, J. (1998). *Understanding by design.* Alexandria, VA: Association for Supervision and Curriculum Development. (Note: the 2nd ed. of this book was published in 2005.)

Wiggins, G. P. (1993). *Assessing student performance: Exploring the purpose and limits of testing.* San Francisco: Jossey-Bass Publishers.

Wormeli, R. (2006). *Fair isn't always equal: Assessing & grading in the differentiated classroom.* Portland, ME: Stenhouse Publishers.

Index

Association Listings

Visit individual association websites for other publications,
newsletters, online journals, blogs, and services.

- **American Educational Research Association (AERA) www.aera.net**
  1430 K Street NW, Suite 1200, Washington, D.C. 20005, Phone: (202) 238-3200
  Journals: *American Education Research Journal*
                 Journal of Educational and Behavioral Statistics
                 Educational Researcher
                 Review of Educational Research

- **American Federation of Teachers (AFT) www.aft.org**
  555 New Jersey Avenue NW, Washington, D.C. 20001, Phone: (202) 879-4400
  Journals: *American Teacher*
                 American Educator

- **Association for Middle Level Education (AMLE) www.amle.org**
  4151 Executive Parkway, Suite 300, Westerville, OH 43081, Phone: (614) 895-4750
  Journal: *Middle School Journal*
                 Research in Middle Level Education Online

- **Association for Supervision and Curriculum Development (ASCD) www.ascd.org**
  1703 North Beauregard Street, Alexandria, VA 22311, Phone: (703) 578-9600
  Journal: *Educational Leadership*

- **Council for Exceptional Children (CEC) www.cec.sped.org**
  2900 Crystal Drive, Suite 1000 Arlington, VA 22202, Phone: (888) 232-7733
  Journals: *Exceptional Children*
                 Teaching Exceptional Children

- **International Reading Association (IRA) www.reading.org**
  800 Barksdale Road, Box 8139, Newark, DE 19714, Phone: (302) 731-1600
  Journals: *Journal of Adolescent and Adult Literacy*
                 The Reading Teacher
                 Reading Research Quarterly
                 Reading Today

- **Learning Forward www.learningforward.org**
  504 South Locust Street, Oxford, OH 45056, Phone: (513) 523-0638
  Journal: *Journal of Staff Development (JSD)*

- **Music Teachers National Association (MTNA) www.mtna.org**
  441 Vine Street, Suite 3100, Cincinnati, OH 45202, Phone: (513) 421-1420
  Journal: *American Music Teacher*

- **National Art Education Association (NAEA) www.arteducators.org**
  1806 Robert Fulton Drive, Suite 300, Reston, VA 20191, Phone: (703) 860-8000
  Journal: *Art Education*

- **National Association of Secondary School Principals (NASSP)**
www.nassp.org
  1904 Association Drive, Reston, VA 20191, Phone: (703) 860-0200
  Journal: *Principal Leadership*

- **National Association of Special Education Teachers (NASET) www.naset.org**
  1250 Connecticut Ave. NW, Suite 2000, Washington, D.C. 20036, Phone (800) 754-4421
  Journal: *Journal of the American Academy of Special Education Professionals*

- **National Council for the Social Studies (NCSS) www.socialstudies.org**
  8555 16th Street, Suite 500, Silver Springs, MD 20910, Phone: (301) 588-1800
  Journals: *Social Education*
  Middle Level Learning

- **National Council of Teachers of English (NCTE) www.ncte.org**
  1111 Kenyon Road, Urbana, IL 61801, Phone: (217) 328-3870
  Journals: *English Journal*
  English Education
  Language Arts
  English Leadership Quarterly
  Voices from the Middle

- **National Council of Teachers of Mathematics (NCTM) www.nctm.org**
  1906 Association Drive, Reston, VA 20191, Phone: (703) 620-9840
  Journals: *Teaching Children Mathematics*
  Mathematics Teacher
  Journal for Research in Mathematics Education
  Mathematics Teaching in the Middle School

- **National Education Association (NEA) www.nea.org**
  1201 16th Street NW, Suite 310, Washington, D.C. 20036, Phone: (202) 833-4000
  Journal: *NEA Today*

- **National Middle School Association (NMSA) www.nmsa.org**
  4151 Executive Parkway, Suite 300, Westerville, OH 43081, Phone: (614) 895-4750
  Journals: *Middle School Journal*
  Middle Ground

- **National Science Teachers Association (NSTA) www.nsta.org**
  1840 Wilson Boulevard, Arlington, VA 22201, Phone: (703) 243-7100
  Journals: *Science and Children*
  Science Scope
  The Science Teacher

- **Phi Delta Kappa International (PDK) www.pdkintl.org**
  1525 Wilson Boulevard, Suite 605, Arlington, VA 22209, Phone: (812) 339-0018
  Journal: *Phi Delta Kappan*